Fighting for the Soviet
Motherland

Fighting for the Soviet Motherland

Recollections from
the Eastern Front
Hero of the Soviet Union
Dmitriy Loza

Edited and translated by

James F. Gebhardt

University
of Nebraska Press
Lincoln & London

⊚ The paper in this book meets the minimum requirements
of American National Standard for Information Sciences—
Permanence of Paper for Printed Library Materials,
ANSI Z39.48-1984.
Library of Congress Cataloging-in-Publication Data
Loza, D. F. (Dmitriĭ Fedorovich)
Fighting for the Soviet motherland : recollections from the Eastern
Front / Dmitriy Loza ; edited and translated by James F. Gebhardt.
   p.   cm.
Translated from manuscript.
Includes bibliographical references and index.
ISBN 0-8032-2929-1 (cl : alk. paper)
1. Loza, D. F. (Dmitriĭ Fedorovich) 2. World War, 1939–1945—Tank
warfare. 3. Sherman tank. 4. World War, 1939–1945—Personal
narratives, Russian. 5. Soviet Union. Raboche-Krest ĭanskaĭa
Krasnaĭa Armiĭa—Biography. 6. Soldiers—Soviet Union—
Biography. I. Gebhardt, James F., 1948- . II. Title.
D793.L685 1999
940.54'8147—dc21   98-11253
                                                            CIP

Contents

v

Illustrations

Translator's Foreword

To **undertake** to translate the wartime experiences of World War II Red Army veterans for an American audience is a daunting task. One must overcome not only the language and cultural obstacles but also the psychological barrier of more than fifty years of all things Soviet being regarded as communist and therefore as inherently evil.

This is a task I welcome, however, because I have a duty to history. The picture of the war on the Eastern Front that emerges from this account is foreign to most American readers. It contains strange images, unfamiliar places, indecipherable names, and a view of the Red Army wholly contrary to the one that most American readers have previously encountered. This sense of estrangement is to be expected, given the fact that Americans have viewed the war on this distant front primarily through the prism of German accounts.

When in the course of my own military service I had the opportunity to study the performance of the Soviet Armed Forces in World War II in greater detail, I realized that their contribution to the defeat of Germany and, to a lesser degree, of Japan was far greater than has ever been acknowledged in our history books. Having gained proficiency in the Russian language, I was able to read writings by and about the great battle captains of the Red Army and Red Navy. The more I studied, the greater became my desire to understand the Eastern Front war at the personal level. Then came the collapse of the Soviet Union and with it the opening of a new window on the history of World War II.

The light coming through this newly opened window consists of the memoirs of Dmitriy Loza and other Soviet Army veterans like him, who fought in and survived World War II and the Cold War. Colonel Loza was born in 1922 in a Ukrainian village, entered the Red Army in 1940, and graduated from Saratov Tank School in 1942. The unit to which he was first assigned was equipped with British Matilda tanks, seven hundred fifty of which had reached the Soviet Union from Great Britain early in the war.[1] Lieutenant Loza was seriously wounded on a Matilda tank in fighting in late September 1943.

When he rejoined his unit after several weeks of hospitalization, the Matildas had been exchanged for the diesel-engined American Sherman M4A2 tank. The Soviets received slightly more than seven thousand light and medium tanks from the United States of America during the war, the approximate equivalent to six months' Soviet domestic tank production.[2] These first Shermans were equipped with the M3 75-mm gun. Later Shermans, those delivered after July 1944, were equipped with the slightly larger and more powerful M4A1 or M4A2 76.2-mm gun. Loza's first memoir, *Commanding the Red Army's Sherman Tanks*, recounts his wartime experiences beginning with his introduction to the Sherman tank in the fall of 1943 and ending with the capitulation of Japanese forces in Manchuria in August 1945.

Dmitriy Loza has cast his net wider in this second volume, drawing upon not only his own war experiences but also those of acquaintances, to cover a broader space of time and subject matter. In his original manuscript Colonel Loza employed a number of terms unfamiliar to American readers that both he and I have explained using footnotes. To differentiate my own notes from Colonel Loza's, I have attached my initials in brackets [JC] to my insertions, leaving Colonel Loza's annotations unmarked. The maps that accompany five of the stories have been prepared on the basis of Colonel Loza's own drawings.

To further the reader's understanding of how the Soviet military lived during World War II and how Russia now honors its World War II heroes, I have attached four appendixes to this memoir. The first is the military oath taken by all Soviet enlisted personnel upon completion of initial military training, along with the instructions for administering this oath. The second appendix is a translation of the famous "Not one step backward" order, read (but not published as a text) to the Soviet Armed Forces in late July 1942. The third appendix is a list of common Soviet combat decorations of World War II in order of precedence. The last appendix is a translation of the law signed by President Boris Yeltsin on 15 January 1993 codifying the rights and entitlements of recipients of the Soviet Union's, and now Russia's, highest military awards.

I would like to acknowledge here the encouragement and assistance given me by several persons and institutions in the completion of this manuscript. Lieutenant Colonel Barney King, USA (Retired), and Major John Donovan, USA, read and offered valuable suggestions for improving the text. The staff of the U.S. Army Signal Corps Museum at Fort Gordon, Georgia, assisted me in tracking down information on the SCR-399-A radio set. The staff of the Aberdeen Proving Ground Museum in Maryland provided me with important technical information on ammunition for the Sherman's 76.2-mm cannon and its storage within the hull. My wife, Deborah, spent many hours alone in one part of our house without hint of complaint while I worked on this project in another. Finally, Colonel Dmitriy Loza, from his distant residence in Moscow, Russia, in addition to supplying the basic manuscript and maps, answered my numerous written queries with swiftness and enthusiasm. To him and his Red Army comrades I dedicate my contribution to this work.

Author's Introduction

The Great Patriotic War lasted 1,418 days and nights.[1] These wartime years were filled with tragic and heroic events. Not all of them have been described in books and magazines, published in photographs, or projected onto the theater screen. One must agree that without the stories of those faraway days of the Russian front, a complete truth about the dark and difficult conflict with fascist Germany cannot exist.

The duty of veterans is to make their own personal contribution to filling in the blank pages of the history of the greatest battles of the twentieth century. Each frontline veteran is the repository of the "small change" of battles, often events of an unusual nature. It would be a great pity if their accounts did not become accessible to the broad populace of all former combatant nations but instead sank into oblivion.

The materials presented in this second volume of my wartime memoirs come from my personal experiences or were told to me by friends and fellow veterans of the war. Soviet soldiers fought with the enemy not for life but against death. It was win or be killed. There was no third choice, particularly after mid–1943, when the Stalingrad and Kursk battles had been fought and won. The Soviet Army was inexorably driving the Germans westward. Our soldiers, sergeants, and officers already had substantial combat experience. In a majority of cases, frontline soldiers took risks, often dangerous ones, boldly. They did not think only about themselves. I can even say that by this time in the war, tankers in particular displayed unmatched valor. In both offense and defense they operated in a fashion so unanticipated that it frequently forced the enemy into a difficult situation.

Further, the Soviet people fought the Germans not out of fear but out of conscience, not for rank or awards but for the liberation of the Motherland from German occupation. These were the principal motivations of hundreds and thousands of unusual feats by Soviet soldiers that surprised the world. There were, of course, many other motives, but those are a subject for discussion at another time and place.

Audacity and Intuition

Five months of the most fierce combat with the enemy was behind us. Stubborn defensive battles had halted the German forces on the approaches to Moscow. The counteroffensive of Soviet troops around the capital began on 5 December 1941.

As they had before, units of 1st Guards Rifle Division showed exemplary combat proficiency. This division, the first to earn the title of Guards, carried this much-celebrated banner high. Its unit commanders displayed bravery not daily but hourly, and they acquired expertise in conducting modern combined-arms combat. The 1st Guards, having begun to drive the enemy back, made the transition to actual attack on the night of 7 December.

Forward detachments assaulted enemy nodes of resistance.[1] The officers leading these units effectively utilized a combination of key factors: the complex meteorological conditions, their own excellent knowledge of the terrain, and the peculiarities of the behavior of enemy troops.

Winter in the Moscow environs had begun in an exceptionally severe fashion, for which the Western Europeans were completely unprepared. The mercury column in the thermometer plummeted to $-25°$ C during the day and to $-35°$ C at night [$-13°$ and $-31°$ F respectively], and the snow cover reached a meter in depth. In these harsh weather conditions enemy units and formations, especially tank units, were largely restricted to the roads, and thus their lateral maneuver along the front was greatly complicated.

German combat and logistic equipment functioned only intermittently in this weather. A large percentage of the troops, most of whom were dressed in summer clothing, suffered from illness or weather-related injuries. The German high command's plan to conclude their "march to the East" in a lightning-fast manner had utterly collapsed. Thousands of soldiers and officers paid in blood for the reckless daring of the German ruling elite. General Gunther Blumentritt, the former chief of staff of the German

1

Fourth Army, later wrote, "Now, even in Hitler's headquarters, they suddenly understood that the war in Russia was just beginning."

Soviet commanders of all ranks took one fundamental circumstance into consideration during all of their decision making in the offensive: because the brutal Russian winter had forced the German troops into the villages to seek shelter against the freezing cold, only a guard force was placed around occupied villages in the Moscow area at night.

Hero of the Russian Federation Colonel Georgiy Dmitrievich Ionin, now retired, remembers well the battles of those long-ago days.[2] [The remainder of this story is told in the voice of Colonel Ionin.]

The enemy was totally unprepared for the attack of our 1st Guards Division. The German command had not given the slightest thought to a possible Soviet offensive in such severe weather conditions. Clearly, the enemy had forgotten that the deep winter snow and the bitter cold were neither frightening nor unusual to the soldiers of the Red Army, who were dressed in warm sheepskin coats, felt boots, and well-made mittens.

These factors were important, but they are not the sole explanation for our success. The soldier (in the broad sense of this word) is the creator of victory. In the Great Patriotic War, the heaviest burden of military combat rested on his shoulders.

The first hours of night combat brought good results. We captured scores of prisoners, who gave us exceptionally valuable information, along with some infantry weapons and mortars. The forward detachment of 85th Rifle Regiment, commanded by Captain Aleksandr Nikolaevich Krinetskiy, was particularly effective. Having learned from the prisoners that a battalion of enemy submachine gunners was located in Apukhtino, the commander ordered his unit to move noiselessly toward the village under cover of darkness. With a battalion of submachine gunners under his own command, Krinetskiy knew that given the size of the enemy force he could achieve success by launching an attack on the Germans from several directions. To accomplish that purpose, he had his unit encircle the village quickly and stealthily, deploy rapidly, and then suddenly burst into the enemy garrison.

They took out the guard force without firing a shot. The first two companies then moved on skis among the trees and shallow ravines to the western and northern outskirts of Apukhtino. Having thus covered the possible paths of German retreat, Krinetskiy himself led the third company to drive the enemy soldiers out of the houses and into the bitter cold.

The forward detachment's main body reached their designated start positions. Under the captain's leadership, the soldiers surreptitiously crept into the village and quickly surrounded each house. On command, they threw grenades into the windows. And then it began: the hapless Germans, many of them half-dressed, fled into the streets and immediately fell in the hail of bullets. Soviet units attacking from the west and north gunned down those few enemy soldiers who had managed to escape from Apukhtino. The shrewd combination of storming the houses in the village while simultaneously attacking it from outside with significant forward detachment forces quickly defeated the German troops, who were equal to the Soviets in number.

By the end of 7 December, 1st Guards Division had advanced from four to fourteen kilometers and had liberated thirteen villages from German occupation. The offensive continued nonstop until the middle of January. The division's other regiment, the 4th Rifle Regiment, operated no less successfully in these battles. Its commander was Colonel Mikhail Emelyanovich Vaytsekhovskiy.

To this day I recall one instructive episode. The artillery battery that I was commanding had been subordinated to 4th Rifle Regiment. My 76-mm guns were deployed in firing positions two kilometers from the enemy along a road leading toward the forward edge. I arrived at the rifle regiment command post. Colonel Vaytsekhovskiy, having learned from my brief report where the artillery was located and how many guns we had, ordered me to move the firing platoons and occupy positions adjacent to his command post. This unusual instruction surprised me greatly. Even as an academy student, I knew that it was absolutely against regulation to position artillery near important installations and facilities, let alone among them. I therefore decided to warn the colonel concerning that fact—even though he was a much older and more experienced officer than I, a mere nineteen-year-old lieutenant. Mikhail Emelyanovich had commanded a regiment, a brigade, and combined detachments during the Civil War.[3] His courageous combat leadership had earned him two Orders of the Red Banner.[4]

I told him that the enemy might discover the artillery battery by resection and, in firing counterbattery fire on us, inflict damage on his command post. Not responding to my words, the colonel demanded that I proceed immediately to carry out his order. Within twenty minutes I reported to him that the battery had occupied firing positions near his command post and was prepared to execute fire missions. Only then did the commander respond to my warning. "I had to choose the lesser of two evils," he said. "In this complex and unclear situation, when there is no stable front line and subordinate units are fighting a tough battle with variable success in limited visibility, it is far better for the personnel of the command post to be subjected to artillery shelling than to have to conduct a close-in fight with enemy tanks and infantry. They have already been put in this kind of danger once. So that your battery does not expose itself, you will fire only when necessary and only with my permission."

This seasoned veteran knew what he was talking about. The situation he had described to me is exactly what took place. Not an hour had passed when the silhouettes of three enemy tanks with infantry aboard appeared in the foggy haze some four hundred meters to the right of the command post. They were moving toward us but not firing. Clearly, their leader did not know about the presence of artillery in the command-post area.

The order was given to commence firing. We fired round after round at the enemy using direct lay [aiming the guns directly at the targets and not at aiming stakes as during indirect firing]. Each solid-shot projectile struck its target. The enemy tanks froze in place without any return fire. Our cannons spoke again, this time with fragmentation shells aimed at the troop targets. The battle was brief, but it produced ample results. Three Panzer IV tanks and dozens of bodies of enemy soldiers and officers remained on the approaches to the command post. Only a few Germans managed to save themselves by fleeing.

After offering sincere thanks to the artillerymen for their outstanding effort, Colonel Vaytsekhovskiy shook my hand firmly, looked me squarely in the eye, and wryly smiled. He had taught me a cogent lesson. I well understood what combat experience was all about, what it meant to act not by rote but by giving thoughtful consideration of all nuances of a developing situation.

Lyuba the Tank Killer

The war came to our land. As the poet Sergey Vikulov said, "They have thrown down the glove to Russia."[1] Not only men but also women picked up this glove. We men might have thought their hands were too weak for weapons, but there were women soldiers who did not wish to stand on the sidelines at this grave time for the Motherland. This account centers in one of the hundreds of thousands of women who entered military service during World War II.

Lyuba Zemska was born in 1923 in Kharkov, about 400 miles south of Moscow, in my own native Ukraine. We had a terrible famine there in 1933, and the young girl was orphaned.[2] She was still living in an orphanage when the Germans invaded the Soviet Union. Determined to do her part, Lyuba made her way to the local military commission and insisted that they send her to the front.[3] The commission instead sent her off to a medical training facility, where she took an accelerated course to become a medic. She went to the active army, to the medical battalion of 100th Rifle Division, which was soon to become 1st Guards Division.[4]

However, the work of a medic did not satisfy Lyuba Zemska. Her passionate desire was to kill the enemy with her own hands. Yet her frequent requests for transfer were ignored. The commission responsible for personnel reassignments would not release Lyuba from her medical specialty because soldiers with her level of medical training and skill were urgently needed on the front lines. She was conscientious, skillful in her profession, and physically strong. Undaunted by the lack of response to her transfer request and still determined to participate more actively in combat, she continued to work toward her goal.

The fires of war had been burning on our land for three months when Lyuba's long-sought opportunity arrived. A new antitank rifle, designed by Sergei Gavrilovich Simonov and known as the *PTRS*, had been issued to the Red Army,[5] and frequently the wounded men whom Lyuba treated would make favorable comments about the weapon. She knew that units in her division were now being screened for the best and bravest soldiers, the most level-headed and battle-tested, to become antitank gunners with this new rifle. Their mission was to destroy enemy tanks.

Lyuba Zemska was one of the first to submit a written request to be sent for training as a tank killer. Her immediate supervisor had serious doubts as to whether this young woman had the physical strength for such an arduous and dangerous specialty as that of tank killer. Considering it his personal duty to dissuade her from a hasty decision, he twice deferred Lyuba's request.

With no intention of being thwarted from her goal, Lyuba appealed to the next higher level in her chain of command. Made wise by life and experience, the colonel recognized the young *Komsomolka's* determination to serve in combat and granted her request for reassignment.[6]

The former medic traveled to one of the frontline towns where a tank-killer school was training future *PTRS* gunners. Seasoned soldiers—who knew from personal combat experience how difficult and dangerous the role of the antitank gunner is—frequently attempted to talk Lyuba into returning to her previous line of duty. But she paid no attention to these soldiers' exhortations. Energetically, with a visible fighting instinct, she continued to develop in her new role.

Toward the end of her training period, Lyuba had become an exceptionally accurate gunner, a fact that aroused an admiring envy in her comrades in the school. The time came for graduation examinations. On the day of record fire, a snowstorm arose, and the thermometer dropped to the –30° C [–22° F] mark. Despite these difficult weather conditions, Lyuba Zemska completed all the exercises with excellent marks and earned the congratulations of the school commandant.

Lyuba returned to the 1st Guards Division and was subsequently reassigned to the 85th Rifle Regiment, having realized her dream. She now possessed an effective weapon for destroying German medium tanks—that is, tanks whose armor was thirty to fifty millimeters thick on the front slope and twenty to thirty millimeters on the turret and sides. "Now everything depends on me personally. When I engage an enemy armored vehicle, not one of my muscles will quiver! I vow it!" Zemska repeated to herself. This tank killer, now thoroughly familiar with enemy tanks and armored troop transporters, knew well their particular areas of vulnerability, and she could deliver swift and deadly fire into these soft spots.

During the last part of January 1942, the 1st Guards Division was fighting with some success northeast of Kursk. By the morning of the twenty-first, the division's units had liberated twelve villages, taking valuable trophies in the process.[7] The decisive movement of the *gvardeytsy* toward the south threatened the Germans in the area of the town of Shchigry with encirclement.[8] The German response to this threat was to launch a series of fierce counterattacks.[9]

A particularly tense situation was developing that day in the attack zone of 85th Regiment. Having captured the village of Uderovo, the regiment's battalions were continuing to move successfully toward Kryukovo and Parmenovka. The Germans brought up fresh reserves to this important axis and launched a counterattack into the regiment's flanks. Eleven tanks on the right flank and seven on the left were supported by significant infantry forces.

The fierce engagement that developed became the battle that christened Lyuba Zemska as a tank killer. It was also the first serious test of her devotion to duty and her combat ability.

The regimental commander, Lieutenant Colonel Nikolay Kozin, must be given his due. During a brief lull between engagements, he ordered a review of all the regiment's fire-support units and then promptly redistributed their personnel so that each gun, mortar, and antitank rifle crew or team included some combat-experienced soldiers. Seasoned veterans, reliable examples to soldiers recently arrived at the front, would thus guide the novices in their first battle. For this reason Sergeant Viktor Maslov was paired with Lyuba Zemska in the PTRS crew.

Any battle is difficult, but one's first is especially so. Fate brought the untested young woman together with enemy tanks on the firing line for the first time on 21 January. She could easily see the five steel monsters crawling toward her position near an old poplar tree, the distance between her and them decreasing with each minute. The *peteerovtsy* nervously waited.[10] "Let them come closer!" Maslov exhorted his partner. Powdered snow raised by their tracks swirled in front of the tanks, obscuring the precise outline of the vehicles. The tank main guns and machine guns were silent. Each vehicle contained five enemy crewmen, protected by armor. Twenty-five against two in a foxhole. The *gvardeytsy* calmly estimated the range, looking for the desired 300 meters at which the armor-piercing incendiary bullet would most likely penetrate the German tank.

Then the ground trembled and the air was torn by the simultaneous firing of enemy tank main guns. They fired round after round at the village as they moved toward it. Finally the tanks closed to the effective range of the antitank rifles.

Sergeant Maslov drew back the bolt on his rifle to load it while Lyuba lay next to him, holding rounds for reloading the PTRS magazine. A shudder suddenly passed through her gunner's body, and his head fell sharply to his chest. The former medic turned to help him, but her aid was already unnecessary. A bullet had struck him straight in the chest, killing him instantly. Lyuba remained alone in the position at this critical moment in the battle. The armored wave continued to roll toward her, hurling kilograms of death-dealing metal every second.

The advice of her school instructor flashed across her mind: "Do not hesitate! Seconds will decide if you live or die! If you delay, you will be ground up in the tank's tracks. Shoot at the right moment, and don't miss!"

Lyuba carefully placed the body of her combat comrade aside on the ground and then prepared herself for battle. The rifle's stock still held the warmth of the dead sergeant's hand. She took aim. The tanks were moving closer and closer, the lead machine now clearly visible. She could see the muzzle opening of the main gun and the barrel of the coaxial machine gun. Both weapons were firing continuously. Bullets were raising fountains of earth and snow around her position. Lyuba was calm and showed no fear.

The enemy tanks were now only 150 meters away, moving at not more than ten kilometers per hour. In just a few moments they would reach the old poplar tree. It was time to fire! She squeezed the trigger smoothly. She did not hear the shot but felt the recoil in her shoulder. The bullet's tracer flashed through the air and burrowed into the lead tank. Black smoke enveloped the vehicle, and it stopped. Without hesitation Lyuba shifted her fire to a second tank. She squeezed the trigger three times and saw red tongues of flame erupt from the tank's engine compartment. She brought a third vehicle, an armored troop carrier, into her sights and carefully aimed at its vulnerable spot. At the instant she began to squeeze the trigger, several bullets struck her. Medics managed to crawl over to the antitank gunner, but they could not help her.

The battalions and companies of 85th Rifle Regiment fought off the enemy counterattack almost the entire day. They did not surrender to the enemy the position they had captured earlier. When the battle was over, the men lifted the body of the brave tank killer and, placing it in a poncho, carried it to the rear. They found an unfinished letter in her pocket. The addressee was unknown. "Ukraine, my Ukraine!" Lyuba had written, "I am your daughter. . . . I pledge to you in memory of all my dead brothers and sisters that I will take cruel, merciless vengeance on the fascists."

Lyuba Zemska was posthumously awarded the Order of the Red Banner. Her life was brief but brilliant, like a flash of lightning. In one battle, one fierce engagement with enemy tanks, she brought the hour of final victory closer.

Spalling

The spray of an ocean storm, the splash of water during a swim in the river, the diffusion of the rays of a rising sun, even the effervescent plume that shoots forth from an uncorked bottle of champagne—they are all so vividly appealing in their display. From the end of 1941 and throughout almost the entire subsequent twelve months, however, T-34 tankers were involuntarily subjected to a far less invigorating kind of spray—the spalling of the armor of their own tanks.

From the beginning of the Great Patriotic War, the Soviet government was faced with the enormous problem of evacuating countless industrial enterprises from the country's western regions to its eastern regions. The relocated defense plants, as the chairman of the Council of Ministers [J. V. Stalin] reported, "began production at their new sites some seven or eight months later. This [lapse in production] has led to a weakening of our defense capability and has placed the Soviet Union in mortal danger."[1]

The Red Army's failures during the initial period of the war allowed the enemy to capture a number of mineral-rich regions of Ukraine and Belorussia. As a result of the Soviets' having lost control of these regions, a complicated situation developed in the plants that manufactured the armor for their tanks. Because these factories had received insufficient quantities of some of the smelted metals required to ensure the necessary toughness of armor, the armor plate they produced turned out to be somewhat brittle in its composition—and, of course, there were negative consequences on the battlefield.

For quality-control reasons alone, the distribution of this brittle armor should have been halted immediately. The plant directors repeatedly raised this issue to high government officials. But the front demanded weapons and more weapons, including tanks! It was a perilous time. The plants poured and rolled their clearly defective product and sent it out to the tank-building factories.

The T-34s assembled with this defective armor arrived as equipment for units of 45th Brigade, 4th Tank Corps, in June 1942. They were brand-new tanks, just off the assembly line, still bearing their factory paint.

The brittle-armored tanks of the brigade fought their first battle in the defense at Voronezh the month following their delivery. It was a fierce engagement with the enemy. Almost immediately the unit commander had begun to receive radio messages with strange contents. Despite the failure of enemy shells to penetrate the T-34 tanks' armor, crew members were being wounded inside their turrets, primarily in the exposed areas of the body—the hands and arms, the face, and, in the case of some commander-gunners, the eyes.[2]

With the first lull in the battle, the Soviet troops began to investigate these mysterious wounds. It soon became clear to them that the steep slope angle of the T-34 turret's exterior surfaces was allowing enemy solid-shot rounds generally to ricochet when they struck that area. But when such a round did indeed hit the turret's outer wall, pieces of the tank's armor itself flew off the inner wall at extremely high velocities—a rate that seemed to vary according to the kinetic energy of round at the moment of impact. In general, if the enemy round struck on the left side of the tank, the commander-gunner—whose crew position was closest to the left inner wall of the turret—was being injured by the fragmenting armor of the vehicle wall. If the round hit on the right side, the armor spalling was striking the loader, whose crew position was on that side. The size of the fragments ranged from microscopic to several millimeters in diameter.

From the moment they became aware of the situation, SMERSH personnel busied themselves in the investigation.[3] Coming rapidly to the conclusion that the spalling was evidence of sabotage in the factory production line, they filled their counterintelligence communications channels with messages to higher headquarters.

The eye wounds sustained by the commander-gunners presented the greatest difficulty to doctors in the army hospitals. Having never before encountered wounds of this type, these physicians lacked both the experience in surgical technique and the special instruments that they needed to handle the problem. Did the new surgical approaches that the doctors were thus forced to devise under these circumstances perhaps constitute their introduction to microsurgery?[4]

In the hospital, in response to their doctors' questions concerning the cause of their eye injuries, some patients recited a tankers' ditty: "*Tanka rodnaya bronya ne poshchadila menya. Zadeli oskolki 'stalnogo dozhdya'!*" [My tank's armor showed me no mercy. It wounded me with pieces of "steel rain"!] This response was absolutely incomprehensible to the "white coats." Then the wounded men went on to explain in greater detail the misadventure that had occurred.

We tankers in the rear and at the front found out about this "sickness" of the Soviet-made combat vehicles through various channels (unofficial, of course)—stories told by the wounded returning from hospitals and letters from friends in the active army.

This serious deficiency in the combat worthiness of the T-34 was finally eliminated in early 1943. It was the tankers of the older generation—soldiers and officers who had gone through training before the Great Patriotic War and come into the active army in the first months of that conflict—who experienced the situation firsthand.

I will openly admit that when our 233d Tank Brigade of 5th Mechanized Corps first received Sherman tanks in the last months of 1943, we combat veterans, in studying their tactical-technical characteristics, recalled the possibility of armor spalling in the fighting compartment if enemy armor-piercing rounds were to strike it. We thought that the M4A2 might be afflicted with the same "illness," though its armor was somewhat thicker than that of the T-34 (100 versus 90 millimeters).

We did not hide this negative frontline experience from our younger generation of tankers. In fact, we talked freely about it in preparing the enlisted personnel for the upcoming battles. We were guided by the rule that combat comrades should know about the experiences of their forebears, both good and bad. We did not want the new soldiers to lose heart or panic if some "surprise" should arise on the battlefield.

Our concerns were put to rest in the January 1944 battles on the flat fields of right-bank Ukraine, however.[5] The Shermans took more than a few direct hits on the turret and did not manifest the infirmity that had plagued the early T-34s. Enemy rounds failed to penetrate their armor, and not one bit of spray erupted inside the fighting compartments. Instead, at the places where the enemy antitank solid-shot rounds had struck the exterior surfaces of the tanks, there were marks—spots of various diameter and depth, which were frequently accompanied by hanging "icicles" of melted turret steel. An unquestionable sign of the high tensile strength of the armor, these marks were dubbed "Hitler's kisses" by our tanker comedians.

Not by Rote but by Sk...

Housed in the memories of Great Patrio...
ans and in the archival documents are countless exam...
military skill and discipline demonstrated by soldiers a...
and of the combat actions successfully carried out by vari...
military units under many different conditions. Yet the war a...
saw a number of unusual engagements with the enemy that we...
not conducted within the constraints of existing field regulations.
Such events could not be made public during the period in which
they took place, nor could they be used as examples in the curriculum at military academies. But one is indeed prompted to
ask whether these incidents, secondary though they may have
been, were not stepping stones to the coming victory. Here is an
account of one such unacknowledged encounter.

In March 1942 two regiments of 1st Guards Division were
holding a bridgehead on the left bank of the Northern Donets
River (see map 1). The bridgehead was twelve kilometers wide and
six to eight kilometers deep.[1] A significant portion of the defended
area was forested. The remaining terrain was open, trafficable by
tanks. The ice on the river still had sufficient thickness to support
combat vehicles weighing up to forty tons.

Early on the morning of 2 March, after an artillery preparation,
the enemy launched an attack on a narrow front with virtually an
entire regiment of infantry supported by twenty tanks. Though
they suffered great losses in personnel and had six of their tanks
disabled, the German forces managed to overcome the resistance
of the Soviet troops, who had been weakened by earlier engagements and were defending in open terrain. By 1300 hours the
enemy had captured the village of Rubezhnoye and reached the
north bank of the river.

The situation demanded the launch of a counterattack, the destruction of the enemy force that had penetrated into the defense,
and the reestablishment of the initial situation. A rifle regiment
of a second-echelon division was being prepared to carry out the

an absolute superiority
t's success. The division
v, had earlier reported
ad requested that he
1e 22d Tank Brigade,
on of the *gvardeytsy*
he deputy brigade
1ter to become clear,
1ad been in many

·r was so steeply
land only in the
seemed the wisest

·eaking through
ir main attacking
..., ınto the village—the important
... the bridgehead. Once they had captured Rubezhnoye,
the Germans left the majority of their Panzer IV tanks there in
the village center and positioned only a modest number of tanks
along the street that led down to the river. A small number of
infantrymen were positioned in the houses next to the water.
Three machine guns and an artillery battery were set up on the
northern outskirts of the village.

During the process of refining the Soviet counterattack plan,
the division artillery chief, Guards Lieutenant Colonel Aleksandr
Sveshnikov, recommended the firing of a brief artillery preparation according to the following sequence: a four-minute barrage
on firing points in the Rubezhnoye area, then a five-minute barrage on the infantry positions, and finally a three-minute barrage
on the targets fired in the first barrage. The primary purpose of
this preparation was to suppress the enemy artillery battery that
the Soviets had detected. Artillery support of the counterattack
was to be executed against individual targets on request.

This sequence of artillery firings to defeat the enemy both during the artillery preparation and during the actual counterattack
itself was completely in line with official Soviet military doctrine
as it then existed. But Major Skornov resolutely maintained that
changes be made in the sequence as the artillery chief had outlined it. Skornov advised that in their artillery preparation as well

as in their support of the counterattack, Soviet forces concentrate the principal mass of fire at the enemy tanks and that they fire continuously until the attacking forces reached the danger-close line.[3] Lieutenant Colonel Svechnikov objected, explaining that indirect artillery fire was ineffective against tanks and would not inflict any significant damage on them.

While expressing his agreement with the lieutenant colonel's assessment, Major Skornov defended his own recommendation. Enemy tanks, he asserted, were the only thing that would be able to disrupt the counterattack—and indeed, by all indications, there were twice as many of them as friendly tanks. The fact that the Germans had not brought the tanks up to the limit of their advance—that is, all the way to the river—was testimony that they had still not dug in on the captured terrain. The major proceeded to remind his superiors that it was now lunch time and doubtless the Germans were celebrating their recent victory: infantrymen and tankers, having left their vehicles, had dispersed into the houses and were probably drinking schnapps.

In this favorable situation, dense artillery fire into the area where the tanks were parked would prevent the Panzer crews from mounting their vehicles and preparing them for combat. The Soviet attackers, not having to battle against tank fires, would destroy them. Though the Soviet side had a smaller number of armored vehicles, they were nonetheless the backbone of the counterattack. Therefore, the Soviet artillery should operate foremost of all in the interests of the small Soviet tank force. The enemy machine gunners and infantry on the river bank, Major Skornov contended, did not represent a serious threat to the tanks. Of course, it was in the interest of the counterattacking infantry also to suppress the enemy infantry, but not at the expense of firing at the Panzer IVs.

The deputy brigade commander's arguments were so convincing that not only the division commander but also the chief of artillery agreed with him. The necessary instructions were thus immediately issued to change the artillery preparation.

The artillery cannons were fired at the scheduled moment. Our tanks rushed to the river, with infantry following close behind them. Easing down onto the ice at marked sites along the near riverbank, the tanks then sped toward Rubezhnoye, firing their main guns as they moved under the cover of our own artillery-shell explosions. From the very outset the counterattack on the opposite bank developed rapidly. The scenario played out exactly as Major Skornov had predicted. Encountering no effective tank main-gun resistance, our tankers shot up seven enemy combat vehicles on the streets of the village and captured six vehicles intact. Only one Panzer IV managed to make a break for German lines. Leaving the many bodies of their soldiers and officers lying in the bridgehead, the wounded but surviving enemy units hurriedly withdrew to their starting positions.[4]

Having brilliantly accomplished the assigned mission and taking with them the captured enemy tanks, the troops of 22d Brigade departed to their assembly area.[5]

The second-echelon division's counterattacking force had been operating by unwritten rules, but their orders had been based on both an in-depth analysis of the situation and a thorough knowledge of enemy habits. The Soviet force thus managed, with almost no losses, to overcome an enemy that was superior to it in manpower and equipment and to achieve victory not by rote but by skill.

Friendly Fire

The Spas-Demensk operation was conducted from 7 to 20 August 1943. Its purpose was to defeat the enemy's forces on the Spas-Demensk axis and create conditions for a subsequent offensive toward Roslavl. This operation was part of the Smolensk offensive operation.

The enemy had a solid, deeply echeloned defense. The Soviet command's concept was to launch a strike north of Spas-Demensk with 10th Guards and 33d Armies and south of Spas-Demensk with 10th Army in order to break through the enemy defense and, in coordination with 49th Army, to surround and destroy the enemy's Spas-Demensk grouping. Soviet forces were subsequently to develop the offensive into the flank and rear of German troops operating against Bryansk *Front*.[1]

On 7 August 1943, forces of 10th Guards and 33d Armies

launched their attack. They failed to surprise the Germans, and the battles on the enemy's main line of defense were prolonged. To accelerate the breakthrough, a portion of the *front* second echelon was introduced into the fight in the form of combat units and equipment of 68th Army. On 9 and 10 August the enemy rushed from the Orlov axis two infantry divisions and one panzer division to the breakthrough sector. New enemy formations continued to arrive in subsequent days.

On 10 August, forces of 10th Army struck north of Kirov; after the second day they had moved some ten kilometers into the depth, enveloping the enemy's Spas-Demensk grouping from the south. This situation forced the German command, after of a number of unsuccessful counterattacks and counterstrokes, to begin withdrawing its forces from the Spas-Demensk bulge on 12 August. The next day, 49th Army in conjunction with 33d Army formations liberated the town of Spas-Demensk.

In the Spas-Demensk operation, it was initially intended to use 5th Mechanized Corps in the zone of the offensive of 10th Guards Army. By 11 August, however, it had become clear to the commander of West *Front*, Colonel-General V. D. Sokolovskiy, that it would not be effective to introduce this formation into the battle in the manner that was planned. The Germans were directing their counterattack grouping against the *front*'s right wing (10th Guards and 33d Armies).

In connection with this German initiative, General Sokolovskiy decided to commit 5th Mechanized Corps to the south, around Kirov, to reinforce the forces of 10th Army. On 12 August its units executed a ninety-kilometer march and assembled northwest of Kirov, in preparation for enlarging the success of the army's formations on the opposite bank of the Bolva River the following day.

Two events will make me remember 13 August 1943 until my dying day: my battle christening (my first enemy encounter) and the tragedy I witnessed as our artillery fired on our own tanks. I was to see the effects of friendly fire again in January 1944 in Zvenigorodka, when the tanks of First and Second Ukrainian *Fronts* met, joining the encirclement ring around the enemy's Korsun-Shevchenkovskiy grouping.

These unfortunate events occurred because the troops were generally ignorant of the fact that in the particular sector of the two sides' line of contact, Soviet Army units were equipped with foreign tanks (in the first instance British Matildas, in the second American Shermans). Both here, and later in Ukraine, the foreign-made tanks were mistaken for enemy tanks, with dreadful consequences.

It was early morning. Our 233d Tank Brigade had been assembled in a mixed forest since the evening of 12 August. The brigade's 1st Battalion was stretched out along the west edge of the green expanse. My 1st Company was on the left flank, 200 meters from a country road, beyond which was a broad buckwheat field.

From out in front of us came the growing din of battle. The front line was not more than two kilometers away. Unfortunately the situation that was unfolding at the forward edge had not yet been reported to us at the lower tactical level.

About an hour passed. The sounds of all types of weapons fire were reaching us with increasing intensity. The roar of a terrible battle grew closer. Soon we saw on the road a column of artillery prime movers approaching from our rear at great speed and towing 76-mm cannons. The tank destroyers deployed from the march on the other side of the country road, left of the forest occupied by our brigade. In this manner they were covering the open area between the two wooded salients. They quickly camouflaged their guns with available vegetation and prepared them for battle. The men had been ordered to man their crew stations. And, as before, there was no information regarding the situation on the Bolva River line.

As a young, still-green lieutenant I was somewhat nervous. The unknown always arouses concern. A superior officer showed up in the battalion position; he was not from our brigade. We continued to sit in our Matildas, catching the sound of the nearby battle. We were looking in that direction as well. Enemy bombers had appeared over the forward edge. They went into a steep dive, and a series of aerial bomb explosions tore the air. The antiaircraft crews were firing continuously, and a single Ju-88 bomber careened into the ground.

About an hour later the scene that lay before me and my subordinates changed sharply, transposed into something that one could not imagine in his worst nightmare. Small groups of soldiers appeared in the buckwheat field some 900 meters ahead.

They were running toward us, clearly intending to seek cover in the forest. Some were carrying weapons, but the majority were unarmed. One need not be a military genius to understand that a Soviet Army infantry unit, unable to withstand the powerful enemy attack, had abandoned its positions. This was the first time I had ever witnessed such an unusual event. I had no idea what to do in such situations.

Several minutes later I received categorical instructions: fire at the retreating Soviet troops! I broke out in a feverish sweat. How could this be? Shoot at our own troops? The battalion commander came running up to my tank, and again he ordered, "Fire! fire with machine guns!"

An order is an order. It has to be carried out. With a breaking voice I gave the command. "First platoon, fire over the heads of the infantry! Second platoon, set up a fire screen in front of the retreating soldiers!

It came to me reflexively (perhaps I read it somewhere) that we could create a situation that would force the fleeing soldiers to stop running and hit the ground. This would give them time to catch their breath, look around, come to themselves, and finally recall their soldier's oath and analyze their actions.[2] The soldiers undoubtedly would be embarrassed by their display of weakness, after which it would not be particularly difficult for the commander to turn them around.

Six Bren coaxial machine guns tore the air with long bursts.[3] The stream of tracer bullets whistled over the unorganized formation of retreating troops. It started out high, then dropped lower and lower, pressing the troops downward. In front of the fleeing troops was a "fence" of mangled greenery and clods of dirt that had been created by the machine gun bursts. To fall into the beaten zone [the area upon which the cone of fire falls] would be a quick and certain death. The Brens chattered, and a leaden wind swept over the field. Like it or not, the soldiers had to stop running.

In the blink of an eye the panicked troops were forced to take cover by falling flat on the earth. That is what was required. I commanded, "Cease fire!" Quiet ensued; then suddenly several soldiers stood up and once again plunged toward the rear. First platoon's Brens barked in short bursts. The running soldiers flopped down again in the buckwheat. Several minutes passed with no signs of movement in the field. Then, finally, they understood that another step to the rear meant death. The infantry commanders appeared on the scene and barked out brusque commands. The infantrymen got up and made their way back toward the river in a straggling formation. As we discovered later, the tank machine-gun fire had struck seven soldiers, whom we left at their last, inglorious frontline position. This is the kind of death that came to some of the Soviet soldiers in that war.

My nerves were frazzled, and my head ached. I would not wish such a condition on my enemy. Half a century has passed since that incident, but every moment of the experience is deeply etched in my memory. By the will of fate and the order of Stalin, we had to execute the role of a barrier detachment: we were forced to use our weapons against our fellow soldiers.[4]

Replenishing our ammunition in the afternoon of that day, we carried out that routine task in complete silence. Words stuck in our throats because of what had just occurred. Our nerves were not yet fully relaxed. We needed time.

Then quickly came a new, second shock. What else would this day bring? Information came in, albeit late, concerning the situation on the Bolva River line. The enemy had launched a counterattack with significant forces, intending to hurl back our infantry units that had forced the water obstacle a short time earlier. The counterattacking forces not only had liquidated our small, unreinforced bridgehead but had also managed to rapidly cross the river line and capture a sector of the eastern bank. The panicked withdrawal of several infantry units described above was one of the sad outcomes of the battle.

The Germans immediately began engineer preparation of the terrain they had just seized—digging positions, emplacing mines, bringing up antitank guns. Our command made the decision to disrupt the enemy's plan, to destroy the German troops before they had substantially reinforced and prevent them from withdrawing to the opposite bank. The 2d Brigade of 5th Mechanized Corps, also Matilda-equipped, was assigned this mission.

By 1700 hours, the battle had flared up with renewed force. *Shturmoviki* made several bomb and cannon attacks against the Germans.[5] Artillery fired a barrage. Advancing along the river from north to south, motorized infantry and tanks of 2d Mechanized Brigade attacked the enemy's hurriedly occupied defense positions.

The sudden appearance of Soviet tanks and the rapidity of their actions had an immediate effect. The Germans, having realized the impending threat that their units on the east bank would be cut off from their main forces, began a hurried withdrawal of personnel and equipment to the west. But they ran out of time. Only an insignificant number of defending forces managed to accomplish this evacuation. The remaining Germans were defeated and captured.

Second Brigade received the order to return to its previously occupied assembly area. The brigade commander ordered his units to move independently to their earlier-held positions. He did not assemble them into a common march column. His directive was fully justified because it saved a significant amount of time—especially since the distance involved was short, all of two or three kilometers.

The company of Senior Lieutenant Knyazev was on the tank brigade formation's left flank during the counterattack.[6] This unit's most direct return route to its assembly area was across the buckwheat field, past the artillery unit and our own position. The company commander led his unit into harm's way by this shortest route.

The three lead Matildas appeared from behind a hillock and came straight across the field. A minute later we were staggered by what we saw: the muzzle flashes of artillery fire and two burning tanks. The guns were firing direct lay.[7] Three men from my company rushed over to the artillery unit. While they were running in that direction, the artillery unit managed to fire off a second volley. A third Matilda was stopped in its tracks, the rounds having disabled its suspension. The crews of Knyazev's company reacted appropriately, firing high-explosive rounds. Two artillery pieces were turned into twisted heaps of metal, their crews killed.

How long this senseless duel continued is difficult to say. We began to fire green rockets to signal "friendly troops." The artillery unit ceased firing. The tank cannons were also silenced. The exchange of fire was costly to both units: ten dead personnel, three tanks disabled, and two artillery pieces destroyed.

The artillery battery commander was beside himself. What

kind of shame for his unit—they had fired on their own troops! They had mistaken the Matildas for enemy tanks. The gun crews were not familiar with the silhouettes of the foreign vehicles that were present here. It was an enormous error on the part of higher headquarters.

At 1300 on 28 January 1944 a meeting of tankers of First and Second Ukrainian *Fronts* was convened in the center of Zvenigorodka. The goal of the operation—encirclement of a large enemy grouping in the Korsun-Shevchenkovskiy bulge—had been achieved.

For us Sherman tankers of 1st Battalion, 233d Tank Brigade, however, the joy of this great success was overshadowed by another event. Our battalion commander, Nikolay Maslyukov, had died. He was an excellent, experienced officer and a charming man. He had been killed instantly by a Soviet tank main-gun round.

This is how it happened. Maslyukov's Shermans were moving toward the town from the northwest. They had penetrated enemy defensive positions and advanced across an eighty-kilometer expanse of muddy chernozem fields and roads. Heavy main-gun fire eliminated the weak enemy infantry-artillery cover of the gravel road leading into Zvenigorodka. Maslyukov's men did not conserve ammunition. The situation demanded the most rapid arrival at the attack's final objective line.

Bursting into the town they used their tracks to crush the enemy and fired their machine guns in long bursts. Having seen enough of destroyed towns and villages, they attempted to minimize the damage done to buildings.

At this same time T-34s of 155th Brigade, 20th Tank Corps, Second Ukrainian *Front*, were rushing toward Zvenigorodka from the southeast. The crews of this unit had never laid eyes on a Sherman tank, nor had they ever heard the sound made by these vehicles that were now surging toward them. This was inexcusable negligence on the part of the staffs of the two *fronts*. Not much effort would have been required to inform the tankers of Second Ukrainian *Front* and provide them photographs or sketches of the M4A2. And the tragedy that resulted here might never have happened.

Six Shermans, all that remained of 1st Battalion, 233d Tank

Brigade, reached Zvenigorodka. Maslyukov sent them with their *avtomatchiki* along two parallel streets in order to attack the Germans on a broader front rather than from one axis only.[8]

Captain Maslyukov's tank and two tanks from Junior Lieutenant Petr Alimov's platoon skidded into the town's central square. Two T-34s rushed in from the opposite side. Maslyukov was exultant—the linkup of forward units of forces coming to meet each other had been accomplished. A distance of 800 meters separated the two units. Our 1st Battalion's commander began to report his current situation to the brigade commander. But as he uttered the words into his handset, communications were interrupted. An 85-mm antitank round, fired by one of the T-34s, passed right through the side of the Sherman. The tank erupted in fire. The captain and two members of the crew were killed.

The drama that had just been played out was a direct result of the T-34 crews' lack of awareness. They had not known that units of an adjacent *front* were equipped with foreign-made tanks. They had mistaken the Shermans for German tanks and opened fire.

Our Sherman crews shared some responsibility for the tragedy that occurred. Having seen the T-34s, they should have given the mutual recognition signal of two red rockets immediately, and not after the incident. Their mistake cost Maslyukov his life.

In the ideal situation, forces attacking in various directions toward the same point, or objective, should have radio procedures for mutual identification and reporting. By these means they can periodically exchange information regarding what line one or the other unit or formation has reached. This capability existed in the circumstance described here, for tankers of both *fronts*. But unfortunately they ignored it, and unjustifiable losses were the result.

Delayed Retribution

It was winter 1947, the second cold season of my service on Section 74 of the Transbaykal Railroad. I had submitted a request to attend the Frunze Military Academy and was awaiting the call for the selection examination.[1] After passing the exam, I would be put on the list of selectees for this prestigious institution of higher military learning.

One February day I received an unexpected telephone call from Guards Captain Ivan Reshnyak, the Chief of SMERSH of our 46th Guards Tank Brigade. Like me, he was a veteran of the unit. We had fought together in both Europe and the Far East. For someone who headed up this atypical organization, he was a remarkable man by everyday standards and a good comrade. He could resolve any issue, even the most complex and diverse—frequently without resorting to the use of the full legal authority of his office.[2] In all of this he did not use the "punishing sword" of the NKVD but was guided by common sense.[3] He loved to repeat the maxim that "Each man is needed for combat. Save him!"

"Dmitriy, drop by and see me, please!"

So I went. And speculated. *Why does he want to talk to me? Perhaps it is connected to a report on training.*

I stopped by Reshnyak's small office. He greeted me with a warm smile and a firm handshake. Then immediately he got down to business. "Dmitriy, do you remember a Senior Lieutenant Sergey Orlov who served as a platoon commander in your company in 1943?"

His question surprised me greatly. "How did you know this, Ivan, and why are you interested in this person?"

"He turned up recently, living in Ukraine. Listen to what information we have received in the brigade through our counterintelligence channels. They are asking you to corroborate what Orlov says. In late 1946 Senior Lieutenant Orlov went to a local military commission, presented his military identification documents that he had managed to retain in German PW [prisoner of war] camps, and told the following story:

"During the battles in September 1943 around the town of Roslavl [Smolensk oblast],[4] Orlov was a platoon commander in 1st Company [commanded by Dmitriy Loza] of 1st Battalion, 233d Tank Brigade, 5th Mechanized Corps. His Matilda tank was destroyed. The crew perished, and Orlov, though seriously wounded, was captured.

"Orlov was held in several different German concentration camps, but he escaped with a group of seven military personnel in March 1944. The Germans pursued them, killing four of the prisoners. The remaining three managed to survive. Orlov, one of these survivors, crossed the front line and made his way to the village of Rizino in Ukraine, where he stayed and lived as a regular citizen. His two fellow escaped prisoners returned to their homes. We have their addresses. Because Orlov's leg had been so seriously wounded that he could not bend it at the knee, he was no longer subject to be drafted into the army.[5]

"To the question as to why he had kept quiet for two years and had not contacted the military commission to report all this,[6] the senior lieutenant replied, 'I felt very bad. I did not believe I would live long. My wounds bothered me a great deal. I did not have the strength to conceal my past any longer. I came to lay out the whole truth about myself. It's up to you to decide my fate now.'"

I listened to Orlov's account and grew angry. Talking about enduring hardships, my former subordinate had suggested that after such a long and horrific war, probably no witnesses—not one officer or sergeant of his frontline tank unit—remained alive. How could these men have survived such a bloody battle using Matilda tanks, which had a maximum armor thickness of sixty to eighty millimeters? And he strongly conveyed this confidence that none of his former crewmates were alive to contradict his story. But in fact there were two witnesses. They knew the whole truth about those battles around Roslavl. And they recalled how this former platoon commander had conducted himself.

"What is your response to what you have heard, Dmitriy?"

"The dirty [unprintable, untranslatable obscenity] bastard!" I was hardly able to get the words out, but I continued to curse him.

Here is the incident I was compelled to recount in response to Ivan Reshnyak's question. There was only a small kernel of truth in Orlov's cock-and-bull story—the place and time of the battle, and the brigade and battalion designations. And he did not forget my full name and rank. All the rest was 100 percent lies.

On 17 September 1943, 233d Tank Brigade was committed to battle on the right bank of the Desna River. The offensive on Roslavl was developing slowly for two reasons: the enemy was offering stubborn resistance, and the Matilda tank turned out to be totally unsuitable for combat in swampy, forested terrain. These vehicles were intended for use in the deserts of Africa or other dry regions. Some not particularly smart thinker in Moscow decided to send 5th Mechanized Corps into terrain for which their equipment was absolutely inappropriate. Surely this person had no knowledge of the tactical and technical characteristics of the British tank.

In fact the Matilda's suspension was completely covered by side skirts that had a series of rectangular openings in the upper part. In the desert, the sand fell away from the tank through these holes. In the Smolensk forests and swamps, mud and tree parts became jammed together behind these skirts. The track was then practically immobilized by this congealed mixture. Even the tank's engine noise was muffled. We had to stop every four or five kilometers to clean out the suspension parts with a shovel or a stick.

We reached the village of Gobika, thirty-seven kilometers east of Roslavl, on the afternoon of 18 September. We got into a fierce fight at this settlement. Supported by my tank, our *desantniki* seized a portion of Gobika. The Germans were dug in on a hillock in the northern part of the settlement. We could not drive them out with the available forces, so we stopped and waited for reinforcements to be brought up.

Orlov's Matilda had settled into a marshy depression in one of the field gardens during the attack and was unable to recover itself. The vehicle was in the neutral zone between the German and the Soviet positions. We tried to get a tow cable out to the tank, but the enemy bracketed the recovery team with mortar fire, wounding two men. We had to abandon these efforts until the onset of darkness.

I ordered the senior lieutenant to set up an all-around defense for his tank while we awaited nightfall. I also ordered him to stay in continuous radio communication with my tank. Orlov followed my instructions to the letter, according to radio operator Sergeant Pavel Nichnik, who stood radio watch in Orlov's tank.

When evening came, we prepared a long towing line by hooking several tank tow cables together. With the arrival of darkness, this cable would be attached to Orlov's Matilda and another tank would quickly pull it from the soft ground. Everything was prepared for the recovery operation.

But firing suddenly broke out in the area of the mired tank: a Bren machine gun was being discharged in long bursts until an entire disk of cartridges was emptied, literally in only a few seconds. Then the firing stopped, as suddenly as it had begun.

I ordered my radio operator to call Orlov and find out what was happening with him and the reason that the machine gun had been fired—something so unusual for this situation. But Sergeant Nizhnik, who was standing radio watch in the turret of Orlov's tank, did not answer any of our calls. Then, several minutes later, Nizhnik called to my tank and reported something that made my hair stand up: "The commander has deserted to the Germans!"

He repeated this stunning phrase three times. I immediately reported this extraordinary incident to the battalion commander, and we quickly recovered the platoon commander's Matilda from the mud. The battalion counterintelligence officer then arrested the tank's crew. An investigation, which was initiated at that moment, revealed the following:

After receiving the company commander's order to establish immediate security of the mired tank, Orlov had the Bren machine gun removed from the turret. When dismounted from the tank, the Bren was placed on its own bipod, making it a good light machine gun for ground use. Each tank carried several loaded 100-round disks.

Orlov and the gun commander, Junior Sergeant Yakov Stroynov, moved some ten meters toward the enemy and took up a firing position behind a mound. The platoon commander ordered the driver-mechanic to remain behind the hull of the Matilda with his submachine gun. His sector of observation and fire was the left and right flanks of the tank. Sergeant Nizhnik, as earlier, stood radio watch in the tank's turret.

Gun commander Stroynov provided us more detail in his statement. After the machine gun had been positioned, Orlov ordered him to crawl back to the tank and return with two additional disks, indicating that the two they had brought with them were insufficient. Carrying out the commander's instructions, Stroynov made it to the tank and asked Nizhnik to hand down two disks. After he was given them, he turned toward the machine gun position in order to lay down on the ground and crawl toward the gun. The sky was beginning to darken.

He was dumbfounded by what he saw: the platoon commander was running toward the German positions with his arms raised. Stroynov immediately threw both magazines to the grass and rushed headlong to the machine gun. The enemy appeared to have fired several bursts at Orlov but missed—it's not so easy to hit a man zigzagging at a sprint. Stroynov dropped alongside the Bren from a dead run and pulled the charging handle back to commence firing. But the bolt was missing. He began to search frantically around the immediate area, and found the bolt ahead and to the right of the gun, on top of the ground.

He grabbed it and quickly reinstalled it. By this time, the platoon commander was approaching the enemy positions, with his arms still raised in the air. Stroynov squeezed the trigger and struck his target with a long burst. Orlov collapsed into a German outpost. In his nervousness Stroynov continued to squeeze the trigger until the machine gun fell silent, the disk empty of rounds.

The crew was removed from the tank and broken up. They were guilty of failing to prevent their commander's flight. But how could they have done so? The scoundrel had planned everything and dispersed his subordinates in such a manner that they could not see the initiation of his traitorous actions. He made only one stupid mistake—with the bolt. Had he taken it with him, Stroynov would have been totally disarmed.

Ivan Reshnyak listened attentively, not once interrupting my account. When I finished, he asked, "Dmitriy, do you know the subsequent fate of Orlov's crew? It would be good to find one witness!"

I smiled, a response that somewhat upset the captain. "I don't find this to be humorous! This is a serious matter. It will decide a person's fate!"

"Your service has done a good job. After so many years, they

tracked down a former tank company commander from 1943. I
have outlined for you, Ivan, the honest truth about that day so
unfortunate for my unit. We had just begun our combat path. But
I can provide you a witness, right now."

Reshnyak looked at me in surprise. "From where?"

"Pavel Nizhnik, the radio operator in Orlov's crew, is still in
the battalion today. He is the senior headquarters clerk."

"Call him in!" the captain almost shouted.

Five minutes later Guards Senior Sergeant Pavel Nizhnik
entered the office of the brigade SMERSH representative. Having
familiarized him with the documents he had earlier read to me,
Reshnyak asked Nizhnik to talk about what he knew concerning
the circumstances surrounding Orlov's desertion to the enemy.

There were no significant discrepancies between our accounts.
Reshnyak was satisfied. He made one request of us: to put down
in writing everything we had recounted to him and to provide it
to him within three or four days. This we did.

Some four to six weeks later Ivan Gregorevich called me.
"Dmitriy, get Nizhnik, and both of you come to my office. We
have interesting information about your former subordinate."

When we had seated ourselves in Reshnyak's office, he briefed
us from new materials obtained by brigade counterintelligence.
When they had showed Orlov our witnesses' statements, and he
then read them for himself, he turned white. He was silent for
several minutes, having lost the gift of speech. He understood
that he had been exposed. Credible, serious eyewitnesses had
been found. He was now in a hopeless position. Knowing what
kind of punishment awaited a traitor to the Motherland, he no
longer attempted to hide his "traitor's biography."

Sergey Orlov had been captured in mid-1942. The Germans
recruited him and sent him to an intelligence center near Berlin
for the necessary training. At the end of that same year he was
inserted into the Soviet Union through Iran. He arrived in Gorkiy
with documents from a hospital and was then sent to our 233d
Tank Brigade.

After surrendering on 18 September 1943, he was treated in a
German hospital for the wounds caused by Stroynov's machine
gun. For the subsequent eight months Orlov was trained in a
school for the preparation of intelligence agents designated for
postwar activation. A month later he was inserted into a con-

centration camp, from which his handlers organized his flight with a group of war prisoners. Several of the escapees were killed in the course of the pursuit, and three were left alive. This was testimony to the "courage" of this act by the officer-tanker, who had managed to break out of the German torture chambers and to assist several fellow countrymen in doing the same.

They had instructed Orlov to set up a living arrangement anywhere in the Soviet Union. Work extremely hard, they had told him. After the war was over, he was to report to a military commission and explain his capture as the result of his having been seriously wounded. Perhaps the Soviet officials would send him to a special camp for verification.[7] Having attained freedom, he was to continue to work honestly and sincerely. He would receive the appropriate orders telling him when he was to initiate his intelligence operation and specifying its nature.

Orlov's hour of retribution had arrived. Having betrayed his military oath and committed treason to the Motherland, he received the punishment established by law.

Shooting the Moon

The attack on Roslavl continued. The flight of Senior Lieutenant Sergey Orlov to the Germans weighed heavily on me. Counterintelligence personnel, meanwhile, continued to investigate Orlov's crew. My turn would come later. Perhaps continuous combat would prevent the summoning of a company commander to brigade headquarters.

It was 22 September. As we slowly advanced northward, 233d Tank Brigade units drove the enemy out of two small settlements that were important nodes of the German defense. Our continuing struggle for mobility in the soft terrain was not the only problem facing us. As the result of some twisted notion or oversight on the part of the logistic system, only armor-piercing rounds (solid-shot) were being brought forward for the Matilda's 40-mm main gun. The closest ammunition supply dumps did not have high-explosive rounds. Consequently we were unable to carry any of this type of ammunition in our basic load, and our units' combat capability was sharply reduced. With the main gun we could successfully engage only armored targets—and infantry targets only at the effective range of the machine guns. The Germans had no doubt been informed by the recently deserted Orlov concerning this significant tactical limitation in our units.

The picture on the battlefield unfolded almost humorously. Enemy infantry were being forced to the north along a country path across a potato field. My tank platoons continued to pursue them at slow speed, stopping frequently to clean mud, grass, and roots from our suspensions.

The distance between the Matildas and the enemy grew to somewhere between 800 and 900 meters. Tank machine guns were of little effect at this range. The situation was unique. The opposing sides were almost like peaceful neighbors to one another. The Germans were unhurriedly withdrawing into the depth of their lines without suffering losses from our fire. We were advancing behind them at a walking pace. Because of the terrain, we simply could not push our equipment any harder.

This "slow dance" could have continued for an indefinite number of kilometers. But the German troops soon accelerated the course of events.

A group of approximately ten Germans was walking along the field on the left side of the road. Two lanky soldiers from among them stopped and, dropping their trousers, began to display their pale white buttocks to us. It was as if to say, "You can't get us! Try to range us with the machine gun. You won't fire the main gun, Ivan, because all you have is armor-piercing rounds!"

This little display was acted out more than once. In bending over, a tall, skinny German even managed to thrust his head between his outstretched legs and curse at us with laughter.

In Ukraine this type of display of body parts where the legs begin is an insult of the highest order. Perhaps the tall, skinny soldier knew from Orlov that the tank company commander was a Ukrainian and had decided to provoke him to wrath, to make him seethe in anger.

My gun commander, Sergeant Yuriy Sloboda, repeatedly requested permission to teach the Germans a lesson. Each time I had to restrain him: "You can't shoot an armor-piercing round at every dismount! We have fifteen or sixteen rounds left in the tank and do not know when our next resupply will occur. Stay calm!"

Several tank commanders, all of whom were my countrymen, begged: "100 [my call sign], request permission to shoot these bums with main gun." My response remained unchanged: No!

Emboldened by their supposed immunity, the "actors" raised the stakes. They showed us countless views of their exposed parts, both front and rear. My patience was finally exhausted. "Yuriy, fire!" He had long awaited this command, knowing that sooner or later it would come. It would have been a sin not to give these pranksters what they deserved, if only to teach others not to engage in similar insulting behavior.

At the miscreants' next performance (this time there were three of them), Sloboda shouted to the driver-mechanic, "Stop!" The Matilda froze in place. Yuriy placed the crosshairs of his sight on the tallest German, who had a sufficiently broad rear end. The cannon barked. It was a direct hit into the wide area of his posterior. In the blink of an eye, one of the "actors" ceased to exist. Like the lick of a cow's tongue! The formless pieces of his body flew in various directions, concluding the "presentation." The "actors" who remained alive pulled up their trousers as quickly as they could and ran like deer.

We pushed the enemy troops until nightfall. They flowed away from us like a current. Now the German soldiers and officers had seen with their own eyes that it was not smart to taunt Soviet tankers.

The brigade's units renewed the attack on the second day. Roslavl was a stone's throw away. Enemy resistance grew markedly as the Germans managed to bring up reserves. My tank was hit at noon, and I was seriously wounded. I did not return to my unit for three months.

While I was recuperating, I often thought that being wounded allowed me to avoid an uncomfortable conversation and, possibly, punishment for the incident of Orlov's desertion from my company. In fact, despite the incident, the brigade and corps command awarded me the Order of the Patriot War 2d Degree for the ground combat.[1] My first combat decoration came at a high price.

Skill and Daring

It was 24 September 1943. The advancing Soviet forces were fighting their way to Roslavl. Each kilometer of movement required the expenditure of significant effort. The terrain was difficult (forest, swamp, and sparse road network), and the enemy offered fierce resistance, skillfully using the peculiarities of the terrain. The *Matildovtsy* experienced the greatest difficulty.[1] It was almost impossible for them to maneuver to bypass or outflank enemy nodes of resistance. All of these factors forced us to conduct frontal attacks, to attack the strongest aspect of the enemy's defenses. This tactic did not bring rapid success, however, and it was accompanied by appreciable losses.

Occasionally we managed to find a crack, a small break, in the Germans' combat formation. And the tankers, with the mission to move quickly into the rear of enemy strongholds and create a threat of a flank attack on them, hurried into these places without pausing. At the same time, these penetrations facilitated the actions of our own infantry and tanks attacking from the front.

In the afternoon the platoon (two Matildas) of Lieutenant Nikolay Averkiev managed to slip along a narrow, swampy forest road into the rear of an enemy position on a dominating hill. The platoon commander was attempting to penetrate deeper into the enemy-held terrain, to bypass both infantry and artillery positions and then fall upon the defenders from the rear. He coordinated his actions by radio ahead of time with the attack axis of the main body of 1st Battalion, 233d Tank Brigade. Combat practice had affirmed more than once the effectiveness of a daring raid on the enemy from two directions.

Averkiev's two tanks attempted to move stealthily in order to avoid exposing themselves unnecessarily. The abundance of trees, thickets, and bushes permitted such maneuvers. They reached the edge of a birch forest, along which wound a field track. Averkiev stopped his vehicles and ordered that the engines be shut down.

He wanted to study the terrain carefully, to choose a route that would permit them to attack the enemy's rear.

It was quiet all around. Two kilometers to the left was a wood-cutter's house with several smaller structures around it. They were deserted. There was not an enemy soldier in sight, a fact indicating that the Germans' defenses were shallow. Perhaps the enemy had concentrated all its forces and fire support assets in the stronghold on the hill.

The platoon commander caught the sound of an approaching diesel truck. It was coming from the rear toward the forward edge. Averkiev immediately drew up a plan: destroy the vehicle and capture a "tongue."[2] Having interrogated the prisoner, they could clarify the situation in this sector of the defense. But such luck was rare.

The lieutenant gave the necessary instructions to his gun commander for opening fire. He and his driver-mechanic, Sergeant Mikhail Zaika, moved forward from the tank about fifteen meters and lay down in some bushes. They were prepared to rush the vehicle and capture a crewman.

A heavily laden truck rounded a distant curve in the road. A minute or two passed. The target drew even with the commander's ambush point, precipitating a short burst of machine-gun fire from the tank. The three-ton truck's motor immediately burst into flames. The driver and his passenger jumped from the cab and fled into the roadside underbrush, straight into the arms of Averkiev and Zaika.

They began to interrogate the prisoners right there next to the tank. First of all, they demanded that the prisoners point out on a topographic map the disposition of the German units defending on the hill. These men were bringing up ammunition supplies and knew little themselves. But they were able to provide some information about the enemy—and, as everyone agrees, any scrap of information is better than none.

They had to hurry. The crews took their positions and fired up the Matildas' motors. Suddenly an enemy motorcyclist roared up at high speed from somewhere on the left. He shot past the tanks like an arrow and headed toward the front line. Averkiev cursed in anger. This unexpected observer had escaped, and surely he had seen the tanks. The planned surprise attack on the enemy's rear had been compromised.

In the developing situation the platoon commander made the only correct decision. Without wasting time, they had to move toward the enemy stronghold and attack it before the motor-cyclist's report reached the enemy headquarters and troops and before the defenders could undertake appropriate countermeasures.

Averkiev's two-tank platoon had not managed to move even 1,500 meters when three Ju-87 dive-bombers appeared in the sky above them, immediately flying toward the Soviet tanks. Undoubtedly the enemy pilots had complete information on the nature and the exact location of the targets. An unequal duel soon began—the maneuvering Ju-87s and the slow-moving Matildas. The tanks lacked any antiaircraft machine guns.

The lieutenant reported by radio to the 1st Battalion commander on the developing situation and his planned subsequent actions. With such a disproportion of forces, it was no longer feasible to consider attacking the enemy from the rear. Surprise had been completely lost. The number-one mission now facing the Matildas was to burrow into the forest as rapidly as possible and make it difficult for the German pilots to aim their bombs.

The Soviet troops would wait there under the green canopy until the German aircraft ran low on fuel. Of course, the dive-bombers would drop their bombs. But this would be an area strike and not a pinpoint attack on the target—a tank.

The tanks turned to the right on Averkiev's command. It was clear from the rapid reaction of the aircraft that these were experienced pilots. The enemy flight commander immediately discerned the tankers' intent. He dived his aircraft toward the ground to cut them off.

Showers of earth and debris from the high-explosive ordnance landing close by rained down on the front of the platoon commander's Matilda. The "Englishman" began turning in place to the left and then stopped.[3] Nikolay understood—the left track was broken. They could not repair it while under air attack. The second tank continued its flight toward the safety of the wood line, now thirty or forty meters away. A powerful explosion hurled the lieutenant to the turret floor, and he lost consciousness.

Dusk was beginning to fall when Averkiev regained consciousness. Something heavy was pressing on his chest. It was Sergeant Dmitriy Zelentsov. Nikolay carefully pushed the lifeless body out of the way. He took several deep breaths, then raised himself up. He wanted to help his fellow crewman, but the gun commander was dead. The platoon commander struggled to his feet with difficulty. Multicolored circles floated in his eyes. Leaning on the main-gun breech for support, he felt a sharp pain shoot through his left forearm, and his head was aching. Nikolay decided not to turn to the side for fear of losing consciousness again. Making a quick glance to the left, he saw a long wound, oozing blood, through the torn sleeve of his coveralls. Carefully sitting down, he pulled out his individual first-aid packet and tore it open with his teeth. He then found the end of the bandage and began to wrap his wounded arm. Such a simple task, one would imagine. But it took the platoon commander some time and much effort. He broke out in a sweat.

Averkiev stood up slowly, moved to his crew position in the commander's hatch, and raised his head outside the turret. He looked around. His glance fell on the hull of his Matilda. It was a horrible sight. Everything was smashed. Pieces of armor and engine had been thrown to the side. The second tank stood at the edge of the forest. The entire right-side suspension was gone. The grills had been blown upward. The vehicle had not managed to reach the green cover of the trees to hide there. "A direct hit from one, possibly two fragmentation bombs," the commander thought dejectedly.

His heart ached heavily at the sight as the ringing in his head grew louder. At times it seemed that grindstones were at work inside his skull. His thoughts were confused. Averkiev struggled to bring separate words together into a coherent chain of logic, not always successfully. He was nervous and remained quite confused. Nikolay learned later that he had suffered a concussion.

Suddenly he was overcome with worry. Where are the other two members of my crew, the driver and the radio operator? Concern for his combat comrades forced his brain to function more clearly. He could not see anyone. Without raising his head, the lieutenant called Mikhail Zaika's name. No one answered.

It was still somewhat light outside. Nikolay decided for the time being not to abandon the cover of the bombed-out tank. He did not want to give himself away. He would await the coming of night and then try to find some signs of his men. For now, he dropped down in the turret, where he retrieved a pair of binoculars. Once again he carefully stuck his head up and trained the binoculars on the woodcutter's house. Near the porch of the house he saw a German soldier, armed with a submachine gun, walking unhurriedly from the front of the house toward a small shed. It slowly dawned on him. A sentry! Nikolay inspected the area surrounding the woodcutter's house with the eight-power lenses but detected nothing of note. Once again he directed the field glasses to the house of the forest guardian, and he then almost dropped them. The door of the house opened abruptly, and a human form was thrown out onto the ground. The figure raised himself up to his feet. Mikhail Zaika!

Averkiev took a deep breath and became dizzy, even a bit nauseated. After gathering his strength, he continued to observe. An officer appeared on the threshold of the hut and gave an order to the guard, who then ran quickly over to Mikhail, poked him with the submachine gun barrel, and pointed with his hand to the shed. The Soviet driver-mechanic, still trying to find his legs, moved toward the structure and then disappeared inside it.

They have captured Mikhail! was the thought that flashed through Averkiev's mind. *They have tortured him, and now his life is in danger!*

These realizations, heavy as stones, in one moment pushed everything that had concerned the commander far into the background. He forgot about his wounded arm, and his headache subsided somewhat.

How can I help him? How can I get him out of harm's way? If only there were a pair of *Matildovtsy* nearby, then it would be possible to risk an attack on the woodcutter's house.

While he could still distinguish objects, Nikolay did not take the binoculars from his eyes but instead inspected all the corners of the forest worker's homestead and the approaches to it. For what reason? He did not know why himself. A car had already driven up to the house in the oncoming darkness and let out an officer. Two others accompanied him, and together they went into the building. The same guard with submachine gun remained at his post.

Averkiev conceived, considered, and rehearsed various scenarios of his actions. The forces were unequal. He had one substantial superiority, however: he knew almost everything about the enemy (where and how many there were), but the enemy were in total ignorance of him. This significantly reduced their superiority. To this fact had to be added the advantages of the night cover and the suddenness of his attack. As he laid them out, all these realizations led the lieutenant to the decision to attempt to save Zaika.

From this deciding moment, all the platoon commander's actions were directed at one thing—to prepare as quickly as possible for the task at hand. He had to secure his combat knife, find additional magazines for his TT pistol, and three "lemon" grenades.[4] He took some sugar and several pieces of sausage from the emergency ration supply—nourishment that he would need both to execute the intended mission and, in the event of its success, to bolster the strength of the driver-mechanic.

Averkiev hurried, forgetting his wound. Then, feeling some weakness and dizziness, he had to sit down and take a break. As much as possible, he had to conserve his energy. He still had to crawl over to the tank of Junior Lieutenant Viktor Shalov. Averkiev had found only one grenade in his own tank, and he could locate no spare magazines for the pistol—though he recalled that there had been some. They had disappeared somewhere. It was likely that the explosions of the aircraft bombs had thrown everything into disarray.

The lieutenant jumped to the ground and did not hear his feet touch the soil. He stomped his heel, yet his ears did not catch a sound. He carried out one more test. He placed his ear against the hull of the Matilda and tapped on the armor with the knife handle. Silence. A sad discovery—he was deaf! A substantial new obstacle had arisen. Even in this critical state, however, the platoon commander experienced no thought of changing the decision he had made.

Given the circumstances created by his deafness, he was forced to utilize the hunting skills he had mastered in his youth under the tutelage of his father. He needed them now as he had never needed them before.

Nikolay's father had been a tank officer. Captain Nikolay Petrovich Averkiev had served in many far-eastern garrisons in the prewar period. He was an ardent hunter and fisherman. As a rule, on his leave period he went into the taiga and hunted for wild game or fished in one of the countless rivers of the region. His constant companion in all of the expeditions was his son. Nikolay the senior took great delight in handing down the subtleties of hunting and fishing to his beloved son.

Major Nikolay Averkiev died in 1940 in the Soviet-Finnish War. Having finished secondary school and having decided to follow the same difficult path into combat that his late father had forged, Nikolay the junior entered First Saratov Tank Academy.

Hunting demands a cautious, quiet approach that does not disturb the vegetation. Averkiev might also have to wait some time to overpower the guard. *Don't hurry. Be patient.* When the moment came, he had to strike quickly and silently and then withdraw without leaving a trail for the enemy to follow. Night finally brought total darkness. The sky was overcast, and a gusty wind blew. The conditions were favorable for the venture to the woodcutter's house.

Before he set off toward Viktor Shalov's tank for grenades and pistol cartridges, the platoon commander decided to make a circle around his own Matilda to confirm the magnitude of the damage it had suffered. The conditions for inspection were the absolute worst—darkness. Literally in his first step Nikolay stumbled over the body of a man whose lower torso was under the tank's hull. He bent down, turned the corpse face up, and sighed. It was his radio operator, Sergeant Anatoliy Starykh. Alongside him lay his PPSh-41 submachine gun,[5] apparently destroyed by a grenade explosion, as well as scores of fired cases—physical evidence of the fierce fire exchange that had occurred here. Averkiev understood without any difficulty. Starykh and Zaika had fought with the enemy at the Matilda. Starykh had perished, and Zaika, no doubt wounded, had fallen into German hands.

The platoon commander conducted a quick inspection of his destroyed tank, then hurried over to Shalov's tank. The picture there was even more depressing. The engine and fighting compartments had been distorted by an explosion. None of the crew members remained alive. It was hopeless to look for anything in the tank. Everything had been scrambled by the bombs or blown outside the tank.

Thus had the platoon commander collected confirmed data for his daily report: two Matildas were unrecoverable losses, six tankers were killed and one captured, one solitary "active bayonet" remained in the combat formation.[6] It was unpleasant arithmetic.

Defeat in battle depresses people who are weak in spirit. They throw up their hands. In contrast, defeat mobilizes strong people. It forces them to consider and analyze the cause of the miscalculation or mistake that has occurred and in the future to undertake measures that will prevent a similar situation from arising in an engagement with the enemy. Averkiev belonged to the second category of frontline soldiers.

He immediately closed the book on this problem and began mentally to make time calculations. It was the last week of September. Night lasted for eight hours. He had already used about ninety minutes in contemplating and preparing for the execution of his plan. Six and one-half hours of limited visibility remained. He had to anticipate that he would spend no less than half of that time in reaching the location, studying the situation there, and completing the action itself: taking out the guard and liberating Mikhail. If this most critical part of his work were to be drawn out for any reason, that would not be so terrible. Dawn would not arrive quickly.

Averkiev took a compass heading to the woodcutter's house and set off. He went deep into the woods and somewhat to the right in order to approach the homestead from the side where the wind would blow from the enemy into his face. He moved along in a somewhat subdued manner, not creating even the smallest noise with his footfalls or breathing.

At last he was about fifty meters from the home site, in the final departure position. Had Nikolay not become deaf, from here he could have listened for everything. In his present condition, however, his hope lay in his sight. Yet at this distance and in the darkness he could see little. He lay down and rested. The first task was to await the changing of the guard. He did not know when the current guard had assumed the post. And until he did, he could not launch his attack.

Like a grass snake, he moved on his stomach toward the shed where his driver-mechanic was being held. From here he could well see the whole area of the yard. One thing remained—patience, the iron self-possession to wait, clenching his teeth, for the decisive moment. He would attack in the first minutes of the new guard's watch. Averkiev studied his route. There was an additional factor in his favor. The man coming out of the building would need a bit of time for his eyes to adapt to the darkness. The platoon commander would select a place for the attack on the German that took all of this into account. He would bring down the guard with one precise blow with a silent weapon, his combat knife. His hand had not lost the skill it acquired long ago.

It was as if time had stopped. The wind gusts strengthened. Even the weather was helping to execute Averkiev's plan. The lieutenant was calm, vigilantly monitoring the steps of the German near the house. The guard was looking at his watch more frequently now, a sure sign that he would soon be replaced.

Time was up! The house door opened, and beams of diffused light fell on the porch floor. Out came a soldier with a submachine gun. He was below average in height. After exchanging a few words with the guard on duty, he assumed the post, and the relieved guard disappeared into the house.

The new guard continued to stand in place. He seemed to be thinking about something. After several minutes he headed toward the shed with an unsteady stride. Averkiev remarked to himself that Fritz had been sipping schnapps.[7] All the better!

The German looked back at the house and then went around the corner of the shed. He stopped and began to prepare to urinate. He turned his face toward Nikolay, away from the wind so he would not spray on himself. The submachine gun hung loosely on his shoulder. The guard's position was not advantageous to a sudden attack. Averkiev needed to wait a bit longer, until the German turned his back. Then, with an almost noiseless rush in two steps, Averkiev would grab the guard's neck with his left hand and thrust the knife under his left shoulder blade. Finally the new guard finished his business and turned around slowly to walk into the yard. The platoon commander counted the seconds and then dispatched the guard. He now held the German submachine gun and two loaded magazines in his hands—it was crucial firepower reinforcement.

The Soviet lieutenant's subsequent actions occurred at a rapid tempo. He crawled to the shed doors. Finding a small crack in them, he quietly but clearly whispered, "Misha, it's me, Nikolay.[8] Listen to me closely. Do not answer. I cannot hear you because I am deaf. I have taken the guard out. Take my combat knife [he slipped it under the door]. Try to cut your way free through the [thatch] roof as quickly as possible. I'll be behind the shed to the left. I'll cover you with my trophy submachine gun. Work quietly!"

The tense and worried platoon commander waited thirty, perhaps forty, minutes. He lost track of time. He could do nothing to help his comrade but be on the alert for approaching Germans.

The chance to be free gave the wounded Mikhail, whom the Germans had also tortured, incredible strength. Scraping with the knife and his hands, he managed to cut away a corner of the roof and crawl outside through the resulting hole. He could not drop to the ground directly because of his exhaustion and the pain from the wound in his side. Minutes later he was hanging by his hands, and Averkiev was standing under him. The driver-mechanic sat on the shoulders of his commander, who then lowered him to the ground. After they embraced each other firmly, Nikolay slipped the TT pistol and F-1 grenade into Mikhail's hands. Now both tankers were armed.

"Quick, Misha, let's get out of here. Follow me!"

More than seventy minutes would pass until the next changing of the guard. During this interval Nikolay and Mikhail had to move off into the forest, away from the woodcutter's hut. When they reached a forest thicket, they would decide whether to continue their flight immediately or rest for a time. It depended on the physical condition of them both.

Mikhail determined the direction to the line of contact between the two enemies by the sounds of an artillery barrage that he could hear. It was about four kilometers distant. He had to explain this information to the platoon commander by using his fingers. Moving through unobstructed woods (exclusively through open places), it would take at least two hours for them to walk this distance. If they took a short rest break now, they should be able to make it to the forward edge by dawn. That seemed to be their best option. The lieutenant made all these calculations and musings aloud so that he would not lose valuable time explaining them to Mikhail.

"Misha, no matter how difficult it is because we are both wounded, we cannot stop! Our salvation is in movement. It is better to cross the front line in darkness. Do you agree?"

Zaika nodded his head.

"Then let's get to it! First, let's rebandage each other. Second, we'll eat something—two pieces of sugar and a slice of sausage for each of us. For dessert we'll eat some berries. We can still find them in the woods."

Zaika's wounds looked repulsive. Gangrene was setting in, and his left side was beginning to swell. The commander had a single field-dressing packet, which he gave to his subordinate. For himself, he tore his undershirt for a bandage. As much as they needed the ammunition, they pulled two bullets from German submachine gun cartridges and sprinkled the powder on their wounds. They had no other form of medication to use, and Russian soldiers had done this from time immemorial—gun powder was a good disinfectant.

The two men took not more than ten minutes in treating their wounds and then went back to the task at hand. They could munch on the sugar, eat a slice of sausage, and gather berries on the move. They maintained their azimuth to the forward edge by compass.

The two wounded *Matildovtsy* walked along paths and forced their way through forest thickets. After walking two kilometers they were exhausted but did not slow their pace. Then, sixty or seventy meters ahead of them was a clearing. On the opposite side of it they could make out the silhouette of a van—a mobile repair detachment—and a Panzer IV tank. Averkiev's heart raced and his eyes lit up. Leaning over to his driver-mechanic, he feverishly whispered, "Mikhail, I am not ordering, I am asking you. You have the right to refuse. Can we capture the tank? We could speed across the front line quickly on it!" Zaika agreed with enthusiasm.

"It seems to me that we have to go back into the woods a bit and come around the right side of the field so that we come out on the enemy's downwind side. This will give you the best opportunity to hear the conversations and activities of the German soldiers. Meanwhile, I'll crawl toward the tank on my stomach and inspect it. It may be disabled. In that case, we'll have to change our plan. I'll come back, and we'll continue our travel on foot."

Mikhail heard the squeaking of a door opening at the maintenance site. He grabbed Averkiev's hand and pressed it tightly. The platoon commander stopped talking. A German came out of the van, turned on a flashlight, and headed toward the Panzer IV. He disappeared inside and then shortly went back to the van.

The lieutenant continued explaining his plan. "If the tank is functional, I'll give a signal with the flashlight. Come toward me immediately. Be careful and pay attention! Now, about our actions at the tank. Jump into the driver's position and get ready to fire up the engine. When everything is set, I'll give you a hand signal. I'll be running toward the maintenance van. You start the engine. At that instant I'll open the door to the van and throw in the hand grenade. I'll run back to the tank, climb up on the front slope, and jump into the turret. We'll move out. I'll be prepared to open fire with the submachine gun at anyone who comes out of the maintenance van."

The two men captured the German tank with precision and ease. As it turned out, the tank had arrived at the field maintenance point only a short time earlier, and its engine had not even cooled down yet. Averkiev did not have to fire the trophy submachine gun during their escape: the exploding grenade killed or seriously wounded all the Germans in the maintenance van. No one came through the door.

The *Matildovtsy* understood. The single decisive period of their sojourn in the enemy's rear was approaching. The moment of balancing on the edge of mortal danger had arrived. There was no longer a great threat to them from the enemy entrenchments; the German troops would view these Soviet tankers in a German tank as their own. The problem for Nikolay and Mikhail was how to get across the forward edge so that their own Soviet antitank artillery would not fire at the Panzer IV. It would be ironic for them to die in the last stretch of such an adventure.

Having captured the German tank, the two Soviet tankers undertook some measures to present themselves as Germans. Zaika put on the German driver-mechanic's helmet and extended only the upper portion of his head out of the driver's hatch. Averkiev stayed inside the turret, not exposing himself. He had to get the weapons ready for action: he loaded the main gun with a high-explosive round and put a belt in the coaxial machine gun.

They came out onto a road and headed south toward the forward edge at maximum speed. They encountered heavy and light truck traffic, passing it without incident. The platoon commander inspected the surrounding terrain in the tank commander's periscope. On the left in a depression was a mortar position. On the right on the hill were bunkers. Infantry were walking about.

The density of enemy personnel and combat equipment grew with each hundred meters the two Soviets progressed. Soon they would see the marker separating the opposing sides.

A German soldier suddenly appeared in the curve of the paved country road. He waved his arms and then formed a cross with them. The road beyond this point was closed.

And so the critical moment had arrived. Averkiev and Zaika began a series of unusual actions with the intent of convincing the Soviet antitank gunners up ahead not to open fire on the German Panzer IV coming toward their positions.

Mikhail stepped on the gas, and the tank surged forward. Quickly rotating the turret 180 degrees, Nikolay fired the main gun at the German stronghold. Mass confusion ensued. Someone fired a *panzerfaust* at the fleeing tank, but it missed.[9] The platoon commander then ordered his driver-mechanic to maneuver in a zigzag fashion while he himself fired the coaxial machine gun. As the vehicle slewed right and left, the machine-gun bullets were dispersed over a large area behind the tank.

"The German tank is firing into its own position!" the cry went up in from the Soviet troops. "It's crazy! A deserter!" The Soviet antitank gun crews rushed to their guns, and a command rang out to commence firing. In seconds, there was a salvo. Dense explosions covered the German defensive positions. The artillery battery commander quickly gave instructions to prepare to fire smoke rounds. The next volley created a smoke screen behind the Panzer IV, blinding the enemy antitank gunners.

Seeing the protective cover from the Soviet side, the lieutenant ceased machine-gun fire and came up out of the turret. He began to shout at the top of his lungs, "We are yours! Don't shoot!"

Zaika drove the tank into a gully. Averkiev ordered him to stop and shut down the engine. With heavy mortars the Germans briefly plastered the area where the tank had disappeared from their view. Then quiet descended on the scene. On the German side, the soldiers were probably beginning to search for the crew whose tank had been taken over to the Russians. On our side, after firing had ceased, *avtomatchiki* immediately surrounded the tank. The platoon commander extracted himself from the turret with difficulty and jumped down to the ground. Infantry soldiers looked with amazement at the "German." Nikolay was barely able to talk. "We are Soviet tankers!"

Two commanders—one from the rifle company that was defending this sector and the other from the artillery battery—came running over. These two officers, who had quickly understood the actions of the Panzer IV crew racing toward their position, began to interrogate the lieutenant. "Do not question me. I cannot hear you. I am deaf! We will tell you everything later. But now, help my driver-mechanic crawl out of the tank. We are both wounded and in need of medical attention."

The two German tank thieves were in the regimental aid station all day on 25 September. Medical personnel changed their bandages and fed them. They wanted to send the tankers to a hospital, but Averkiev insisted that the tank brigade commander be informed of their whereabouts. In the evening a brigade light vehicle arrived at the rifle regiment and took the men back to their unit.

When the commander of 5th Mechanized Corps, General Mikhail Volkov, learned of the feat of these two foreign-vehicle tankers,[10] he ordered his staff immediately to draw up award recommendations for both men—for the Order of the Patriotic War 1st Degree. Volkov personally decorated the lieutenant at the battalion aid station. The deputy tank brigade commander, Colonel Pavel Shulmeyster, decorated Zaika in the hospital.

The subsequent fate of the two *Matildovtsy* is worth noting. After his recuperation, Mikhail Zaika did not return to the unit for some reason. At his own request, Nikolay Averkiev went to the corps medical treatment facility. During his two weeks there, in his own words, "I had enough of smelling medications and lying around." He quickly returned to his own 1st Tank Battalion and died in fierce combat around Smolensk in October 1943.

Flamethrower Tanks

One of the lesser-known tools in the arsenal of the Red
Army during the Great Patriotic War was the flamethrower tank.
This weapon, which did not enjoy a long life on the battlefield,
has been treated like a stepchild in the literature of the war.[1]
Flamethrower tanks, however, did make a contribution to the
defeat of the enemy.

The type-1942 automatic tank flamethrower [*ATO-42—avto-
maticheskiy tankovoy ognemet*] was mounted on two types of
tanks. On the T-34 it was contained in the front portion of the
hull, and on the KV-series tanks it was positioned in the turret as
an additional armament. The reservoir with flame mixture was
located inside the hull, taking up about one-half of the storage
space normally given to the basic load of main-gun rounds.

The T-34 flamethrower tank carried two hundred liters of
flame mixture, enabling the tank to fire twenty shots at ten liters
of mixture each. Mounted on the KV-series tanks, the flamethrower had sufficient mixture for fifty-seven shots. Both flamethrowers were capable of firing rapid successive shots, to a maximum range of 100 to 120 meters. The driver-mechanic controlled
the weapon on the T-34, and the gunner on the KV tank. The
ATO-42 was intended for use against exposed or covered enemy
personnel and military equipment.

During the war five separate flamethrower tank battalions and
one separate flamethrower tank brigade were established. Each
battalion was equipped with twenty-one tanks and the brigade
with fifty-nine. Operating under the authority of the Reserve
of the Supreme High Command [*RVGK—reserv verkhovnogo
glavnokomandovaniya*], these units served to reinforce various
formations—as a rule on the axes of main attacks in offensive
operations, but they could also be used in the defense.

Decades have passed since the Great Patriotic War. Lieutenant
General (Retired) Vasiliy Gerasimovich Reznichenko clearly
recalls each battle of that war in which his tanks employed this

weapon.[2] [The remainder of this chapter is told in the voice of Lieutenant General Reznichenko.]

It was early November in 1942. The 511th Separate Flamethrower Tank Battalion was assigned to the 5th Tank Army of Southwest *Front*. The unit was ordered to occupy an assembly area on the south side of the Don River, southwest of Serafimovich (see map 2). Along with 8th Guards Tank Brigade, our flamethrower tank battalion was ordered to support one of the army's rifle divisions. The army's mission was to break through the positions of the defending 3d Romanian Army.

It should be noted that the flamethrower tank battalion was to operate jointly with conventional tanks, comprising the second line of the armored combat formation. It was not considered wise to employ them separately because of their inability to accommodate a regular load of main-gun ammunition. In addition, during this period of the war the tank army contained a mixture of several dismounted rifle divisions in addition to the tank corps. This enormous complement possessed little mobility and was difficult to command and control. Later in the war, all the rifle divisions were removed from the tank army—a measure that greatly improved the maneuverability of the remaining reduced force.

Preparation for the upcoming offensive was conducted with the strictest possible observance of all camouflage and security measures. We were striving for the utmost secrecy.

We received our combat mission on the night of 19 November. In the morning they read to us the proclamation of the Southwest *Front*'s military council.[3] A powerful eighty-minute artillery preparation began at 0730. Amidst the thunder of exploding shells during the unfolding of our unit colors, the tankers and infantry uttered their pledges to defeat the hated enemy. This was the beginning of the long-awaited Stalingrad counteroffensive.

The sudden hurricane of fire, especially from the multiple rocket launchers, demoralized the Romanian soldiers and officers. Soviet infantry units, reinforced by tanks, surged forward. Enemy guns and machine guns, having given away their firing positions with their first volleys, were destroyed. One of the enemy strongholds was offering stubborn resistance. It was equipped with full-profile trenches for the soldiers and good firing positions for its supporting guns. Apparently no great losses of men and equipment had occurred here during the Soviet artillery preparation. The destruction of this entrenchment could become a protracted struggle that, in turn, could slow the tempo of our entire offensive.

The division commander decided to call upon the full power of the flamethrower tank battalion. Carrying out his order, 511th Battalion, supported by eight ground-support aircraft, moved forward a short distance. The tanks covered the enemy positions with two salvos of burning mixture. The effect was staggering. The tanks had set afire everything that could burn. Enemy officers and soldiers who had not been killed on the spot fled in panic and confusion. The offensive then continued at its previous fast pace. The flamethrower battalion lost none of its twenty-one tanks. The attacking force had broken through two enemy defensive positions in a short period of time.

The situation required a strengthening of the force of the main attack and a more rapid penetration of the enemy's tactical defensive zone, however. The army commander committed his mobile group—1st and 26th Tank Corps—to the battle. Their mission, in cooperation with mechanized and tank formations of the neighboring Don *Front*, was to move rapidly in the general direction of Kalach to encircle the enemy's Stalingrad grouping.

The mobile group broke into the enemy disposition to a depth of approximately thirty kilometers on the first day of the offensive. At dawn on 20 November, 26th Tank Corps broke through to Perelazovskiy.

To block the subsequent advance of Soviet forces, the German command launched two counterattacks—one at the right flank with forces of the German 22d Panzer and Romanian 1st Armored Divisions, and the second at the left flank with the German 14th Panzer Division.

Heavy fighting erupted between Medvezhiy and Perelazovskiy. Two rifle divisions, 8th Guards Tank Brigade, and our 511th Flamethrower Tank Battalion were operating here. We became engaged in combat for Bolshaya Donshchina. Unfortunately the difficult situation in this particular sector forced the attack by conventional tanks and flamethrower tanks to be conducted in a disjointed fashion. The result was the rapid loss of eight Soviet flamethrower tanks.

The 5th Tank Army commander, Lieutenant General Pavel

Romanenko, left the infantry by themselves to cover the flank and ordered the separate flamethrower battalion to disengage on the night of 22 November and assemble in the Ust-Medveditskiy *sovkhoz*.[4] We worked over the course of the next several hours to bring our unit strength back up.

Our men knew that this pause would be brief and there might be no rest. We immediately set about repairing our vehicles, checking all joints and connections, and filling our tanks with flame mixture. We worked at full speed, hoping to catch an hour or two of sleep after we had finished. It did not happen.

Artillery and tank main-gun fires rained down on our assembly area at dawn from behind the small hills that surrounded the *sovkhoz* settlement. We responded in kind and quickly began to prepare to defend against the full attack we anticipated.

The battalion command did not have the slightest idea of the enemy's strength. Who was in front of us? How many of them? Where might the enemy appear next? We were totally in the dark, though we knew one thing for sure: by this time the forward units of 26th Tank Corps were arriving at their crossing points on the Don River near Kalach.

We sent out dismounted reconnaissance to the hills and nervously awaited their return. An unknown situation is always troubling. The command was striving to clarify the situation as quickly as possible. The army commander General Romanenko and a member of his military council appeared at the battalion's command post at approximately 0800 hours. Romanenko demanded to know whom we were about to attack. We were unable to provide him with an intelligible answer.

"Could you be engaging some of our own forces?" the general asked. "A tank corps is coming to us from the reserve." He then ordered us to send a tank platoon out on reconnaissance and have it report back to him. He would wait. Being a senior lieutenant, I was ordered to command this reconnaissance.

The army commander issued a last-minute instruction to me: "Do not fire first! They might be our forces."

Our unit had few fully combat-capable tanks. We selected the best we could find, including the tank of the battalion commander, Major Vladimir Trukhanov. I climbed up into the turret. Driving the tank was the experienced driver-mechanic Sergeant Mikhail Kostin. During World War I the phrase was born and often confirmed, "A seasoned soldier is more valuable than a 200-carat diamond!"[5]

Ten minutes later we left on our assigned reconnaissance mission, and almost immediately we ran into trouble. The terrain was covered in high steppe grasses, with a thick layering of snow. As we moved out across this ground, the tracks threw the snow up and all around our tanks in thick white clouds. This snow quickly covered the periscopes, blinding the drivers. I ordered all tank commanders to open their turret hatches and, standing up in their turrets, guide their driver-mechanics using their intercoms. We pushed forward.

We approached the hills, then watched as the lead tank with *desantniki* aboard, still raising clouds of snow all around it, dropped down into a large depression. In front of us was an array of artillery pieces, all in position. We counted the guns—no fewer than a battalion. All the gun crews were wearing white camouflage smocks. *Ours!* I thought. *This is probably the reserve unit that has come forward during the night.*

I was totally mistaken in my deduction, however. The artillerymen fired on us at almost point-blank range. Perhaps the shroud of snow around our tanks prevented their gunners from aiming accurately, or they were not a well-trained unit. But they did not destroy a single tank. Nonetheless it was clear that the troops giving us this "hot" reception were hardly our own.

My own crew did suffer losses. An enemy high-explosive round struck the upper right edge of my turret, sending shrapnel in all directions. One piece killed my loader, and another wounded me on the bridge of my nose. At the moment of impact we both had been standing half-exposed in the open hatch, looking at the terrain and helping Sergeant Kostin drive the tank through the high grass.

On my command, the platoon immediately deployed into a battle line and began firing main guns from short halts. I was able to get off only one shot. My driver-mechanic was begging me for guidance. He could not see where he was going because his vision block was still obscured by the snow. I had to stop firing and give directions to Sergeant Kostin.[6]

Unfortunately, only one of our T-34s had a functional flamethrower. But it played an important role in defeating the enemy as its fiery stream struck the closest enemy gun, burning the crew alive. Panic ensued among other enemy cannoneers, and they fled for their lives in all directions. We used our machine guns and in some cases our tank tracks to finish the fight with them. We captured a seriously wounded Romanian officer. He told me that a group of tanks, an infantry platoon, and the artillery battalion had been left behind to cover the withdrawal of the moderately damaged 1st Romanian Armored Division. The tankers and infantrymen had abandoned the position without orders, leaving the artillerymen to fend for themselves.

Twenty minutes later my platoon returned to Ust-Medvedinskiy. I reported the results of the reconnaissance to the army commander, who thanked us for our rapid and successful execution of the mission. Having ordered the battalion commander to submit award recommendations for my men, he sent me to the aid station.

After the Stalingrad and Kursk battles, the front moved westward, into the Donbas area. The 511th Separate Flamethrower Tank Battalion off-loaded at Rovenka station and assembled in the town of Avrosimovka on 25 August 1943. It was placed at the disposal of the commander, 2d Guards Army, of Southern *Front.* During the period of combat actions, the battalion was further subordinated to 3d Guards Rifle Division, commanded by General Kontemir Aleksandrovich Tsalikov.

By evening of the following day the battalion occupied start positions along the railroad right of way. A belt of trees, planted to keep snow from drifting onto the tracks, extended along both sides of the road bed.

The forward edge of the enemy's defense followed the Mokriy Elanchik River in the zone of the division's attack. The village of Bogachevka was to our right, and the enemy had built a reinforced stronghold in the village of Vasilevka to our left (see map 3).

After a brief artillery preparation at dawn on 27 August, the flamethrower tanks moved out in an attack line with the infantry. Of course it would have been better had they also been accompanied by conventional T-34s. The battalion commander, Captain Dmitriy Savochkin, used a small deception: he ordered his tank commanders to use only their cannons and machine guns against enemy targets and not to employ their flame weapons until he gave the command. This was a wise decision. It preserved the surface and shock of the presence of the flamethrowers, which were most effective at direct-fire ranges of 100 to 120 meters.

Supported by our tank fires, the infantry boldly attacked the enemy's forward positions and broke into the first trench line, quickly suppressing individual nodes of enemy resistance. We slowly ground our way into the depth of the enemy's disposition, to the second and finally the third lines of trenches and dugouts, where the resistance began to stiffen. Now, on command, the tankers utilized their flamethrowers while moving forward. The appearance of these weapons stunned the enemy: a great number of the remaining machine-gun and antitank-gun crews were killed, and though many who remained alive attempted to flee to the rear, bursts of fire from the tanks' Degtyarevs forced them to the ground.[7] We now had broken entirely through the enemy's first position.

Our battalion continued to advance without slowing down. We had to develop the success that we had achieved into the depth of the enemy's defense. At the same time, the enemy was using artillery fire to delay our unit's advance. Frequent shell explosions covered the battalion's left flank (Captain Vasiliy Lvov's company), and cannons fired from the village of Vasilevka. These were enemy tanks firing solid-shot rounds, setting four T-34s on fire. We also suffered personnel losses: the battalion commander and Captain Lvov were wounded, and two platoon commanders, two driver-mechanics, three other crewmen, and the battalion sergeant major were killed. We were paying a high price for the use of flamethrower tanks without conventional tank support. Our tanks, with their limited storage capacity for conventional ammunition, simply could not maintain a high volume of fire for any protracted period of time.

The situation was also worsening on the right flank. Several vehicles of Senior Lieutenant Boris Radchenko's company had become mired at the bank of the Mokriy Elanchik River. The progress of the battalion's combat formation was slowing, threatening to bring the entire attack to a halt. Something had to be done—and quickly: I contacted the artillery forward observers. They determined the location of the targets in Vasilevka, the defending enemy's main node of resistance.

A short time later the contrails of multiple-launched Katyusha rockets marked the sky.[8] Seconds later we heard the sounds of these rockets exploding in Vasilevka and beyond. Conventional supporting artillery also began to pound the target area, enveloping the enemy stronghold in smoke and flames. Several German tanks were set on fire. The remaining German tank crews, fearing another Katyusha salvo, hurriedly abandoned their positions.

After breaking through the German stronghold, we began to push our attack deeper into their territory, though with considerable losses. The combat between the Mius and Kalmius Rivers, and at the Kalmius River itself, was exceptionally fierce.

Infantry units of 3d Guards Division and the flamethrower tank battalion reached the near approaches to Section Five of the "Metallist" *sovkhoz* and the small village of Stalino. The Germans had managed to organize a hasty defense at this line, having deployed a significant number of weapons of various types, the site being the enemy's initial position for covering the approaches to the river line. The river itself, which was a stone's throw away, did not present a serious obstacle for our tanks. They could easily ford it.

During a brief pause in the advance, reconnaissance primarily by observation established the situation. The opposite bank of the river line was high and steep, with an antitank ditch along the bottom land. The broken outline of trenches could be seen on the hills beyond the river. In front of them was barbed wire, probably covering minefields.

Our troops could not overcome defenses like these from the march. We needed time to bring forward to this position all the men and equipment that were required for us to complete the breakthrough and organize a deliberate attack. The regiments of 3d Guards Rifle Division and our battalion began preparation for the upcoming battle on the Kalmius River.

The topography of the land on the opposite bank and the large number of enemy forces in strongholds on the *sovkhoz* and in Stalino did not promise us an easy victory. We had to anticipate that the battle would be protracted and fierce. All the commanders, from the platoon leaders on up, understood this fact well. We had to find some unique, unconventional method of action, and we had to accomplish the mission with the fewest possible losses. Officers of all ranks were required to preserve the lives of the troops to the greatest possible degree.

General Tsalikov found a way out of this difficult situation—the use of deception. The general's divisional reconnaissance had determined that the enemy's left flank was less strongly defended. Tsalikov's plan therefore was to make it appear to the enemy that he was moving his troops and equipment to a new axis of attack, farther to the right. Using the darkness of the night and violating security to some degree, he accomplished this charade by repositioning division second-echelon units, prime movers, and flamethrower tanks whose armaments were inoperative.

The Germans—believing that this movement was an actual redeployment and that the Soviet attack would come against the weak spot in their defense—in turn began to reposition their own men and weaponry to their left flank. In making this counter-move, they weakened the very sector where our commander intended to break through the enemy position. We had accomplished our goal.

The salvos of guns firing a brief artillery preparation along the entire zone of 3d Guards Division's attack broke the relative calm at dawn on 29 August. Infantry units and the flamethrower tanks rushed toward the river. The artillerymen now concentrated the entire weight of their fires on the forward edge, attempting to destroy enemy antitank weapons and machine guns. This would ensure the most rapid forcing of the water obstacle by the attacking echelon.

The dry summer weather caused our artillery rounds to raise up thick clouds of dust when they hit the ground, creating a dense screen in front of the attacking forces. Enemy troops returning fire in the immediate area were completely blinded. The situation also placed Soviet tankers in a difficult position, obscuring their targets.

Having forced the river, the flamethrower units reached their effective range. They fired short bursts again and again, and tongues of flame licked at the first trench line. Rivers of fire raced along the surface of the ground. Flame mixture flowed into the engineer works and burned everyone inside. One had to witness this horrific scene to understand the terror it created among the enemy troops.

When this red and black savagery began to subside somewhat, the battalion commander issued a new order: "Two short bursts!"

A subsequent death-dealing wave of fire struck the second line of trenches and dugouts. The attacking infantry moved carefully behind the flamethrowers, not meeting any resistance. The charred German corpses represented no threat to them now.

The enemy defenses had been broken, a fact that occasioned the decisive moment of the attack. The victory had to be exploited. Without losing valuable time, we had to penetrate into the depth of the enemy disposition. General Tsalikov issued an order. The rifle regiment, flamethrower battalion, and artillery battalion would comprise the division forward detachment. Destroying the enemy's remaining nodes of resistance and pursuing its retreating units, the forward detachment was to capture several sections of the large railroad junction and the station at Volnovakha from the march. This was a difficult mission.

The complication in this particular case lay in the fact that the different components of the forward detachment varied significantly in the speeds at which they were able to move. The tanks and artillery were more or less equal to one another in this regard, but the dismounted infantry was an altogether different story—if a concerted advance were to be attempted, their slower pace would delay the forward detachment's arrival at the objective.

The flamethrower tank battalion commander requested from the infantry regiment commander that his troops be temporarily attached to the tank unit. In a brief time the tanks became the infantry's means of mobility. *Gvardeytsy* would be mounted on the armor, in the turrets, on the artillery prime movers, and even on the guns attached to them. The flamethrower tanks raced toward Volnovakha with their assault troops. The remaining infantry units were loaded onto available wheeled transport to catch up with the forward detachment later.

It was a good decision, the only way to save time. The loss of even ten minutes in a rapidly unfolding battle might mean the difference between victory and defeat.

Having overcome the enemy's last covering positions on the approaches to the town with two volleys of flame, the forward detachment succeeded in gaining a foothold in the town. Had the battalion not been equipped with this most fearsome weapon, the flamethrower, the capture of this portion of Volnovakha would have been much more difficult. We had now secured a viable base from which the division's main forces could carry out the rest of their assault.

By order of the Supreme High Commander, the division was subsequently awarded the honorary title "Volnovakha," after the name of the town.

Terrible Weapon

This story is about the Red Army's most remarkable type of weapon: the BM-8 and BM-13 multiple rocket launchers. Both of these systems—commonly known as "Katyusha"—entered the ground forces' inventory before Germany's attack on the Soviet Union. Units were equipped with multiple rocket launchers beginning in June 1941.[1] Immediately such units were elevated to "guards" status. It was an absolutely new direction in the development of our artillery.

An enumeration of some of the weapon's tactical and technical characteristics is sufficient to justify this distinction. The duration of a BM-8 salvo (twenty-four, thirty-six, or forty-eight rockets) was eight to ten seconds, and of a BM-13 salvo (forty-six rockets) seven to ten seconds. No other type of artillery in the world had such a rate of fire. The loading time for the rocket system was five to ten minutes. Maximum firing ranges were five and one-half and eight and one-half kilometers, respectively.

Multiple rocket launchers were deployed in batteries of four launchers. A battalion in a mechanized corps consisted of two of these batteries, and a battalion in a separate rocket launcher brigade consisted of three of these batteries.

The Katyusha made its presence felt on the battlefield on 14 July 1941. The battery of Guards Captain I. A. Flerov delivered a salvo against an accumulation of enemy trains at the Orsha railroad yard. From this day forward, the Germans began an intense effort to capture one of these unusual and threatening fire-support weapons.

The document "Instructions for Guards Rocket Artillery Units" contained a number of measures intended to protect the secrecy of the Katyusha. Enlisted personnel assigned to these units were specially selected and carefully screened. With the delivery of the highly maneuverable American Studebaker truck to the Soviet Union through the Lend-Lease program, the launcher assembly was mounted exclusively on this chassis. This ensured its high mobility on roads or cross-country. Each Katyusha was rigged for its own demolition: if there were any threat of the weapon's being captured by the enemy, the crew—even if it cost the men their own lives—was to blow up the truck and destroy the rockets.

Along with this defensive mechanism, a special tactic for using the rocket systems was developed and practiced in some units: a single 122-mm towed howitzer was sometimes used to develop the firing data for the BM-8 and BM-13 batteries.[2] The multiple rocket launcher battery itself arrived at the firing position only immediately prior to launching its rockets and quickly departed the firing position after the launch. This enabled the unit commander to protect his critical firing systems from enemy air observation and attack for as long as possible in a given tactical situation.

An additional uniqueness concerning the deployment of guards mortars must be underscored: in order to ensure the unhindered movement of the launchers to their starting (hide) positions, they were accorded movement priority on roads. All other equipment and personnel were required to yield to them.

In any situation (assembly areas, defensive positions, and so on), multiple rocket launcher formations and units were positioned in places reliably protected by other branches of troops. In addition a great deal of attention was paid to camouflaging guards mortars unit positions and providing them with reliable direct security. These tactics significantly reduced the possibility that enemy diversionaries and scouts would be able to penetrate to them.

The summer of 1942 wrote the saddest page in the history of the Katyusha. In a period of heavy defensive battles on the southern wing of the Soviet-German front, the enemy captured one loaded BM-13 launcher. The Germans' dream had finally come true! They had seized an example of the Red Army's threatening secret weapon. My artillery-branch friends have told me that this extraordinary event occurred after the strict demands of the

People's Commissar of Defense Order No. 227 of 18 July 1942 were implemented.[3]

The launcher crew was immediately arrested, and a judicial proceeding was initiated. The accused were charged with being panic mongers and traitors. There were no doubts. The military tribunal would sentence them to the stiffest punishment—the firing squad. Assigning them to a punishment company would have been considered the same as giving them a pardon.

The fact that the enemy had captured of a fully loaded launcher was reported up the chain of command. When the designer of the weapon, I. I. Gvay, learned of the event, the first thing he did was to request that the criminal case against the launcher crew be dropped: "The principal secret of the Katyusha is the rocket itself, and it cannot be disassembled! I guarantee this with my own life."

Though Gvay's attitude totally astonished the responsible authorities, this categorical declaration by the system's principal designer did save the mortarmen's lives. They were subsequently transferred to a conventional artillery unit. This in itself was a stern punishment, affecting both the soldiers' status and their pay.[4]

The frantic events of the summer and fall of 1942 had pushed from memory this sad story of the legendary Katyusha. But it came up again, at the end of 1942 in some *fronts* and at the beginning of 1943 in others. Information appeared—initially semiofficial and later official in nature—that a BM-13 rocket (4.9 kilograms of explosive) had exploded during an attempt to disassemble it at a scientific research laboratory near Berlin. For comparison, the explosive charge of an antitank mine ranged from 1.5 to 7.5 kilograms.

In 1943, already in the active army on the West *Front*, I read a captured document, an order to German troops. In part it instructed them not to take as booty and, above all, not to attempt to dismantle ammunition for the Soviet BM-8 and BM-13 rocket systems. As had been convincingly demonstrated, they were equipped with a self-destruct device and could not be disassembled.

In February 1944 I had the opportunity to see with my own eyes how scrupulously the Germans at the front observed this order. A meeting of forward brigades of the tank armies of First and Second Ukrainian *Fronts* (233d Brigade of 5th Mechanized

Corps, 6th Tank Army, and 155th Brigade of 20th Tank Corps, 5th Guards Tank Army, respectively) occurred in the center of Zvenigorodka on 28 January. The operational goal had been achieved. A large enemy grouping had been trapped in the Korsun-Shevchenkovskiy pocket.

Having regrouped their forces, over the course of the last days of January the Germans undertook counterattacks from the outside toward their encircled grouping. This was reconnaissance by battle in search of the most vulnerable spots in the defense of the Soviet 6th Tank Army units. Later, beginning on 4 February, the enemy launched powerful strikes with the clear intention of linking up with its cut-off troops. Sometimes the Germans committed up to two hundred tanks and two regiments of infantry into battle, supported by artillery fire and massed air strikes. But their attempts were thwarted. The defending Red Army forces stubbornly held their positions.

The battles raged fiercely at times. I remember how the barrels of our coaxial machine guns in companies of 1st Battalion, 233d Tank Brigade, drooped to such a degree from continuous intense firing that the bullets were dropping to the ground only scores of meters in front of the Shermans. We then continued to assault the enemy infantry with bursts from our antiaircraft machine guns or, if the command were given, our hull-mounted machine guns.[5] After a powerful artillery and aviation preparation, the enemy launched an attack against forces defending the outer encirclement ring early on the morning of 11 February. This force included a large number of tanks echeloned in depth, which crushed the Soviet combat formation in the breakthrough sector. By the end of the day, one hundred fifty German tanks, mainly Tigers and Panthers, had managed to penetrate ten to twelve kilometers into the depth of our defenses.

On this day, 35th Guards Mortars Battalion (Katyusha), commanded by Guards Major Pavel Kukushkin, was moved up to hide positions for launching a fire strike. The short rush to the position was extremely difficult. Even the "king of the road" Studebakers were moving at a slow speed across the broken and soft chernozem. While the launchers were assuming their combat formation in preparation to launch, the situation changed dramatically: the enemy literally came within main-gun range of the battalion's units. The guards mortarmen frantically fired the salvos from three launchers and immediately began to abandon the position. They hurried. Oh, how they hurried.

Three of the Katyushas, still loaded with unfired rockets, bogged down in the soggy soil up to the tops of their wheels. While turning around, two of them settled into the roadside ditch. The enemy began to fire at the maneuvering vehicles, and several high-explosive rounds detonated nearby. One of the Studebakers was hit and disabled. The battalion commander had no choice but to leave the three Katyushas and drive his remaining launchers into the depth of our positions so as not to lose all of them.

Having thrown out several smoke pots, the mortarmen managed to get out from under enemy fire. The crews of the two loaded rocket launchers remained to face the Germans one-on-one. The *gvardeytsy* attempted to organize a defense of their Katyushas. But this was a foolish venture. What could they do against tanks with their rifles? Tigers were coming at them! The rocket launcher crews began to withdraw under fire. Three men were killed and two wounded.

Such a dismal outcome was the result of two factors. First, out of either haste or negligence the launchers had not been rigged for demolition in the event it became necessary. Second, the battalion was moved forward and then deployed in combat formation without a reliable cover by infantry or other troops. This was the grossest violation of the appropriate "Instructions on Guards Mortars Units." Each of these turned out to be expensive omissions.

The situation on the battlefield changed frequently. The corps command rushed the remnants of the guards battalion first to one and then to another dangerous sector of the front. Guards Major Pavel Vasilevich Kukushkin did not have time to offer a response to the investigative or counterintelligence organs, although they were seeking an interview with him. Strictly speaking, the complexity of the overall situation in February in the Korsun-Shevchenkovskiy sector protected the guards unit commander against the inevitable unpleasantness.

Two days of intense combat ensued. The enemy continued to fight toward its encircled troops with unbelievable stubbornness. Having suffered defeat in one sector, the German forces quickly attempted to break through in another. Our units and formations holding the outer encirclement ring fought to the death. Over the course of these battles they not only stopped the Germans' advance but hurled them back.

Thus on 13 February the Germans on the Bosov axis were forced to roll back five to seven kilometers. The area where the two BM-13 launchers were mired was in our hands once again. I still recall the picture of this battlefield. The two Studebakers, mired in liquid chernozem, were sitting on the side of a gravel road that had been pummeled by tanks. The rocket rounds, covered with a dusting of snow, were still on the guide rails. They were intact, untouched!

The joy of the guards mortarmen was boundless. The tankers helped recover the Katyushas from their chernozem pits with tow cables. The crews rushed to inspect their vehicles. Strangely, the enemy had decided not to destroy such a dangerous weapon even by fire.

The final chapter of this extraordinary incident was written. The battalion commander was not recommended for a combat award. The surviving crew members were sent to conventional artillery units. The guards mortarmen, in the opinion of many veterans, got off with a light scare in the strict wartime regime.

Death by Fire

During presentations I made to young people, they would often ask me, "Did you ever have moments of fear or times when you thought you would not survive?" I freely acknowledged, "Yes, there were such moments!" Then I would quote the lines of the poet Julia Drunina, "He who says that war is not frightening knows nothing about war."[1]

An incident I experienced in February 1944 was frightening and, it seemed at the time, not survivable. At the end of January the Red Army had undertaken an operation to encircle the enemy's Korsun-Shevchenkovskiy grouping. Continuous, fierce battles had been raging for two days on the Rezino-Lysyanka axis. The enemy was attempting to defeat the defending forces of 6th

Tank Army and 47th Rifle Corps with a powerful tank attack and to break through to trapped German units.

At this time, after returning from the hospital, I was the chief of ammunition supply for 1st Battalion, 233d Tank Brigade. I was a lieutenant. My duties included repair of tank armaments and supplying the line companies with all types of ammunition. The latter was not an easy task. This winter was warm in the Ukraine, with rain falling during the day and wet snow at night. The chernozem was churned up to a depth of almost one-half meter, rendering the roads almost impassable. All this demanded an enormous intensity of effort on the part of my subordinates and me. We had a one-and-a-half-ton GAZ cargo truck, with limited cross-country capability, at our disposal to accomplish our assigned tasks.[2]

During the hauling of ammunition (two or three trips per day), the *gazushka* [GAZ truck] literally traveled on the strength of our shoulders and backs: we pushed it many kilometers and pulled it out of deep mud countless times. Our ammunition supply section well understood that to leave the tankers without shells and cartridges was a crime. We may have had a tough time on the road, but the situation was twice as hard for the tank crews in heated battle with the armored enemy.

Early on the morning of 13 February, we finally had pushed, dragged, and carried our truck with ammunition to the front line. The Sherman tankers were happy to see us. Many of the tanks had only seven to ten main-gun rounds and just a few hundred machine-gun cartridges left on board.[3] The day would bring more intense fighting. Without considering the enormous losses they were suffering, the Germans were surging northward toward their encircled troops. Upon defeat on one axis, they quickly shifted their effort to another. They were using only Tiger tanks and infantry mounted on armored troop carriers in their attacking echelon. These were highly maneuverable units.

Meanwhile there was a brief period of calm at the forward edge. We could not waste these valuable moments. My supply troops were exhausted, but we had to ignore our personal discomfort. The *gazushka* trundled from Sherman to Sherman, and my troops transferred three-packs of main-gun rounds and crates of small arms ammunition from the bed of the truck to the rear decks (engine-compartment covers) of the tanks.[4] The crews unpacked the rounds, opened the wood crates containing metal ammunition cans, and stowed everything in their turrets.

We were hurrying to the last tank of Junior Lieutenant Aleksey Vasin. We would supply him and then retrace our route for another load. At least, this was our intent. However, the rapidly developing situation at the forward edge disrupted our plan in an instant and forced us to endure some frightening, life-threatening moments. Death was breathing down our necks every second. Four Tiger tanks crawled out from behind a long ridge. No one noticed them at first, engaged as we were in unloading ammunition. Then the dreaded sound of a solid-shot round fired by the enemy forced all of us out of our lethargy.

At that instant, a powerful, hammering blow shook the hull of the Sherman. A fire flashed through the engine compartment. The tankers and my ammo bearers jumped down off the M4A2. A second enemy round turned the *gazushka* into a blazing heap in seconds. Its driver, Junior Sergeant Yuriy Udovchenko, died at the wheel. The tank crew rushed to put out the fire in their vehicle, but the fate of the *gazushka* had already been delivered— there was nothing to save. We hurried to assist the tankers. Then a series of enemy mortar rounds landed not far from the tank, seriously wounding the driver-mechanic. A second volley of mortar rounds, more precisely laid, might land at any moment. More men would be wounded or lost.

There were eight of us standing in an open field, with not a bush or a gully in sight. There was no place to hide, no shelter save the burning tank. I gave the command, and we all took cover under the front of the tank. Explosion after explosion raised black fountains within mere meters of the Sherman. Nothing good could come from this, I feared.

And so the entire group of officers and sergeants was caught in a tanker's hell. It was our choice to be killed by incoming artillery and mortar rounds or to die under the hull of the tank from the explosion of the vehicle itself when the engine-compartment fire reached the ammunition stowed in the turret. I was one hundred percent convinced that one or the other would happen—and soon. I knew this from my own painful experience.

In the initial period of the war, explosives-producing factories located in the western regions of the USSR were dismantled and evacuated to the east, where they were reconstructed and put back into production in 1942. The explosives made in these factories for several consecutive months were of inferior quality because the production process did not adequately purge the product of harmful impurities. As a result, tank ammunition produced during this period in 1942 was noted for one undesirable effect: when a T-34 tank burned, its ammunition self-detonated.

An incident of this nature happened to a friend of mine from the armor academy. The tank of company commander Lieutenant Petr Tunin was set on fire in the summer battles of 1942. Two crew members were killed and two others wounded. Bleeding profusely, Tunin was attempting to crawl away from his burning T-34. The main-gun ammunition in its turret exploded when he was fifteen to twenty meters away from the vehicle. Pieces of armor flew in all directions, one of them finding Tunin. They later picked up the lieutenant's cold body in a furrow of the wheat field. A cursory examination revealed that a large metal fragment had split his skull.

We were now fighting the enemy on the fields of Ukraine in January and February 1944 with American tanks we had received in late 1943. This was our first combat test of the new and still not completely mastered equipment. We measured the U.S. tank according to our own yardstick and in these circumstances expected it to perform in a manner not unlike our own T-34.

I understood better than my subordinates the tragedy that was about to envelop us. If the main-gun ammunition on the truck was exploding in the fire, it posed no risk to us. The driver had attempted to position the *gazushka* in a safe place. He had failed, and it was now parked about fifty meters from the tank, still burning. The primary threat to our lives was the main-gun ammunition supply aboard the Sherman.

We lay pressed together under the front of this tank and awaited the detonation of the still-unpacked ammunition containers, both in the turret and on the back deck. My men had already unloaded several three-packs onto the tank when this incident started. Most of what remained outside the tank, however, were metal cans of machine-gun ammunition. Minutes would pass by, perhaps ten or twenty, and then another common grave would be created on the battlefield. We awaited the fateful moment for ourselves. Our bodies shivered involuntarily in fear.

The fire in the tank above us was making its presence felt. The coveralls of those who were closer to the rear of the tank began to give off smoke. We all rolled from side to side, seeking a protective layer of dirt against the heat coming off the hull. Five hundred meters to our south, Tigers and Shermans were engaged in main-gun duels. Unable to withstand his fear of fire and hoping for something better, one of the tankers got up and ran. Two mortar rounds exploded in his path, and he was stretched out on the plowed field. It was clear that the Germans had us under observation. They had us in their sights and were intending to kill us to the last man or force us to be burned alive under the tank.

Ammunition on our truck began to detonate. We heard a muffled shot—the burning powder of a round ejected from its casing—and the slap of the projectile into the ground. One of these rounds fell quite close to our burning Sherman but did not explode.

At the time I believed the ejected round failed to explode simply because it had not encountered a hard object in its trajectory and therefore its explosive charge did not function. This would not be the case, of course, with rounds that prematurely detonated inside the tank. On the contrary, the turret walls themselves were obstacle enough for these rounds to hit.

The culminating moment was approaching. A hissing fire erupted in the middle portion of the tank. The turret hatches were open, feeding fresh oxygen into the fire. The temperature under the M4A2 immediately shot up several degrees. We listened, trying to determine how close the battle was to our position. We were grasping at straws, hoping for rescue. But the enemy had not been driven back. As before, we were still in his sights.

It was becoming unbearably hot under the tank, but we could not abandon its cover. It would be certain death from enemy mortar fire. There were several loud bangs in the turret. A projectile driven from its case had ricocheted around the turret and then fallen to the floor. Then there was quiet.

We had been lucky thus far. It was a solid-shot round.[5] There was no question about what would happen when the propellant charge of a high-explosive round detonated from the heat. The warhead would detonate against the turret wall and immediately set off sympathetic detonations of other similar rounds. This would be the end of us all!

Several agonizing minutes passed. The cacophony of small arms ammunition exploding in the turret grew louder, but we paid no attention to it. We were awaiting other sounds. Finally a whole series of main-gun rounds exploded. We heard loud clanging and metal scraping. Seconds later the absolute worst came— a thunderous explosion! Then nothing. Quiet. Then still more detonations! A clank! And again silence.

Our anticipation of a fatal instant had lasted almost an hour. The fire continued to burn away inside the tank hull, but no more ammunition detonated. There were no further explosions. What had happened?

The cannonade of the nearby fire fight was fading away to the south. A group of dirty hostages—almost insane from the high temperature under the tank hull, poisoned by carbon monoxide gas, and shaking from nervous tension—we crawled out from under the smoking, huffing, blackened Sherman. Our legs unable to hold us, we sat on the ground. A light rain was falling. We lifted our blackened faces up to its cooling spray and breathed in deep gulps of wet, clean air. We rinsed the soot and ash from our faces and hands.

The seven of us had been extremely lucky. We had come out of a fiery oven unharmed. To which saint or what god should we offer thanks?

Until the end of the war in the west, and in the conflict with the Japanese Kwantung Army, there was not a single incident in which the projectile warheads of the main-gun rounds of a burning Sherman exploded. Later, when I was on the faculty at the Frunze Military Academy, ordnance specialists told me the reason for the stability of these warheads: it was the high quality of the explosive charge itself.[6] Unfortunately, for a number of understandable reasons this had not been the case with our own tank ammunition throughout 1942.

The Marshal's Embrace

When he was minister of defense of the USSR (1957–67), Marshal of the Soviet Union Rodion Yakovlevich Malinovskiy ordered all the senior commanders of the armed forces and branches of forces periodically to give lectures and make speeches to the professorial and instructor staffs of military academies.[1] The topics of these presentations were new types of armaments and combat equipment and the issues of tactics and operational art. The speakers were to draw on the rich experience afforded by the Great Patriotic War with regard to the utilization of conventional forces and the conditions under which nuclear weapons could be employed in future wars.

The practice of this lecture series permitted the higher leadership of the Soviet Army to maintain continuous contact with academic institutions—to be involved at a high theoretical level in the teaching of students and in the development of scientific studies, instructional materials, and textbooks.

Rodion Yakovlevich, himself a senior instructor at the M. V. Frunze Military Academy in 1939, decided to give a presentation there. It was in late October 1960 in the academy's assembly hall. The speech of the minister of defense was devoted to an analysis of the preparation and conduct of one of the largest operations of the Great Patriotic War, the Jassy-Kishinev operation, in August 1944.

In the month of July, forces were being assembled. Logistical and equipment resources required for the upcoming offensive were being moved forward in large quantities. And it was all being accomplished at night with the strictest observance of security measures.

Just days remained until the launching of the planned operation. At the end of July, the German-Romanian military command attempted to eliminate the Soviet bridgehead on the right (west) bank of the Prut River. Their intention was to cut off our forces on the right bank of the water obstacle and prevent them from withdrawing to the opposite bank. This was to be accomplished by a powerful attack on a narrow front in the northeast direction.

To execute this concept the enemy secretly amassed a significant concentration of manpower and equipment. Our defensive positions at this time were manned primarily by infantry units and formations, reinforced by artillery and antitank fire support. We had no tanks at the forward edge or in the immediate depth of these positions west of the river. A second factor in the enemy's favor was that its entrenchments were on higher ground overlooking the terrain our forces occupied. Our sector was under enemy observation up to the water obstacle and east of it in some sectors.

I must also focus the reader's attention on the meteorological conditions during this period of time. June and July of 1944 were dry and hot in Moldavia and Romania. The ground was parched and cracked, and the soil in the fields and vineyards that had been plowed up in the spring had acquired a free-flowing consistency similar to sand. This drought and the soil conditions it created were to play havoc with the tanks we had committed to the effort of crushing the enemy assault.

From the very beginning the battles took on an exceptionally fierce nature (see map 4). The advancing enemy forces succeeded in breaking through initial Soviet defensive positions in a short amount of time. There arose the genuine threat of our losing the bridgehead that was so vital to the upcoming offensive.

The developing situation required that we make use of our reserve forces, principally our tanks, to launch a powerful counterattack. But there were no tanks in the bridgehead, the closest ones being those of 5th Mechanized Corps, 6th Tank Army—specifically, its 233d Tank Brigade, which was situated twelve kilometers from the forward edge in the village of Skulyany.

As Marshal Malinovskiy told the audience in the assembly hall that day in 1960, he reported the deteriorating situation to the Supreme High Commander, J. V. Stalin, on the first day of the German offensive. He requested Stalin's permission to use a portion of the tanks from the forces that had been designated for the planned August offensive. Without their participation, the *front* commander asserted, it would be very difficult to restore the bridgehead. But Stalin, refusing to permit the use of a single tank for the purpose, ordered Malinovskiy to accomplish his difficult mission with only the forces of the defending units. He also recommended massing artillery fires and air strikes.

As the minister of defense was to tell his young audience, in the face of great difficulty Soviet forces went on not only to hold their positions in the depth of their defenses but even to recapture areas at the forward edge that had earlier been captured by the enemy and to drive a wedge into the enemy's defenses along the highway to Jassy. The attacking German force having suffered significant losses, the enemy's plan was foiled.

During a break in the lecture session, I walked up to Marshal R. Ya. Malinovskiy and asked permission to clarify one issue. He responded, "I am listening."

"Comrade Minister of Defense, you said that Stalin denied the use of tanks for reestablishing the initial positions on the right bank of the Prut River. I am from 233d Tank Brigade, 5th Mechanized Corps, 6th Tank Army. On your order, on 1 August 1944 our units participated in the conduct of a counterattack. Having accomplished the mission, the brigade was withdrawn back across the Prut River to its previous assembly area."

Rodion Yakovlevich was a bit perturbed. But at that moment he leaned over to me, hugged me by the shoulders, and whispered in my ear, "Don't say a word, Colonel."

"Yes, sir!"

Of course, the marshal did not expect to find in the assembly hall a participant of the events of July–August 1944 on the eve of the Jassy-Kishinev operation, let alone a tanker. My fellow instructors in the assembly hall saw how Rodion Yakovlevich had embraced me.

"Why did the Minister of Defense hug you?"

"During the war I was fortunate to have fought under his command in Second Ukrainian *Front*. We were briefly recalling those days!"

This is how it really was in August 1944. The situation had become more critical by the close of 31 July. On the left flank the enemy had reached the near approaches to the monastery (more correctly, the ruins of the cloister that had been totally destroyed by artillery fire and air strikes). The danger of capture of the highway leading to Jassy was imminent. The fighting continued into the night.

The 1st and 2d Battalions of 233d Tank Brigade were alerted on the following morning. These two units were sent by forced march to starting positions one kilometer from the forward edge, while 3d Battalion remained in Skulyany. Our tanks were to assemble in a forest east of the brick pile that was once the monastery.

At this time I was the chief of staff of 1st Battalion. We had a number of issues to resolve in a very short time—for example, how to supply officers with topographic maps of the area of combat actions. They handed the maps to me on the run at brigade headquarters. Taking a motorcycle with sidecar, I caught up with my column on the road march and, while still moving, passed the topomaps along to commanders of all ranks.

Subordinate units reached their designated positions an hour after being alerted. True, we had been delayed somewhat crossing the Prut River on a pontoon bridge—which, as it turned out, was adequately covered by air-defense fire. Attempts by enemy aviation to conduct air strikes on the crossing and on our units were unsuccessful. Having dropped their bombs without aim, the aircraft turned back. And two flaming torches burrowed into the earth.

The brigade commander, Guards Major Ivan Sazonov, was already waiting for us at the start positions. The tankers were concerned about the situation. The counterattack mission was assigned to the battalions on the map: 2d Battalion was to operate along the highway, with 1st Battalion to the left of the highway.[2] All of forty minutes were allocated to organizing the fight.

It was too little time, and there was much to accomplish: the commanders had to conduct a brief reconnaissance of the terrain and enemy;[3] the details of the mission had to be passed down to each crew, and each Sherman had to be brought undetected to the start line for the counterattack.

The shortage of time forced the battalion commanders clearly to violate an established, required procedure for organizing this kind of activity. The textbook method was to conduct commanders' reconnaissance in small groups (a battalion commander with two company commanders, then the company commanders with their three platoon leaders). Tank officers were supposed to change into the uniforms of the defending Soviet troops in order to blend in. The immediate area of the reconnaissance was to have good local security.

In this particular case, however, all of these established practices had to be ignored because of the short period of time available. The battalion commander led the officers on the reconnaissance in one large group consisting of three company commanders (two tank and one *tankodesantniki*) and six tank platoon commanders.

I have already mentioned that the terrain the enemy occupied dominated over the ground where our forces were entrenched. This elevated position offered the enemy the full opportunity to observe every meter of the defenses of the Soviet units. It could not be discounted that the enemy might double or triple its number of observers in the course of the attack. The most insignificant movement on our side did not go unnoticed by them.

We quickly felt the pressure of this scrutiny. The gaggle of Soviet officers on reconnaissance reached the southwestern edge of the woods to the right of the monastery ruins. Our tankers brought their binoculars up and began to study the terrain in both our own and the enemy dispositions. The axis of the counterattack did not meet with their approval. The Shermans had to operate in unfavorable conditions, attacking enemy units from low ground toward high ground. One thing pleased them, however: the sun would be somewhat behind and to our left at the time of the counterattack. It would not blind our sights and would, at the same time, present considerable interference to the Germans and Romanians.

Time was pressing. The unsuitability of the site selected for the commanders' reconnaissance became extremely clear. To work in sight of the enemy is to risk one's life every second. Tankers understood all of this exceptionally well. They tried to resolve the necessary issues as rapidly as possible and then leave the site, but they were unsuccessful. The enemy struck quickly. The first artillery shells landed in front of the group, lightly wounding two officers with shrapnel. Responding to a command, the entire group rushed deeper into the woods. The second volley killed three officers and seriously wounded a fourth. It was a sad beginning to the battle preparations. Two of the wounded were able to remain in their duty positions, but four officers had to be replaced.

The commanders' reconnaissance group returned to our position carrying their dead and wounded. The battalion commander appointed replacements for the fallen officers: the commander of his own Sherman and of the two company commanders' tanks.[4] The deputy battalion adjutant filled the fourth vacancy.

The time period allocated for preparation of the counterattack was coming to an end. The artillery preparation would be fired in just a matter of minutes. The units were to move to their starting positions for the attack and deploy into battle formation under the artillery's cover.

Captain Aleksandr Kogan, the battalion commander, ordered all company officers (of the battalion and the *tankodesantniki*) to assemble at his tank, where he assigned missions on the map. "At the attack line, look at the terrain again. It's possible I will give someone a correction or adjustment on the radio," he concluded. This was far from the best way of organizing a battle, but the shortage of time forced us to resort to it.

Never during my entire period of service at the front—either before or after this incident—did I witness another so hurried, incomplete, and shallow preparation of one of the most important components of an active defense, the counterattack. For we who would execute it, there remained much that was unknown (or virtually unknown) about the terrain and the enemy. The experience of war over and over again confirmed the old axiom: "A rapidly and incompletely organized battle invariably leads to misfortune, great or small!" In just a short while we would see and feel the truth of these words in more detail.

The artillery located along the forward edge, as well as in the immediate rear and across the Prut River, opened up simultaneously at 1000 hours. The Shermans moved forward. Our 1st Battalion turned left of the highway, 2d Battalion to the right, with hilly terrain dividing the tankers of the two units. Consequently they were counterattacking along independent axes, unable to support each other by fire. It could not have been worse.

Both battalions began the counterattack at 1030. Kogan's 1st Battalion tanks struck at the left flank of the enemy, who had penetrated into our defense on the southwest approaches to the monastery. The attack had to take place on the slope of the foothills that trailed off to the south. This was an unfavorable axis for two reasons: the tanks frequently had to expose their right sides to the fire of enemy weapons situated in the high ground, and the necessity of moving along the trench lines (ours and the enemy's) kept the units from being able to maneuver to the front. This situation was fraught with danger: a Sherman could drop into a defensive fortification (a weapons position, a bunker, a fighting or communications trench), either ours or the enemy's, at any moment. These trenches—which had been dug out since the previous March and had been improved a great deal since then—were but one of the serious obstacles that awaited the counterattacking units.

All of these circumstances strongly affected the tempo at which the companies and platoons were able to move: it remained slow. And tanks moving slowly across the battlefield, without maneuvering to the front, were good targets for enemy antitank weapons and field artillery. It must be recognized that the enemy's system of ground observation was extremely well organized, a fact aided in part by the vantage of the higher terrain.

As the battle unfolded, the counterattacking tanks of 1st Battalion and its attached *tankodesantniki*, along with the defending Soviet infantry, smashed through the first line of the enemy units. The artillerymen gave excellent fire support. They destroyed and set on fire seven enemy tanks in the area south of the monastery. Approximately ten enemy tanks, seeking cover from the accurate fire of antitank artillery, withdrew, covering themselves by utilizing the irregularities of the terrain.

The situation also was developing in our favor on the axis of 2d Tank Battalion. Its companies and platoons confidently built upon the initial success. Captain Kogan moved his Sherman slowly into the depth of the enemy position, steadily firing his main gun and the machine guns. Explosions of tank rounds formed a kind of moving "screen" in front of the companies' combat formations. This complicated the enemy's conduct of aimed fire from antitank systems and tanks that were seeking cover in the folds of the terrain. However, the German-Romanian command quickly adjusted to the developing situation.

The fact that the enemy's observation system was well organized had been driven home to us earlier during the commanders' reconnaissance. In all likelihood, enemy observers at posts established on the flanks of the counterattack sector could well see (but not be seen by) our formation. They began to report the precise coordinates of Sherman tank locations.

Nothing, it seemed, could compromise the somewhat plodding development of our success. But combat is combat, and one's situation can change rapidly and radically. This is exactly what happened to us soon after the start of the counterattack. Long-range artillery shells (not less than 150 millimeters) raised up thick fountains of explosions along our line of tanks. Because the narrow terrain did not permit a large interval between vehicles, a very real threat was hanging over us—one artillery round might damage two Shermans.

The command was issued to disperse, though the opportunities for the Shermans to accomplish this goal were extremely limited. Units began to maneuver, trying more quickly to increase the interval and distance between the tanks. But visibility was poor in the dust and smoke from the geysers of exploding enemy artillery rounds. Two tanks careened into trenches. They attempted to drive out of the traps under their own power but in vain. Their tracks simply dug deeper into the loose, dry soil of the former vineyards. The deputy battalion commander for maintenance, Senior Lieutenant Aleksandr Dubitskiy, and I hurried to the two Shermans' assistance with a tank-recovery vehicle. We drove up to the first one and quickly extended the crew a tow cable. Dubitskiy rushed on foot to the second stuck tank to prepare it for recovery from the trench.

At this time an FW-189 *Rama* appeared in the sky.[5] A short time later the stuck tanks and the recovery vehicle came under artillery fire. The assistant driver-mechanic was wounded. Fortunately our fighters soon shot the wings off the air-controller aircraft, and it plunged to the ground.

I was extremely lucky in this situation. I was standing next to an immobile Sherman, on its left side. The loose dirt of a revetment saved me from certain death. A heavy shell landed one pace behind me and buried itself in the dirt. The explosion was considerably weakened. But then a powerful blow between my shoulder blades bowled me over. I got up with difficulty, looked around, and brushed myself off. A firm, impressively large lump of clay had fallen at my feet. This "bomb" (thank God it was not a shell fragment) had knocked me down.

Matters were developing rapidly. Revving its engine, the recovery vehicle pulled the stuck tank out of the trench. We quickly unhooked the tow cable and headed toward the second tank, but Dubitskiy was waving his arms: the Sherman no longer required our efforts. Enemy fire had damaged its right side suspension components and immobilized it.[6]

We would hurry after the advancing units. Having dropped down into a broad, dry riverbed, they were destroying an enemy stronghold with stationary fires. The panorama of the battle was not a comforting sight. Three Shermans were stuck in gun positions and communications trenches, and two others were engulfed in flames. The battalion's remaining vehicles were attempting to execute a maneuver to the left along the dry riverbed, bypassing the node of resistance. The tankers had thrown out smoke pots in order to cover the combat formation from the right. This blinded both us and the enemy. The wind was calm with a low cloud cover. Firing conditions were adverse for both sides, but enemy fire was weakening.

Taking advantage of the slight degree of ease in the situation, Dubitskiy recovered the three tanks from "trench captivity"—one after the other, in rapid succession. They immediately rejoined the attacking combat formation. The work of the battalion maintenance and recovery team was dangerous but necessary. Forward artillery observers accompanying the battalion transmitted the coordinates of enemy firing positions. The fountains of shell explosions covered these positions a short time later.

Our counterattacking tanks were now approaching the former forward edge of the enemy defense. The tempo of their movement was sharply reduced, and in some places units were stopping altogether and firing their main guns at the enemy. The initial superiority of the counterattack—a powerful strike by twenty-one tanks on a narrow sector of the front—had exhausted itself. We could not bypass the enemy pocket of resistance. The Shermans were halted.

The critical moment of the battle had arrived. Forward movement had stopped, and our stationary combat formation was now on exposed terrain. The German-Romanian artillerymen were not slow to take advantage of this circumstance. Heavy artillery rounds were falling, explosion after explosion. Two were direct hits, and the crews abandoned their vehicles.

The duty of the commander is to monitor the pulse of an engagement at every moment and to undertake whatever measures, often urgent ones, are necessary. This was the time for urgent measures. On the order of such a commander, aviation appeared in the sky. Ten *shturmoviki* flew over from the other side of the Prut River. The spark trails of multiple rocket launcher missiles streaked toward the earth. The enemy artillery bombardment of our battalion ceased immediately. The Il-2s made another circuit. Now they were suppressing the Germans in front of our adjacent unit to the right.

Then another order came down: tanks, conducting fire, withdraw to the start line. It was 1230. We had fought a tough two-hour battle. My 1st Battalion had lost five Shermans, three of them consumed by fire. The previous forward edge of Soviet units had been restored. The serviceable tanks of 233d Brigade moved back to Skulyany, their previous assembly area.

All tank commanders were extremely dissatisfied with the outcome of the fight just concluded—and for good reason. The unit was inadequately prepared to accomplish its mission, and the battalions, particularly 1st Battalion, operated on terrain with limited opportunity to maneuver to the front. "They crammed us into a bottle," complained the *Shermanisti* [Sherman tankers].

In his presentation at Frunze Military Academy in 1960 Marshal Malinovskiy was silent about these events that occurred in the course of our defeating the enemy offensive. And he ordered me not to elaborate on his account.

Regarding J. V. Stalin's denial of the use of tanks for crushing enemy attempts to annihilate our bridgehead on the right bank of the Prut River, I should add yet another conversation of R. Ya. Malinovskiy with the Supreme Commander.

In May 1944, Malinovskiy had just assumed command of Second Ukrainian *Front* and needed to deal with a critical situation developing in one of his subordinate units. The enemy was systematically launching punishing attacks against 52d Army formations. The army commander, K. A. Koroteev, asked the *front* commander quickly to send him one or two divisions.

Rodion Yakavlevich was inclined to assist 52d Army from his

reserve. The *front* chief of staff, General M. V. Zakharov, and other members of the military council held the same opinion. Just the same, Malinovskiy decided to consult with the Supreme High Commander. He reported the developing situation to Stalin, who listened attentively and then asked:

"What do you intend to do, Comrade Malinovskiy?"

"The Germans are pestering us with counterattacks."

"You've already told me that."

"Undoubtedly, the situation of 52d Army suggests concern for the loss of high ground. Therefore, I intend to introduce two divisions into the battle from *front* reserves and beat back the enemy's striving for the high ground."

After an extended pause Stalin said, "I do not recommend this course of action to you."

"Why not? We have sufficient reserves."

"That is precisely why I do not recommend this. Realize, today you will throw one or two divisions into the battle; tomorrow the enemy will also add divisions to this axis. Then you will throw in still more because you have so many reserves, and heavy and stubborn combat will be waged. This is not in our interests. This is why I advise against it and deny you permission to commit *front* reserves."

"I understand, Comrade Stalin."

"Consider that we now will take some forces from you for deployment to a new axis where we are preparing for an offensive."

This conversation occurred on 29 May 1944.[7]

In May 1944 the commander of Second Ukrainian *Front* unhesitatingly carried out the order of the Supreme High Commander, but in August 1944 he ignored Stalin. There were few responsible commanders of that period who were capable of operating with this kind of latitude. I must give Malinovskiy his due: he undertook what he believed to be the most timely and effective measures to reestablish the combat capability of 233d Tank Brigade. By the beginning of the Jassy-Kishinev operation on 20 August, its units were at 100 percent strength in Sherman tanks.

A Peasant Family's Courageous Deed

The Podolsk Central Archive of the Ministry of Defense contains millions of official documents that attest to the heroic combat deeds of soldiers, sergeants, and officers of various branches of the Soviet military during the Great Patriotic War. And accounts of not only military personnel but also many civilians of our country and of foreign countries, appear in these files.

In October 1967 I stumbled upon an interesting report of the military council of 6th Guards Tank Army, which discussed the heroic deed of a Hungarian peasant family in the fall of 1944.[1] The Hungarian's family name had clearly been mistranslated— Uno Digeyzo Dieno. I began a persistent search that ultimately unearthed the following account.

Soviet forces were engaged in fierce battles south of the city of Debrecen at the beginning of October 1944. The 7th Guards Mechanized Corps was slowly achieving success in the northwest direction, toward Budapest. In the afternoon of 6 October the enemy struck a blow at the corps's left flank with fresh reserves just arrived. Conducting heavy defensive fighting, 7th Guards Mechanized Corps units were forced to withdraw behind the Berettyo River.

A tank company of 2d Battalion, 41st Guards Tank Brigade, commanded by Guards Senior Lieutenant Fedor Vasin, was ordered to operate as a covering detachment as of 1600 on 7 October.[2] Guards Lieutenant Grigoriy Vasilevich Slesarev commanded one of the tanks in this company. Holding favorable positions, the tankers supported the organized withdrawal of the brigade's units.

Vasin's subordinates employed a tactical method that had proven effective in the past. The *gvardeytsy* conducted heavy main-gun firing at the enemy from a site on the terrain selected by the commander. This stopped the enemy's advance. While the enemy reacted to the unfolding situation, a portion of the platoons stealthily withdrew to a new position farther to their own rear.

Vasin's *gvardeytsy* held off the advancing enemy forces for approximately ninety minutes. By the time it had begun to get dark, his men had already set five enemy tanks and troop transporters on fire and had lost two of their own tanks.

The next suitable defensive position having been selected, the tankers would have to conduct difficult night combat from that position onward. Vasin issued the necessary instructions to his platoon commanders for the night action. Then an order came in: "Link up your company with the battalion main body!" The T-34s quickly moved out of their positions and moved in the direction of the small village of Andakhazy. Guards Lieutenant Slesarev's crew was bringing up the rear of the march column. They had moved not more than a kilometer when the commander heard the alarmed voice of his driver-mechanic over the tank intercom: "Oil pressure is falling! The engine is pulling poorly!"

Slesarev ordered the driver-mechanic, Guards Sergeant Mikhail Olenin, to reduce engine RPMs. They would have to stop and check everything out carefully in order to find and correct the problem. No doubt this would require some time, but the situation would not allow it. The enemy might appear at any moment.

The tank commander reported his situation to the company commander by radio. He received permission for independent movement to Berettyoujfalu. The company quickly disappeared into the darkness.

Slesarev's T-34 was moving slowly along a field path. They were seeking a small grove of trees. The houses of the village of Andakhazy should soon appear, and then their final destination would be only a short distance farther.

The tank's engine suddenly stopped. Olenin attempted to restart it several times, without success. The starter was unable to rotate the engine even half a revolution. When they opened the grilles of the engine compartment, they were struck in the face by a wave of heat, as though coming from the heart of a well-stoked oven. It was clear that the engine had seized from overheating.

The radio operator continuously transmitted the company commander's call sign. There was no response. The frequency was alive with unbelievable crackling and squealing: the Germans were conducting continuous jamming. There was no way the Soviets would be able to establish contact in these difficult conditions.

Impenetrable darkness enveloped the immobile tank. A piercing cold wind was blowing, with occasional rain showers. The sky to the right was at times illuminated with flashes of fire: a battle was being fought somewhere in that direction. The front line was being pushed ever farther to the south.

This unusual situation demanded from the commander an order with regard to the T-34. A written instruction existed: in any situation, organize a reliable defense of the tank and preserve it for subsequent battles. Only in exceptional circumstances was it permitted to disable the armaments and radios and, if it were possible, blow up the tank or set it on fire. After all of this, the crew had the right to move away from the tank.

Slesarev thought about it. Five years of service in the Red Army had tempered the character of this young officer. He was calm. Various scenarios passed through his mind. The *gvardeytsy* were in an extreme situation. A simple solution suggested itself: disable the T-34 and leave it.

During his year of active fighting at the front, the lieutenant had twice traveled to the rear for new equipment. Having seen how difficult it was at the factory to forge these weapons, he recognized their value. Therefore he was determined to protect for as long as possible the life of this tank that had been entrusted to him for battle with the enemy. Grigoriy Vasilevich believed that the Germans' success in the Debrecen area was a temporary phenomenon. His troops must prepare the tank for destruction, but they must carry out this act only at the last moment, when the enemy threat was imminent. For the time being, he planned something else.

He gave an order: carefully check the submachine guns for reliable firing, and count and divide the ammunition and F-1 "lemon" grenades equally among the crew members. They removed the coaxial machine gun from its mount, along with all of its magazines. The crew prepared the tank for rapid burning by placing diesel-soaked rags in the fighting and engine compartments and by disassembling one main-gun round and pouring its powder charge into the tank's hull under the driver-mechanic's seat.

The lieutenant sent two men to reconnoiter the village of Andakhazy. They quickly returned. Everything was quiet; there were no Germans in sight. Slesarev ordered the gun commander and radio operator to carefully camouflage themselves in the woods about a hundred meters northwest of the tank. Their mission was to prevent a sudden attack from the most likely direction. Grigoriy Vasilevich and the driver-mechanic remained with their tank. They made several attempts to contact the company commander by radio but, as before, were unsuccessful.

Not more than an hour passed while they organized the guarding of the T-34 and prepared to burn it, should that become necessary. The clock was also about to start ticking for one peasant family and the ten-day venture they would undertake.

The tankers initially heard shouting in broken Russian: "*Rusi, Rusi,* don't shoot! We are Hungarian civilians!" Then two unarmed men came walking up to the T-34 out of the darkness. One was wearing the uniform of a railroad man; the other, peasant clothes. The first man spoke a little Russian. It turned out that in 1916 he had been a prisoner in Russia. Now he worked as a railroad-crossing keeper. He did not give his own name but introduced his companion as Geza Onodi. With a great deal of difficulty, the railroad man was able to explain to Slesarev that there was fighting at the Berettyo River.

Offering their services to the Soviet troops, the Hungarians began to ponder the situation when they were told an engine problem had disabled the tank. These many years later, having learned its details, I was genuinely surprised by the simplicity and wisdom of the plan the peasants devised.

After a few moments, Onodi, with the help of his friend, came up with a purely agrarian solution for covering the T-34. The corn had not yet been gathered from his field. They could assemble a stack of cornstalks and conceal the tank inside the stack. They could then harrow the harvested field in order to eliminate the track marks. The crew could remain inside their vehicle. Onodi's family would bring them food under the cover of darkness.

Without hesitation Slesarev accepted the first part of the plan, to camouflage the tank. But as for placing the crew inside the tank—this was a somewhat more serious issue. After considering all aspects of the idea and weighing all the circumstances, with some trepidation he gave the go-ahead.

Work with the cornstalks proceeded at full speed. Only the gun commander remained in the woods, standing guard. The three remaining Soviet soldiers and the two Hungarians did not sit down for a moment. Maintaining strict discipline with regard to lights, no one smoked. Ninety minutes later, the stack was built. The T-34 was well-hidden from all sides. They gathered up the fallen leaves.

All this time Grigoriy thought and thought. He considered various scenarios of the crew's subsequent actions. Could he trust the Hungarians? Why would they get mixed up in this business with the corn? These actions on their part brought with them considerable responsibility. If the Hungarian or German fascists learned of their involvement, the peasants would pay dearly with their own lives and the lives of their families for helping Soviet tankers. Too much was at stake! Grigoriy wanted to believe in their sincerity, but he could not.

Geza Onodi, having brought the last armful of cornstalks, shook himself off and said something to the railroad man. Then he headed straight for the village. He returned ten minutes later, leading a horse by the bridle. The horse was pulling a harrow, the tines turned upward. A tall young man, perhaps fifteen years of age, was walking with Onodi. It was his son, also named Geza— Geza Junior. He was holding the horse's reins in his hand.

The railroad man remained with the tankers as a voluntary hostage. When Geza Senior returned, the Hungarian hurried to his crossing-guard post: the time for his duty shift was fast approaching. Although the "steel highway" had not been functioning in this frontline area for several weeks, the railroad guard still continued to perform the duties he had been assigned.

One of the tank crew members asked, "Why is he doing this now, at such a dangerous time?" The old railroad man replied proudly, "The Germans and Salashisty will leave.[3] They will have to leave under the blows of the Russian forces, and the railroad, our Hungarian railroad, will remain. I should remain with it!"

Upon his departure the crossing guard informed Slesarev of the senior Onodi's desire that his son remain in the tank along with the Soviet soldiers. Many years later Grigoriy Vasilevich recalls: "This decisive step of the Hungarian peasant—voluntarily to leave his son in our hands, as a sort of hostage—removed all of my doubts." Almost a quarter of a century later, Geza Onodi had this to say: "What other means did I have to convince the Soviet tankers that we were not planning anything evil?"

It was a peasant's field, a small plot of land. How many times in his forty-eight years had Geza Onodi plowed and harrowed it? Countless times! But always by day. Now extraordinary circumstances were forcing him to harrow his ancestral field by night. Not only did this work have to be accomplished quickly, but more importantly, it had to be done to the same standard that would apply in the daytime.

Of course a farmer of that era knew his own land like the back of his hand, every dip and rise of it. He had memorized the length and width of the cornfield in paces.

Onodi began harrowing the field without delay. The father and son quickly and quietly accomplished the work that was so routine to them. There were only occasional snatches of conversation, and the rare snorting of the horse. While the field was being raked, the tank crew moved some dirt around under the tank, where they had set up the coaxial machine gun in case they had to fight.

Geza Senior had to return to the village with the horse before dawn. The rays of the rising sun would soon fall on a carefully worked field and on the solitary corn stack standing on it. The tank crew began its first day in the enemy rear. The thought *How long will we be here?* troubled each tanker. Now we know: it was to be ten days.

The tired *gvardeytsy* collapsed in clothing soaked in sweat and rain. As Geza Junior immediately lay down to sleep, the Soviet crew covered him with what was available. There were no blankets or extra clothing of any kind in Slesarev's tank.

Knowing that the enemy could appear at any moment, the lieutenant organized a continuous two-man watch. When not taking their turn on duty, crew members were to sleep. Slesarev ordered observation and listening (this was the primary method at night) to be conducted for one-hour watches initially. When the men had rested somewhat, he could extend the length of a watch.

The commander and driver-mechanic stood the first watch. From under the tank the conditions for observation were not the best. The ideal position was the T-34's turret, so Grigoriy Vasilevich climbed up into the fighting compartment.[4] Carefully moving the cornstalks aside, he set about to use the vision ports. It was a lost cause, however. The depth of the cornstalk camouflage on top of the stack would not allow even a "keyhole view" in any direction. This effort to use the vision ports would have to be put aside at least until early the next morning. Slesarev angrily cursed himself not foreseeing this problem. He, the commander, was supposed to think of everything! In the course of piling on the corn, they should have left openings at the level of the turret roof so they could see out to survey the surrounding terrain.

More complicated, in fact almost unsolvable, was the problem of their wet clothing. The tank's engine had stopped working long ago, and the metal surrounding it had already cooled. The crew did not have a change of clothing. There could be no thought of lighting a fire, and there were only two dry greatcoats for five persons. One coat would be used to cover the resting watch relief, and the second would be shared by the two watch-standers. Only one solution seemed to remain—to dry the wet clothing with their own body heat. But this also was not an easy task. The crew was either in the tank or under it, in an almost immobile posture much of the time. They could not leave the tank, even at night, and run around the haystack to get warm because they could not leave such tracks in the harrowed field.

After the first twenty-four hours in this condition, their clothing had not completely dried. On the second night, they began to feel the bite of the autumn cold. By the morning of the third day, Geza Junior was compelled to run to the village and bring back some items of clothing and two blankets. The crew immediately took precautionary measures, erasing the Hungarian lad's tracks on the harrowed field by raking them over.

At the same time, the situation for the shut-in tankers was becoming more complicated with each hour. The Germans had gotten wind of a Soviet tank's having become disabled somewhere in the vicinity of Andakhazy. The Germans on motorcycles and the local police in wagons were scouring the entire region but without success. They passed by Onodi's field on the country road twice. The unwelcome guests dropped in on the village several times. They questioned Geza Onodi and his wife, Gezan, about Russian tankers, but the peasants shrugged their shoulders and unflinchingly replied, "We have not seen, and we do not know!"

On the morning of 10 October a declaration was posted in several villages: "Anyone who reports the location of the Soviet tankers will receive twenty *kholds* of land."[5] This was no small reward by Hungarian standards. The family of Geza Onodi remained silent, however, and the railroad-crossing guard uttered not a word. No one was enticed by the generous offer of German bounty!

The railroad guard dropped in at Onodi's home at midday on 11 October and told them about a conversation he had recently had with a certain Hungarian: this person had seemed interested in the whereabouts of Geza's son and wondered if the young man was ill.

They discussed the situation. The local authorities might also be interested in Geza Junior. He had, therefore, to be brought back under his parents' roof and the tankers moved closer to Onodi's house, where food could more easily be brought to them. The most suitable place for the Soviet soldiers to be concealed was the straw stack in Onodi's field garden.

How could they inform the tank commander about this new plan? They could not both go out into the cornfield at night, for they might attract someone's attention. They quickly solved this problem by having the old railroad man use his crude Russian to write out Geza Onodi's request on a scrap of paper: return the son home and move the tankers to a new hideout.

The transfer of Slesarev's crew to their new living quarters was accomplished on the night of 12 October. Leaving the cornfield, the *gvardeytsy* did not forget that they needed to erase their tracks leading from the corn stack toward the road, but they did not have worry. First rain and then snow quickly polished the earth, blotting out all signs of the tankers' presence.

A small German logistic unit arrived in Andakhazy on the evening of the twelfth and remained in the village until the eighteenth. Despite the presence of the Germans, someone from the Onodi family (there were three of them) brought food to the tankers almost every day, either early in the morning or late in the evening, when it was time to bring straw to the cattle.

On the morning of 18 October enemy soldiers who had been quartered in the village were stirring about, loading various military equipment onto their vehicles. Then, throwing many things aside, they hurriedly departed in the northwest direction.

An hour after their departure, the farmyard resounded with the loud happy voice of Geza Junior: "Grigoriy, Grigoriy, *Rusi, Rusi zoldat* [Russian soldiers]!" The longed-for liberation had finally arrived!

As it turned out, the first Russian soldiers to enter Andakhazy were scouts from 14th Motorcycle Battalion, 9th Guards Mechanized Corps, 6th Guards Tank Army. Guards Lieutenant Grigoriy Slesarev reported in detail to the commander of this battalion, Major Dmitriy Plotnikov, concerning what had happened with the tank and how the family of Geza Onodi had hidden the crew over the course of ten days. He presented to the battalion commander those who, at the risk of their own lives, had extended a helping hand to the *gvardeytsy* in their hour of need. Major Plotnikov ordered his chief of staff, Guards Captain Sergeev, to issue an appropriate document to the brave Hungarian.

The certificate, which is dated 18 October 1944, reads: "Issued to peasant Geza Onodi in recognition of the fact that he saved our T-34 tank and hid it and also the tank's crew—driver-mechanic Mikhail Matveevich Olenin and the tank commander, Lieutenant Slesarev—over the course of ten days. It is our fervent request and requirement that this named peasant and his family not be harmed and that they be extended every assistance." It is signed "Major Plotnikov, Unit Commander, field post office 31735."

The Onodi family preserved this remarkable document for a quarter century, and no one knew about it. Had I not stumbled upon the report in the archive, the accomplishment of the three Onodis would have remained unknown. The peasant family felt, however, that they had not done any particularly great or courageous deed. When the situation had required it, they simply put into practice their deep respect for these soldiers, their country's liberators.

I thought differently. The Onodi family had risked their lives in an act of courage. They had displayed no fear. Their actions had to be recognized. The Soviet Committee of War Veterans supported my opinion. Its chairman, Marshal of the Soviet Union S. K. Timoshenko, wrote the appropriate recommendation. For the bravery they displayed in rendering assistance to Soviet forces in the period of the Great Patriotic War, on 6 March 1972 the Presidium of the Supreme Soviet of the USSR awarded the Order of the Patriotic War 1st Degree to Geza Onodi and the medal "For Combat Service" to Gezan Onodi, both citizens of the Hungarian People's Republic.[6]

This is the subsequent fate of the people in this story. Two members of Guards Lieutenant Slesarev's crew perished in battle in January 1945. Grigoriy Vasilevich died soon after the war from wounds he received in the fighting. Mikhail Olenin remains healthy to this day. He has managed to visit his rescuers on two occasions (1972 and 1975). Unfortunately, Geza and Gezan Onodi have also passed on; they are survived by their son.

Failure to Coordinate

Forces of Second Ukrainian *Front* launched two consecutive attacks toward Budapest at the end of October 1944, first from the south and then from the east. Despite the enormous efforts of the attacking forces, in neither case were they able to overcome the powerful defensive belts protecting the city. The ends of the German horseshoe-shaped defensive lines were anchored on the Danube River south and northwest of the city. The density of the enemy positions was unusually high.

Front formations renewed the offensive on 5 December after some weeks' pause. The *front* commander's plan envisioned the capture of the Hungarian capital with two outflanking attacks. Forces of the *front*'s center—7th Guards Combined Arms Army, 6th Guards Tank Army, and General I. A. Pliev's Cavalry Mechanized Group—were advancing from the northeast; and 46th Army of the *front*'s left wing launched their offensive from the southwest.[1]

The brigades of 9th Guards Mechanized Corps, 6th Guards Tank Army, began movement to start positions for the upcoming offensive on the afternoon of 4 December.[2] By the close of the day they were concentrated on the northern outskirts of the town of Hatvan. It was here that two misfortunes befell us. With the combined efforts of artillerymen and tankers, we managed to correct the first problem quickly. The second one had an irreversible, tragic outcome, however.

A significant amount of artillery was deployed in the Hatvan area, on the main attack axis of 7th Guards Army. Its mission was to destroy enemy nodes of resistance with a 45-minute artillery preparation and, in so doing, to create the conditions necessary for the infantry to wage a successful offensive.

The telephone was the primary means of communication within the artillery units, which had moved into firing positions days before the beginning of the offensive. During this time, the higher artillery headquarters established a broad network of communications wire along the front and in the rear of subordinate battalions and batteries. As it later became obvious, braids of live wire were hung on poles and, in many places, were simply placed on the ground. All would have been well with the "god of war"— the artillery—had not the Shermans of 9th Guards Mechanized Corps's brigades shown up there that night. Without any malicious intent we had tangled most of the artillery telephone wire in our tracks, destroying the carefully organized communications net in about an hour. The artillerymen fell upon us like dogs on meat. They were running about frantically, cursing us up one side and down the other.

How could this be our fault? What were they thinking about at higher headquarters? Why did they not warn the artillerymen that their tanker neighbors would be arriving in the area shortly? Staff personnel were the real villains in this fiasco.

Now the artillery communications personnel had to pull out all the stops to repair the broken wire during the remainder of the night. Where would they find the several kilometers of wire they needed for the job?

Because we completely understood the predicament they were in, we did not respond in kind to the curses they hurled at us. To the contrary, all of our brigade's tankers jumped in to help them in their efforts. We knew that the success of our own attack on the following day depended on their fire support. We pulled all the commo wire out of our tracks, checked for continuity, spliced the breaks, wrapped tape around splices, and handed it over to the artillery commo personnel, along with all of our own spare wire. We worked together with them throughout the night to repair the damage we had caused. No one in either unit slept. We were dead on our feet by morning, but communications had been restored. The artillery preparation began at 1015, as planned.

There were staff officers in higher headquarters who forgot that all sorts of combat forces—infantry, armor, and artillery—

could not be concentrated in one relatively small geographic area without adequate coordination for terrain utilization.

In this particular instance the failure to coordinate terrain utilization deprived the tankers of the night's rest that was so necessary to them. Prior to this situation and after, commanders attempted to give their troops the maximum available time for sleep before an offensive because they knew that sleep deprivation was a common occurrence in any combat that was continued for a period of several days.

By not properly coordinating the arrival of a tank unit into an area already occupied by an artillery unit, the planning cells planted a "bomb" under established *front* regulations during their preparation for the operation. They were not thinking it through, they did not consider all factors, they did not foresee — and worst of all, they did not warn either the artillerymen or the tankers. This coordination failure placed both units, and others that were depending on them, in an exceptionally difficult situation.

The second, and indeed tragic, event occurred in the sky, on the northwest approaches to Hatvan at ten o'clock in the morning, twenty minutes before the beginning of the artillery preparation for the offensive. The night before, a German Henschel-126 reconnaissance aircraft had landed at an airfield near Debrecen.[3] Its pilot had offered his services to our command, which decided to take advantage of this opportunity before the Germans missed the pilot and changed their mutual recognition signals. Intelligence staff personnel, assisted by aircraft technicians, quickly prepared a camera for photographing objectives in the enemy rear, and a flight plan and route were carefully drawn up for the reconnaissance mission.

The deputy chief of intelligence of Second Ukrainian *Front*, Lieutenant Colonel Gavriil Zlochevskiy, was ordered to command this unusual sortie. Both the German pilot and the Soviet aircraft commander donned parachutes. At the last minute, Zlochevskiy received a strict order: in the event of anything untoward happening with the aircraft, attempt to land on our side of the forward edge.

The Henschel took off before first light and crossed the frontline trace north of Hatvan. The two men flew all around the German-Hungarian positions, using the German mutual-recognition signal in two of the more dangerous areas. They flew over and photographed enemy positions and terrain on the right bank of the Danube, all the way to the Austrian border. Ten times they turned their camera on and photographed various objectives and defensive lines. When it was time to fly back to our lines, they took a return heading. As the aircraft began to approach Hatvan from the northwest, it sharply reduced altitude and came under our antiaircraft umbrella. Our PVO was reliably covering the town against enemy air attacks.[4]

One of the antiaircraft batteries occupying a position not far from our 1st Battalion, 46th Guards Tank Brigade, suddenly opened up a barrage of fire. The Henschel fired red and green flares, signaling "I am your aircraft" and immediately climbed steeply, trying to get out of the zone of dense fire. The gun crews just as quickly corrected their aim and again brought the Henschel into the beaten zone [the area in the sky where the antiaircraft fires were concentrated]. The aircraft displayed the proper identification signal once more.

"You German fool! Trying to pass yourself off as one of ours. We'll show you!"

The antiaircraft gun crews continued to ignore the aircraft's signals and fired burst after burst into the sky. The He-126 burst into flames. The pilot attempted to put them out with a few rotations of a spin but was unsuccessful. Two figures separated from the aircraft as it began to lose altitude, and parachute canopies immediately blossomed above them. Moments later, however, the parachutists drifted into mortal danger—our infantrymen were firing at them with submachine guns. One of the parachutists quickly absorbed a burst of fire. The second parachutist was dropping into my 1st Battalion's position. We heard his loud voice, "Cease fire!" And right behind it, a long string of curses.

Tankers ran toward the firers at full speed, intending to stop the fusillade. The surviving "German," meanwhile, landed. I ran over to him with several *gvardeytsy* in order to protect him from the infantry who, no doubt, would try to shoot him on the ground. We knew that a live "tongue" was a thousand times more useful than a dead one.

"Who are you?" was our first question to the unknown parachutist. "Are you wounded?"

"I am the *front* deputy chief of intelligence, Lieutenant Colonel Zlochevskiy. You ask if I am wounded? You tried to kill me, you idiots! What material you destroyed!" And he sobbed convulsively, unabashed by the soldiers standing around him.

His right trouser leg and left sleeve were soaked in blood. I ordered the medic who had come running up to give the wounded officer immediate medical attention. Zlochevskiy allowed himself to be bandaged. However, he could not talk because he was weeping so hard; the stress on his nervous system from what he had just lived through had not yet subsided. Our brigade commander, Guards Lieutenant Colonel Nikolay Mikhno, came over. I reported the rank and duty position of the parachutist to him.

After a short time, the commander of the antiaircraft battery came running up to us, asking the tankers to sign a statement to the effect that his gun crews had shot down a German reconnaissance aircraft.[5]

Having heard the air defense artilleryman's request, the *front* deputy chief of intelligence regained the gift of speech and let loose with a long, animated tirade: "You will immediately be brought up on charges! [Several strong curse words.] This is the way I think it should be! Why did you not heed the signal 'I am your aircraft?' We gave it twice, but it didn't slow you down a bit! You morons ruined a most valuable package of aerial reconnaissance material!"

Mikhno gave orders: Detain the antiaircraft artillery officer, summon the brigade counterintelligence chief to deal with the incident, and prepare a medical vehicle to evacuate the wounded to the corps medical battalion.

During the time of my service in the active army, on three occasions I had to witness how, by the neglect of higher staff officers, main-gun fire was initiated against our own tanks, or how aircraft that had rendered the correct mutual recognition signals were shot down. Although these lapses in staff coordination were not the norm, they did occur at the front. The results of these failures, and others such as those that occurred with the artillery units' communications wire, were always painful to the subordinate commanders and their soldiers.

Night Raid

From the first days of the Great Patriotic War, infantry officer Guards Captain Petr Nikitovich Avramenko walked many frontline roads.[1] He made one of his walks in December 1944, from Vanyarc to Galgaguta, fifty kilometers northeast of Budapest in Hungary.

Our advancing forces had reached the approaches to Vanyarc by the close of 5 December (see map 5). The area was somewhat difficult for combat operations, replete with tree-covered hills that greatly limited the maneuverability of the mechanized units. Tanks and other vehicles were forced to conduct their attacks primarily along roads. The Germans had skillfully used the characteristics of the terrain, creating hardened nodes of defense along main roads and in villages. The enemy covered these defensive positions with large quantities of mine and explosive obstacles. To attack these strongholds frontally meant to suffer significant, as well as unnecessary, losses.

Guards Lieutenant Colonel Aleksandr Mikhailovich Ovcharov, commander of 18th Guards Mechanized Brigade, 9th Mechanized Corps, decided to employ a maneuver with dismounted infantry forces. He designated 3d Motorized Rifle Battalion, commanded by Captain Avramenko, as the bypassing detachment.[2] Using the cover of the night, they were to move across the hills and, in a surprise attack at dawn on 6 December, seize Galgaguta, an important railroad and highway junction.

Aleksandr Mikhailovich pointed out to the battalion commander possible movement axes of his subordinate units. The exact area of crossing the front line and specific route of march would be determined after the receipt of intelligence data.

The depth of the detachment's mission was approximately eight to ten difficult kilometers. A majority of it was cross-country, along muddy December fields and through wet forests, avoiding populated areas.

The mission was received at 2100 hours, and the time of the

attack was 0100, four hours having been set aside for preparation for the night raid. There was much work for leaders to accomplish in the companies and platoons in order to be able to execute such an important mission.

The battalion staff was responsible for preparing copies of the map of the area of operations—drawing the movement azimuth on it, along with the exact location of the passage of lines. Previous experience had confirmed that such a document helped the companies and platoons to hold rigidly to the designated route of march during periods of darkness.

Work of another type was in full swing in the companies, who were exempted from all other activities that did not prepare them for combat. Each soldier, sergeant, and officer received three times the normal issue of ammunition. In addition, five captured horses would carry pack-loads of ammunition, mortar shells, and hand grenades. The battalion commander had bitter past experience with ammunition shortages.

In March of the same year [1944], his units had surged far ahead and were the first to enter the city of Mogilev-Podolskiy [on the Dniester River at the Ukrainian-Moldavian border]. They captured its center, expending all their ammunition. They were then encircled by the enemy—who, fortunately, had left abandoned in the city a large quantity of weapons and ammunition. Captain Avramenko ordered his subordinates and the local citizenry to arm themselves with trophy rifles and submachine guns, and it was thanks to these weapons that they managed to defeat multiple enemy counterattacks and keep their hold on the city. The captain had no intention of falling into another predicament caused by ammunition shortages in the present battle.

After the completion of their preparatory tasks, the men were fed another hot meal and then allowed to rest for two hours. With the onset of darkness, brigade reconnaissance began to conduct searches on a broad front, looking for breaks in the enemy's combat formation. The detachment, without engaging in combat, would penetrate through these breaks into the enemy-held area and begin movement toward Galgaguta.

The brigade commander summoned the battalion commander at approximately 2400 and specified to him the battalion's route of march. Reconnaissance had found a sector in the area of Hill

297, one kilometer east of Vanyarc, that was unoccupied by the enemy. Avramenko fixed his gaze on the map coordinates, studying the contour of the terrain. The brigade commander remained silent, allowing his subordinate time for this study.

The detachment commander watched as the picture unfolded before him. A thick forest covered the reverse [north] slopes of Hill 297. The highway leading from Sirak to Vanyarc passed along its northern edge. The close proximity of the road to the forest was in the Soviets' favor because it would enable the battalion to move up to the road with some degree of security. Without exposing themselves, the troops would be able to study the density of enemy movement on the road, and, using this information, determine the method of crossing the road. Subsequently the companies and platoons would move almost 1,500 meters across an open field, cross an unnamed stream, and then intersect a second highway leading from Bercel to Vanyarc. The approaches to this road provided no natural cover. Frequent enemy traffic moving toward the front and the rear could be anticipated along this road.

Open terrain also extended west of this lateral road for a kilometer. The remaining three kilometers of the battalion's route segments lay along the northern and southern slopes of Hills 338 and 287, in thick woods. Two rivers flowed southward on the east side of Galgaguta—the Galga and the Golya. In order that troops not have to cross both rivers, it was decided to attack the southeastern outskirts of Galgaguta.

Ovcharov's voice drew Avramenko's attention away from the map. "Don't frown, Petr. This is not the first time you have gone into the enemy's rear!" He added, "I have decided to attack the enemy at 0040 on the line of the separate grove of trees 300 meters east of Vanyarc toward the outskirts of Vanyarc. This local action will draw the defender's attention and provide favorable conditions for your *gvardeytsy* to cross the front line."

After receiving the brigade commander's guidance, Avramenko headed off to his own headquarters. He continued to visualize the route of march to the final objective. The battalion commander analyzed the situation. The nature of the terrain from the assembly area to Galgaguta, the anticipated crossing of the Galga River, and the subsequent likelihood of combat in the built-up area required that each rifle company have sufficient independent fire-power. This fire-support strength would go far toward ensuring success.

In addition to three rifle companies, Avramenko's battalion had a machine-gun company (nine Maxim machine guns), an antitank company (eighteen antitank rifles), an antitank gun battery (four 45-mm cannons), and a mortar battery (six 82-mm mortars). To his great regret, his troops would not be able to drag the antitank guns along—they had to be left in the rear. The remaining fire-support assets would be distributed in the following manner: 1st and 2d Rifle Companies would each receive a mortar platoon (two tubes in each) and five antitank rifles; the third mortar platoon would be in reserve; 3d Rifle Company would be reinforced with eight antitank rifles; and each company would receive three Maxim machine guns.

The battalion commander still had to decide one important issue: what platoon should he designate as the point platoon? Following the precise azimuth, this unit would lead the main body of troops. When required, it would accept the enemy's first strike, thus creating the conditions for introducing the battalion's first echelon into the fight.

Avramenko knew his subordinates well and thus knew that he had to take this platoon from the lead company—a unit that had one good, a second not-bad, and a third outstanding platoon leader. He chose Guards Senior Lieutenant Evgeniy Mushkin, a young officer who had shown himself a skilled and intelligent leader in previous fights, having earned the Order of the Red Star.[3] Mushkin's two squad leaders, Guards Sergeant Petr Kulev and Guards Junior Sergeant Ivan Kororyanets, were experienced soldiers.

Everyone had gathered at the battalion headquarters, awaiting Petr Nikitich's return from the brigade command post. The battalion commander took the chief of staff's map and quickly drew on it the detachment's route of march. After that, he dictated the apportionment of fire-support assets among the companies. Immediately beginning their work with the map, the officers determined the azimuths of the battalion's movement from the start point and beyond into the enemy's dispositions. Then, having completed these calculations, they carefully rechecked their work. All of the data were transferred to paper overlays prepared for the battalion commander, company commanders, point platoon commander, and staff.

Petr Avramenko quickly assigned his subordinates missions on the map and issued instructions on the sequence of departure to the start line, the southern slope of Hill 297. Then he ordered everyone to rest.

Everyone stood to at 0030 on 6 December.[4] Squad and platoon commanders checked the rigging of every weapon and piece of equipment on each soldier. To keep from giving away the detachment's movement, there could not be a single banging of an entrenching tool or clinking of a rifle. The platoons and companies were ready to move out in thirty minutes. The strictest order was given forbidding smoking.

The night was dark and windy. Nature itself favored our soldiers. The wind was blowing from the north. Any sound or noise from the enemy positions would be heard in the detachment. While this fact might seem insignificant, it was an important consideration on this particular night.

Combat flared up in the Vanyarc area at the exact hour specified by the brigade commander, 0040. The 76-mm cannons pounded away, joined by the 45-mm antitank guns. The mortars were not silent, either. This intensive fire from our side was to convince the enemy of the seriousness of the attackers' intentions. The wind quickly carried the fleeting rattles of submachine guns and then the loud shouts of "Ura" from many voices. Their comrades were fighting in support of the bypassing detachment.

The hands of the clock approached the start time of the night raid. Brigade scouts reported, "The enemy is quiet in the battalion's crossing sector!" The battalion commander gave the command, "Forward!"

Mushkin's platoon stepped out smartly toward Hill 297, and behind him was the entire 1st Company of Captain Vladimir Ostrovskiy. After a short interval came the battalion commander with his headquarters personnel. Behind them followed 2d Rifle Company, commanded by Guards Senior Lieutenant Aleksandr Iskakov. The five captured horses carrying ammunition were also in the line of march.

The pitch darkness and the absence of enemy resistance permitted the battalion to move in a compressed column, which was advancing quickly in its plunge into the enemy's disposition.

They would move through the forest to the northwest slopes of Hill 297 and there prepare for their next rush—across the highway that led toward Vanyarc from the east.

During actions in the enemy rear, the most important thing was always to use the masking characteristics of the terrain and the time of day for troops to remain undetected as long as possible. For this reason, the detachment would avoid passing through any village and would attempt to cross any roads they encountered unnoticed. There were four roads on the battalion's eight-kilometer route—no small number!

Not more than twenty minutes after departure, the detachment was in the woods adjacent to the first highway. The soldiers lay on the ground. Brigade scouts, who were moving with the point platoon, had been ordered to accompany the detachment to a depth of two and a half kilometers. They were divided into two groups and, with Avramenko's permission, moved out to the right and left up to the road. Their mission was to cover the road-crossing sector from the east and west, providing early warning to the main body about any approaching enemy vehicles.

Quickly one group and then the other gave the prearranged signal: the main body could begin crossing the highway. When the short command was issued, the companies and platoons hurried across the road one behind the other. The battalion commander remained in the forest with his staff, allowing the detachment to pass by them.

Two companies were already across the road. Specially designated observers were intently looking in the direction where the scouts were concealed. Suddenly the right-side group gave the signal—a circle made by a blue flashlight, indicating the approach of an enemy vehicle. The 3d Rifle Company, who were prepared for the rush across the highway, immediately led their pack horses into the nearest cover. Tense moments passed. Finally, two heavily laden covered trucks rumbled past, moving toward Vanyarc.

Quiet ruled once again. The signal came from the right side scout group—"All clear!" Then, quick as a shot, "Forward!" and the 3d Company, Avramenko with his headquarters, and the pack horses slipped across the road in one movement.

Now a signal passed from the detachment to the scouts, and they rejoined the battalion. Companies and platoons rapidly resumed movement on an azimuth of 300 degrees. The length of the second route segment was 1,500 meters. They increased the pace immediately, through a cornfield and into a vineyard. The footing grew worse, and the movement slowed down. There might be a field trail nearby, but no one had time to look around for it.

In the point platoon, Guards Sergeant Petr Kulev's squad was ensuring that his unit held to the specified azimuth. Guards Junior Sergeant Ivan Kororyanets' squad was counting paces traveled and, from time to time, announcing the numbers. "Six hundred meters! . . . Eight hundred meters!"

By 0200 the battalion had reached the Vanyarc River, one kilometer north of Vanyarc. The river was approximately six meters wide and over one meter deep at this point. With two obstacles in succession, the river and a highway, this was the most difficult portion of the route. The highway doubtless was one of the main roads in the enemy disposition. The troops could take some comfort in the fact that it was now the middle of the night—soldiers in combat and logistic units were normally resting at this time and so there would not be much movement on the road.

The detachment commander pondered how to cross the river. A shallow spot would be the quickest place to ford it, if they could find one. But they still had more than an hour's movement ahead of them, the attack on Galgaguta, and then the stubborn effort to hold on to the captured objective for a prolonged period of time. There was no possibility of drying their clothing. A ford was not practical.

They would have to find some materials to construct makeshift rafts for crossing the river. But what was available? They began to search. The soldiers combed every patch of land in a radius of 500 meters. The results were disappointing. There was not a single structure in the area, only three piles of brushwood and a stack of straw. Avramenko then made the decision to create rafts from the brushwood and straw. They accomplished this purpose by taking a double armful of straw, enclosing it in several wraps of twine, and then covering it with a poncho. The sections of straw were then bound together with twine or rope to create a sufficiently bulky floating bundle. Finally two or three of these bundles were joined together with poles. A raft of any capacity could now be constructed from these segments.

All the companies and platoons set about constructing the makeshift rafts. Guard posts were established around the area where the battalion had halted. Being forced to observe strict regulations against noise and light, the men were working under exceptionally difficult conditions.

Approximately an hour was consumed in the construction of the rafts. When the first one was completed, the scouts used it to cross to the opposite bank and then stealthily dispersed to the outer edges of the sector intended for crossing the highway and began to observe enemy traffic patterns on the road. Mushkin's point platoon crossed next, followed by the battalion commander and his headquarters personnel. The commander wanted to control the companies and platoons as they crossed and to distribute them out over a 200-meter zone on the opposite bank. From here they would make their jump across the next road.

It took another forty minutes for everyone to cross the river, though everything proceeded normally. The horses were left on the east bank for the time being because they were too large for the rafts and too difficult to conceal on the narrow strip of open ground on the other side. The ammunition they were carrying was unloaded and ferried across, to be deposited on the far bank. The unladen horses would be moved across the river as soon as the main body had crossed the highway. The soldiers in the companies quickly disassembled the rafts and carried the ponchos and straw bundles with them.

There was still another river, the Galga, to cross up ahead. It was Avramenko's plan that Guards Senior Lieutenant Iskakov's 2d Company would cross this river south of Galgaguta. But there was also the possibility that Captain Ostrovskiy's 1st Company would have to cross the river as well. The detachment would attempt to capture intact the bridge east of the town. But anything could happen, and the enemy might succeed in destroying the bridge. The troops carried their makeshift raft materials with them as insurance.

A report came in from the scouts: "Enemy movement on the Vanyarc-Bercel road is insignificant." The situation dictated a fast crossing of the highway. The command went out: "Prepare to move quickly across the road!" To reduce the exposure time of the companies, the battalion crossed in two places, approximately 150 meters apart. Companies then moved away from the road into the forest southeast of Fundushpusta without delay. Having accomplished their mission, at this time the brigade scouts returned to the brigade location.

The battalion did not tarry long in the woods. Company and platoon leaders accounted for all their personnel and weapons. The detachment's "rear"—the pack horses—quietly munched oats. The broad expanse of the forest and broken terrain would now permit the units to move unseen to the near approaches to their final objective. The companies plunged into the woods, renewing their progress due west, in the direction of the saddle between Hills 287 and 338. The going was difficult for the soldiers: they were walking uphill in the dark, and fatigue from their previous exertions began to take its effect on them. But the climb lasted only a kilometer. Now they were on the western slope of the hill mass, and the ground inclined downward all the way to Galgaguta.

The detachment entered its last cover and concealment on the route, a patch of woods east of Fundushpusta. The commander allowed the men thirty minutes of rest. Personnel and weapons were accounted for once again. Everyone was preparing for the upcoming fight. It was still quiet in the enemy-held town. Avramenko quickly assembled his subordinate commanders to refine their missions. He sent Evgeniy Mushkin's point platoon forward to capture the bridge. This would ensure the rapid crossing of the Galga River by Ostrovskiy's 1st Company. Platoons from Iskakov's 2d Company would make the crossing on their poncho rafts. After this, the battalion main body would seize the town with a simultaneous attack from the south and east, capturing first the southern portion of Galgaguta and then the railroad station. The Soviet troops would expand their position to the remainder of the town without delay.

Mushkin's platoon began moving along the west edge of the forest grove toward the bridge. Bypassing Fundushpusta on the west side, the platoon was halted by the challenge of a sentry. The unit's leader did not hesitate, immediately responding to the guard in German: "ss! Special mission!" Quietly commanding his platoon to halt, he moved forward with Sergeant Kulev toward the sentry, mumbling some indistinct words in the enemy's language. When the enemy soldier was just several steps away, Mushkin turned on his flashlight. The bright beam struck the German in the eyes. At this moment Kulev abruptly knocked the German's submachine gun from his hands and dropped him to the ground with a short stroke of a knife.

The platoon leader quickly formed his men into a file and led them forward. The size and nature of the enemy objective were unknown to the unit: it had to seize as large an area as possible.

Approximately 100 meters ahead the *gvardeytsy* came upon an antiaircraft gun battery position. They awoke its crews in two dugouts with loud commands of *"Ruki vverkh* [Hands up]!" They disarmed the Germans, brought all of them to one dugout, and posted a guard. Mushkin sent a report to the battalion commander about the capture of the enemy antiaircraft gun crews and then led his men down the hill toward the river. When they were not more than 150 meters from the bridge, a machine gun opened up somewhere to their right. Its crew were firing at the sound of soldiers' boots, without seeing their target. Bullets whistled around Mushkin's platoon, wounding two soldiers.

Mushkin barked out an order: "Lie down!" But the platoon had already sought the cover of the ground. A moment later the platoon leader ordered Guards Sergeant Kulev to crawl with his squad to the right and Guards Junior Sergeant Kororyanets to take his squad to the left. They converged on the enemy firing position. The Germans periodically fired bursts into the darkness, giving away their exact location. The detonations of several hand grenades ripped the air simultaneously, their echo reverberating along the banks of the river. Mushkin led his men into the attack on the bridge. Reaching it quickly, they raced across and then fired the signal for its capture—a green star-cluster.

As they had been detected by the enemy, the battalion's point squad could not now reach Galgaguta undetected. Quick action became necessary. Avramenko thought for a few moments. His initial plan to cross the Galga River with Ostrovskiy's company on the bridge and Iskakov's company on makeshift rafts south of Galgaguta was no longer viable. It would require too much time. A simultaneous attack on the town from two directions was no longer possible.

While the Germans were still attempting to clarify the situation, Soviet forces had to conduct a powerful and rapid strike to seize the initiative and further confuse them. The detachment commander decided to rush Ostrovskiy's 1st Company and Domushchiy's 3d Company into Galgaguta across the bridge. The 1st Company would attack the center of the town and 3d Company the southern blocks that intersected the highway. Iskakov's 2d Company would attack toward Fundushpusta, and Mushkin's point platoon would remain in reserve.

This decision was announced in the form of fragmentary orders, and the battalion commander led his units into the attack. The *gvardeytsy* of 1st and 3d Companies rushed toward the bridge. The attack on Galgaguta had begun. The enemy offered stubborn resistance in the center of town, engaging in heated combat. A short time later a fierce engagement broke out in the southern outskirts. The enemy began to illuminate with flares the approaches to the southeast edge of town.

A report arrived from Iskakov: "We have taken Fundushpusta from the march. We have captured three wheeled vehicles and a large quantity of antiaircraft ammunition. A logistic unit there did not offer the slightest resistance. They have run away!"

Avramenko moved with his headquarters out of the woods to the northern outskirts of Fundushpusta. His signalers established wire communications with Ostrovskiy's 1st Company. He reported that he had captured four blocks in the enemy stronghold and had reached the main-road intersection in the town. The defenders were putting up stiff resistance.

Several minutes later 3d Company commander Domushchiy reported by telephone: "We are fighting at the highway and moving toward the railroad station."

The battalion commander reported the initial successes on the approaches to and in Galgaguta to the brigade commander by radio and then ordered his command-observation post to displace forward. He needed to be closer to the first echelon. The enemy might counterattack at dawn, now just about ninety minutes away.

Ostrovskiy's 1st Company was slowly moving along the highway through the center of town to the north, fighting for each building. The men of Domushchiy's 3d Company were having particular success. They quickly captured the railroad station, where they found two trains with ammunition and fuel. The company commander, with the battalion commander's permission, left the platoon of Guards Lieutenant Nikolay Samoylenko at the station and launched an attack along the northwest and northern outskirts of Galgaguta with the company's remaining forces.

This important enemy stronghold was completely in the detachment's hands by 0900 on 6 December. They had accomplished the assigned mission.

Our 46th Guards Tank Brigade, followed by the main body of 18th Guards Mechanized Brigade, arrived from Bercel at midday. We launched our attack on the independent axis Nezha-Keseg-Ozagard-Tolmach on the morning of 7 December.[5]

Thank You, Ice

For every veteran of every war there is a village, settlement, town, hill, or section of rural path or urban highway where that veteran's own courage and patriotism were severely tested by the combat situation, where he or she may even have shed blood. Such a place will remain in a veteran's memory for life.

Recalling this kind of experience many decades later, most men and women are thankful for the mercy that was granted to them by the random and deadly fate of war. Even if they were seriously wounded at such a place, they still remain among the living while many of their comrades have been laid to rest. I have a few of these places in my own memory, both in the west and in the far east. This story is about one of these places—and for me, a most unusual one.

It was the last winter of the war. Soviet forces were threatening the Germans in northern Hungary and southern Czechoslovakia. Second Ukrainian *Front* formations were moving slowly but inexorably to the northwest, tightening the encirclement ring around the German-Hungarian grouping in Budapest.

Considering that 7th Guards Army's 24th and 25th Rifle Corps were not having success on the army's right flank, on 21 December 1944 Marshal of the Soviet Union R. Ya. Malinovskiy, the *front* commander, assigned a mission to 6th Guards Tank Army (see map 6): covered by a portion of forces from the north and northwest on the line between Levice and Shalov, the unit was to launch an attack with main forces south along the Hron River and, in cooperation with 7th Guards Army, destroy the enemy in the sector between the Ipel and Hron Rivers.[1]

Carrying out the assigned mission, the tank army's shock grouping of two tank and two mechanized brigades changed their axes of advance 180 degrees and began moving to the south by the close of 21 December. Of the units designated for accomplishing the assigned combat mission, 46th Brigade happened to be the least engaged with the enemy on the approaches to Batovce. It quickly disengaged completely.

The brigade commander, Guards Lieutenant Colonel Nikolay Mikhno, assembled the battalion commanders and briefed them on the new mission. He ordered me once again, as he had several days earlier, to lead a small forward detachment—this time, to move rapidly on the axis Sadnitse-Zalaba, capture Salka from the march, and hold it in order to protect the brigade's right flank. The detachment consisted of a tank company, a platoon of *tanko-desantniki* mounted on the tanks, and a sapper squad. We were to depart in forty minutes.

The battalion commander, Guards Captain Ivan Yakushkin, ordered the subordinates of Guards Senior Lieutenant Grigoriy Danilchenko to prepare for execution of the forward detachment mission. I was pleased by this selection—one could move mountains with this experienced, decisive, and intelligent company commander who knew how to listen to the advice of others. I had traveled thousands of frontline kilometers with Danilchenko from the fields of our native Ukraine.

Time was pressing. We quickly took inventory and replenished our ammunition. Then we set out into the pitch-black night. All tank commanders sat on the left fender of their Shermans next to the driver-mechanic to be able to see the road with four eyes. We always did this in inclement weather and at night.

We passed Sadnitse and, four kilometers south of this settlement, smashed through a checkpoint of some defending enemy unit. It was impossible in the limited visibility for us to discern what kind of enemy forces were opposing us. I reported the situation to the brigade command, and we rushed on toward Zalaba.

Two tanks led by Guards Lieutenant Grigoriy Krikun with *desantniki* on board went forward as the combat reconnaissance patrol.[2]

Going as fast as road conditions would allow, 46th Guards Brigade's main body was moving along the forward detachment's route of march. A distance of five, at times seven, kilometers separated us. At this same time (this information became known to us somewhat later), the Germans, attempting to disrupt our upcoming offensive, concentrated separate units of 6th, 8th, and 3d Panzer Divisions (up to 160 combat vehicles) in the Sokolec area on the night of 21–22 December and launched a powerful strike against the right flank of 7th Guards Army. Due to a poorly organized reconnaissance, Soviet forces had not anticipated the attack.

Our detachment surged toward Zalaba, its left flank securely protected by the Ipel River and Berzhen Hills. Night was our friend and ally. We were falling on the Germans like snow on a bare head. Our main focus was not to delay. We destroyed the Germans with our tracks and by fire. Our crews, as in the past, proved themselves worthy of their "guards" designation. Instill fear and destroy! Fear itself is a valuable weapon against an enemy.

As it turned out, Zalaba held a large German logistical installation. Our reconnaissance was now operating quite successfully. The patrol approached the northern outskirts of the town undetected. Krikun immediately sent out five *tankodesantniki* as dismounted reconnaissance. They slipped through field gardens into the yard of one of the homes on the edge of town and looked around. Several loaded trucks were parked on the street. All was quiet. This was the enemy's immediate rear. The forward edge as it existed that evening was fifteen to twenty kilometers to the north.

The incoming reconnaissance data dictated the course of action that would ensure victory: a rapid attack on the enemy in Zalaba by the forward detachment in column. Crush, disperse, shoot, and capture documents and prisoners in a brief period. Then, without delay, move on to the endpoint of the combat mission, to Salka.

Grigoriy Danilchenko asked me, "Can we turn on our sirens?"

His request pleased me. "We haven't used them for quite a while. Have they become rusty?"

The company commander, it seemed to me, responded with offense in his voice. "Not in my unit! Each one is operating like a good watch."

"Grigoriy, don't be offended. I'm joking."

Krikun met us on the approaches to the settlement. He reported: "All remains quiet in the enemy dispositions. It would be difficult to think of better conditions for an attack!"

I spent several minutes explaining the nature of the upcoming actions. Platoon and tank commanders ran back to their own vehicles. Motors revved. An "armored ram" was launched into the enemy.[3] The powerful shrieks of the sirens assailed our eardrums. The surging, fire-breathing night raid with Shermans is difficult to describe with words. One had to witness the carnage, to experience these adrenaline-filled minutes, the stupefying speed. The M4A2s crushed and then pushed aside everything they encountered along the route of their movement, including cargo trucks and buses. We ran over crates, barrels, field kitchens, and light wagons with our tanks and poured machine-gun fire into supply troops rushing out of the buildings.

An ostentatious staff car stood in the courtyard of the third house on the right—a clear sign an important personage was there. *Tankodesantniki* quickly surrounded the domicile and outbuildings. I went into the house with several *gvardeytsy*. I walked past two rooms to a third room—the bedroom, where a woman lay in the bed. The uniform of a German colonel was on the back of a chair. Where was the uniform's owner? We found him under the bed, where he had attempted to hide. I ordered him to crawl out and get dressed. He was a good catch!

A runner from Danilchenko came in. They had captured a quartermaster general officer in the neighboring courtyard. This was indeed a good haul—two important "tongues." They probably knew a great deal. We would question them later. I hurried the tankers, demanding that we not be held up in Zalaba. The big commotion had given us away. We had to hurry on to our final objective at Salka.

The last houses of the southern outskirts of the village we had just captured were now behind us. Krikun's reconnaissance had moved forward some time ago, undetected by the enemy. The situation still favored our accomplishing the assigned mission, though quickness was essential. Considering the dark conditions, we tried to force more speed out of our Shermans. But, God help us, in doing this we had to remember something else: not to race the *Emcha* into road curves or on icy road stretches.[4] In our situation each combat vehicle was worth its weight in gold. We did not have much combat power, and we were plunging deep into the enemy disposition. In the event of a problem, the crew could rely only on themselves. Help would not come quickly.

We placed the prisoners in my tank, sitting them on the floor of my fighting compartment. "Excuse me, sirs, your colonel and general officer kid-glove handling is over!" Now the detachment commander's Sherman was transporting ten men (its normal five-man crew plus five prisoners).

Another five kilometers down the road we suddenly received an order. Change of mission! Turn around! Move northeast to Lontov, capture it from the march, and hold it until the arrival of the main body. What caused such a radical change in the mission? We had no idea.

As I was to learn later, the brigade had already stopped and reoriented to the new axis of advance. Detachment, stop! We turned around 180 degrees and entered Zalaba a second time, but now from the south. We had to hurry to another sector, toward Lontov. Some quite serious change in the frontline trace of the sides had caused the command to make a new decision, radically altering the direction of our actions. Here is why.

The enemy, developing success to the north, had reached the dominating heights at Sahy by the morning of 22 December. In the situation that had unfolded, the *front* commander planned to launch a strike into the flank and rear of the enemy grouping. He intended to use 21st, 22d, and 46th Guards Tank Brigades, which by this hour had reached the area of Trginya.

For this reason Lieutenant Colonel Mikhno quickly redirected the forward detachment under my command to a new sector of the front. Before morning Guards Junior Lieutenant Aleksandr Sokolov's combat reconnaissance patrol reported that it had made the right turn toward Lontov. The detachment main body was moving at a dangerous speed of approximately thirty KPH. The driving surface of the road was wet and in many places icy.

We reached the fork in the road, and there the accident occurred. My experienced driver-mechanic, Guards Senior Sergeant Aleksey Klyuev, committed an inexcusable error: he had not slowed down for the curve. Unfortunately, exactly at this moment the Sherman struck a patch of ice. It slewed from side to side. The left track struck some kind of surface irregularity on the road, and in seconds the tank was lying on its side. Without stopping, three *Emchas* skidded past and headed toward Lontov. Only Danilchenko's tank stopped, to help recover my tank.

Little good could come from this tip-over. Though we tankers were no strangers to hard knocks, this accident slammed us around inside the tank pretty thoroughly. My passengers were somewhat shaken as well. We were delayed at the accident scene no more than fifteen minutes, however. I handed off the general and the colonel to brigade reconnaissance personnel while my tank was being righted. The prisoners were no longer in our way. It was dark and quiet inside the tank. Now I needed to supervise the actions of the detachment.

My tank had to be checked out thoroughly before it could move — something could have cracked or broken during the impact. I transferred to another tank, and several of the detachment's Shermans headed off to the east, toward the objective we had been ordered to seize.

During that same time a great tragedy was unfolding in Lontov and on the approaches to it. Perhaps because of the increasingly heavy snowfall, reconnaissance had not detected the enemy. But more likely the Germans had taken special care not to touch the patrol, instead allowing it to enter the village, where it was destroyed by enemy troops. The *Emchisti* [M4 tankers] had plunged into an enemy ambush at full speed. Three Shermans were knocked out by point-blank *panzerfaust* shots. A portion of their crews had been killed, and those who survived had been captured. The Germans tied up prisoners with commo wire, poured gasoline on them, and set them afire. We came upon this heartbreaking scene when we captured Lontov on the afternoon of 22 December. Subsequently we knew this village by no other name than "Black Lontov."

The vehicles that had driven around my overturned *Emcha* had driven into an ambush (the same ambush that had allowed the patrol to pass) on the approaches to Lontov. The lead tank was pierced by *panzerfaust* rounds and immediately set on fire. None of the crew survived. The remaining tanks of Junior Lieutenant Nikolay Baboshkin's platoon stopped instantly and unleashed a storm of main-gun fire at the enemy. By the time we arrived, they had put down the German ambush and moved forward somewhat. We encountered the enemy main body two kilometers west of Lontov. The detachment deployed and began to attack. The enemy met us with dense fires from the west outskirts of the village.

We were unable to overcome the defenders with the forces we had on hand (six Shermans and about forty *avtomatchiki*). I reported my assessment to the brigade commander, who ordered us to hold our present position in order to support the deployment and transition into the attack of the brigade main body.

We tankers buried the charred remains of our combat comrades with heavy hearts. In these sad moments the thought came to me, *Had my Sherman not tipped over at the fork in the road, I would have suffered a fate similar to these men. Thank you, ice, for rolling my tank onto its side.*

Fate plays with a person. Occasionally it brings one such a surprise that one can do nothing except throw up one's hands. Twenty years after the events described here, Madam Fate brought together two soldiers who had stood on opposite sides of the front line on that night.

It was 1964. I was a senior instructor with the tactics faculty of the Frunze Military Academy. I had a group of officers from the National People's Army of the German Democratic Republic in a summer training camp. We were developing the theme, "tank regiment in the forward detachment." After the exercise, as we were returning to the base, one of the officers asked me to talk about similar actions of tank units during the Great Patriotic War. We were on the road about an hour, quite enough time for reminiscing.

I gave them several examples from successful battles of 233d Tank Brigade (as forward detachment of 5th Mechanized Corps) in the Jassy-Kishinev operation (Romania, 1944). I emphasized that later, in Hungary and Czechoslovakia (October 1944–April 1945) combat operations were particularly fluid, involving frequent maneuver. During this period, forward (raid) detachments had fewer forces—or, in other words, less strength.

I continued by telling them about the forward detachments I

had led, which consisted of tank and *tankodesantniki* companies on the eastern approaches to the town of Sahy and then south of this town—the actions already described in this chapter. I was silent, of course, about the tragedy that occurred in Lontov. One of the students, a Captain Zeitler, spoke: "I was there. I was a soldier in a tank-killer unit. I remember those heavy battles well."

After our return to Moscow, I looked up the personnel record of this officer. Indeed he had fought on the approaches to Budapest. Another surprise: Zeitler had been decorated with a medal "For Destruction of Russian Tanks" in the battles in December 1944. This information cut like a dagger to my heart. After so many years two former enemies had come together in one place.

Of course I understood that he had been fulfilling his duty to his country. But just the same, I was now required to teach him the tactics of contemporary combat. The German was a good student, receiving high marks and excelling in all his courses. Yet some heaviness remained in my heart. I am speaking about it openly: I did not hold any hatred toward him, there was no malice in me, but a degree of enmity did come to the surface.

Two circumstances gave me comfort. I would not be conducting any more exercises with this particular group of students. They were moving on to the third course, and the instructors of the operational art faculty would become their leaders now. In addition, I was leaving for an assignment as a deputy divisional commander. The Soviet Army had instituted a regulation that after ten years of teaching at an academic institution, an instructor was required to fulfill a one-year assignment with troops. So the parting between the former tank hunter, now a student, and the former forward detachment commander, now an instructor, was unavoidable.

At the end of December 1944, 6th Guards Tank Army was placed in the *front* reserve. Its units and formations were brought up to full strength in personnel and combat equipment and were being prepared for upcoming battles. The tank army remained in the *front* reserve until March 1945. True, when the Germans launched a third attack for the purpose of breaking out of their surrounded Budapest grouping, 9th Guards Mechanized Corps was rapidly moved to the left bank of the Danube River south of

Budapest. If enemy troops had succeeded in forcing the Danube, the Soviets' mechanized corps units would have engaged them in battle. Fortunately this did not occur.

A Slight Error

From my school days I recall this amusing anecdote in the history of my country. Our teacher told us the story during our study of the reign of Russian Empress Catherine II, the era in which the incident took place. As everyone knows, Her Royal Highness was well educated. Just the same, however. . . .

A high court found some citizen-noble of Russia (his name has been forgotten) guilty of committing a dastardly crime and sentenced him to death. One of the sovereign's court grandees requested that Catherine II delay imposition of the sentence and order a supplementary investigation of the case. He assured her that the innocence of the accused would be proven. The empress listened to his presentation but undertook no actions of the requested nature.

The day having arrived for the punishment to be imposed, the persistent aristocrat decided to appeal his case to Her Highness once more. His petitioner having made the request known to her, Catherine II quietly took a sheet of paper and wrote *"Pomilovat nelzya kaznit!"* After signing it in her own hand, she gave the paper to the petitioner, who read the note, bowed low, and then withdrew.

Catherine's intended response to his petition was "Cannot pardon, execute!" She should have written *Pomilovat nelzya, kaznit!* However, she neglected to insert the comma that is required by Russian punctuation rules for this meaning of the two imperative clauses.

Some time later the tsarina learned that the punishment had not been implemented. She demanded an explanation. Her advisors showed her the instruction, which was now in the following form: *Pomilovat, nelzya kaznit!*—"Pardon, do not execute!" The petitioner had cleverly inserted the comma that Catherine II omitted, but in such a way as completely to reverse her decision. Witnesses say that Catherine II merely smiled.

And so a small symbol—in this case a comma, inserted into a document by someone else's hand—saved a man's life.

Now I will tell another story. During the Great Patriotic War each division, corps, and army had its own newspaper. The publication was small in size, and its content was devoted primarily to the particular unit's operational activities. The paper published various orders of the Supreme High Commander [Stalin] and recollections of frontline soldiers on various themes. It provided information on the lives of the people back home, and it reported *Sovinformburo* summaries.[1] Occasionally one could find sketches or photographs of new types of enemy armaments—tanks or aircraft, for example—on the pages of the division newspaper, with the required arrow pointing to the most vulnerable spots, where best to strike the equipment item with a shell, and where to aim incendiary bullets. Jokingly the troops referred to the publication as "our trench *Pravda*."[2]

Honestly speaking, I will say that frontline officers and soldiers loved their newspaper. They especially befriended the photo correspondents. Under the difficult wartime conditions, soldiers eagerly sought the opportunity to be photographed so they then could send the priceless snapshots to their girlfriends and parents. The joy was twofold, both at the front line and in their homes far away.

On 7 November 1944 the division newspaper *Sovetskiy voin* (Soviet fighting man) published the holiday order of the Supreme High Commander, J. V. Stalin. Through an oversight of both the proofreader and the editor, the letter *l* was omitted from the word *glavno-komanduyushchiy*.[3] The meaning of the title thus became "insulter in chief."[4] The newspaper issue containing this error was published in an increased-circulation edition in connection with the upcoming twenty-seventh anniversary of the Great October Socialist Revolution. The division paper had been delivered to units early so that the Supreme Commander's speech could be read at meetings honoring the holiday occasion.

This special edition had also been passed down already to troop units in some regiments. This distribution was a direct responsibility of the political officers and their subordinates.

Soldiers in one battalion detected the typographical error about thirty minutes before their unit's meeting and reported it to the chain of command. A hurricane of enormous force swept through the ranks. The entire officer component of the division was alerted and thrown into the task of collecting up and then destroying the newspapers.

No explanation was offered to anyone. What evoked this action regarding a division newspaper whose ink was still wet? What caused the publication of this edition to be elevated to the class of a "criminal act"? These same measures were taken when the leaflets dropped by enemy aircraft over our troop dispositions were gathered up and burned. And now our own "trench *Pravda*" was being subjected to a similar stern punishment.

The division commander understood perfectly that this typographical error would not be advantageous to his health. He angrily sought an explanation: "How did this happen? You have reduced the Supreme High Commander to the lowest level! The Germans ridicule the integrity and achievement of J. V. Stalin in their leaflets, but never have they stooped to this level!"

With the release of this special issue to countless readers, the prevailing mood in the *Sovetskiy voin* offices was lighthearted and upbeat. They had made their deadline! Overall it was an interesting issue. They had prepared the holiday edition several days in advance, leaving space for Stalin's speech. Having nervously awaited the TASS transmission of Stalin's order on the evening of 6 November, a small group of newspaper staff members had worked the night before the holiday to prepare the important document for printing. But now the laborious, intensive hours of getting out the "soldiers' friend and advisor" were behind them. The editor in chief of *Sovetskiy voin*, Captain Igor Berezkin, let out a deep breath.

His wake-up call came about thirty minutes later. The captain could only sigh: his subordinates—and this also meant their supervisor—had carried out an arch-criminal act. They had denigrated, slandered, even defecated on the name of the Father of the Peoples, the Generalissimus.[5]

The division SMERSH chief with two *avtomatchiki* strode into the spotless Hungarian house where the editorial staff had set up shop. Berezkin greeted them. They replied with a curt response like a pistol shot, "You are under arrest!"

Two days later the military tribunal's sentence was announced: "For discrediting the name of the Great Stalin, for . . . [a lengthy list of similar charges—for aiding and abetting the enemy, attempting to subvert the soldiers' faith in the justice of our cause, and so on]," Captain Berezkin was reduced to private, stripped of all decorations, and sent to a punishment battalion for three months. In that faraway time, which we hope will never return, they knew how to attach a false accusation to someone and make it stick.

The editorial staff did not escape unnoticed: the chief of the division political department disbanded them. Its male personnel were sent out to troop units, and the proofreader, a woman, was discharged from the army and sent home. *Shtrafnik* Igor Berezkin perished in the fierce fighting around Budapest in November 1944.[6]

Two mistakes in texts. Thanks to the lightning-quick thinking of a nobleman and his inarguable boldness (he had the courage to insert a comma in the writing of Her Imperial Majesty), the first error saved the life of a condemned man. The second one was fatal: for it, the editor in chief of a division newspaper was sentenced to the fullest extent of wartime military law, and the punishment destroyed him.

The Unknown Steppe

Formations and units of 6th Guards Tank Army closed on their assembly areas west, south, and southeast of the city of Choybalsan in the Mongolian People's Republic at the end of June 1945. We Sherman tankers of 46th Guards Tank Brigade, 9th Guards Mechanized Corps, now found ourselves in a region where everything was new to us.

We now had to train in—and be trained to live in—the desert-steppe terrain, with its significant daily temperature variations and low humidity. We had to learn to move by azimuth without roads, to observe water conservation strictly, and to protect ourselves against the sun's scorching rays. And no matter what aspect of servicing the force or what military issue was involved, we had to build almost everything from scratch.

One thing comforted us, however. The rich, all-encompassing experience we gained in Europe would help us *gvardeytsy* find our way in this unusual Asian situation. The natives of the Transbaykal region also generously shared their resources with us and thus enabled us to adapt more quickly to local conditions.

From the first day of our presence in Mongolia, our highest priority was attached to the problem of billeting. Tents were set up for officers and crews. The enlisted personnel of the logistical units were housed in their assigned trucks or buses. And as it later became known, several of the sergeants and privates had been sleeping on the ground next to or underneath their vehicles. The troops bivouacked in this fashion for a week, and then disaster struck. They all were to become casualties of the Mongolian steppe and the high likelihood of infectious diseases it offered.

Three men in my 1st Battalion came down with encephalitis. Similar cases rapidly developed in other corps units. The source of the infection was an encephalitic tick, whose bite was dangerous in June and July. We westerners had not been given advance warning about this tick, nor had we been told how to protect ourselves against it as the local predator of the steppes.

Army doctors of all ranks were rushed in. Transbaykal-area natives conducted a rapid series of briefings, and the preventive measures they recommended to the physicians turned out to be amusingly simple. The living space inside the tents and around them, as well the areas under vehicles and around them, had to be either burned over by fire or soaked in diesel fuel. Another recommended measure was to cover the ground with tarpaulins whose edges had been daubed with fuel oil, or to pour fuel oil on the ground around the edges of the laid-out tarps.

Setting fire to the grass required special care—for it was also possible to set fire to equipment. We used soldering torches in tents that had already been erected or to set fire to grass, but few of these devices were available to us.

Tons of fuel were required for the safer, alternative method of soaking the ground or wetting down our tarpaulins. Unit commanders did not hesitate for a moment to use fuel in this man-

ner. The combat readiness of the soldiers was the most important issue.

Strict observation of these measures prevented any further
outbreaks of encephalitis. After all that had happened, we firmly
desired that lightning strike the local doctors to punish them for
their initial silence concerning this serious disease and its cause.

High-ranking Reconnaissance

In the June–July period of 1945, the Trans-Siberian
Railroad operated in one direction. Trains were moving in a dense
flow (at intervals of two to three kilometers) toward the Far East,
carrying the forces of four *fronts* (First and Third Belorussian,
Second Ukrainian, and Leningrad *Fronts*, as well as several for-
mations from the Moscow military district and directly from
Stavka VGK reserves) for participation in the defeat of imperialist
Japan.[1] During this time, over 400,000 personnel; 2,119 tanks and
SAUs; and 7,137 guns and mortars, including 600 multiple rocket
launchers, were moved.[2]

Such a massive repositioning of forces could not have gone
unnoticed by Japanese intelligence. My assertion is based on the
fact that a Japanese consulate was located in the city of Irkutsk
during the period of time in question. I saw the consul sitting on
the shore of Lake Baykal, fishing. Of course he had not been sent
there to catch fish—fishing was his cover. His principal task was
to observe the movement of troop trains.

Our own train stopped near the "fisherman." The track bed
passed along the lake's southern shore. The tankers began to
mock the diplomat: "Share your catch with us! We don't have
time to sit with a fishing rod. You have the time!" Loud laughter
ensued. The Japanese official merely glared, offering not a word in
response.

Beginning in April 1945, apparently, the possibility of Soviet
forces engaging in combat actions in the Far East became obvious
to the leadership of the land of the rising sun. The basis for this

conclusion was the Soviet government's abrogation of the Soviet-Japanese Neutrality Pact on 5 April 1945.[3] The declaration of the government of the USSR pointed out that there were serious reasons for this action. Japan, aligned with Germany, was aiding Germany in its war against the Soviet Union and also waging war against the United States and Great Britain, who were allies of the USSR. In this situation, the declaration stated, the pact that had been signed at an appropriate time had lost its justification, and its continuation in force had become impossible.[4]

All doubt that the Soviet Union would initiate hostilities with Japan had been erased since June. One question troubled the higher Japanese leadership: how soon? In sum, there could be no strategic surprise to Tokyo in the initiation of the military conflict. Only operational surprise—the month and day—was a possibility.

A somewhat verbose statement was issued expounding on the points made by our side, with a single purpose: to show that the command and forces of the Japanese Army knew of the approaching combat actions. In connection with this statement, broad measures were employed to raise the combat readiness of formations and units of the Kwantung Army's first line of defense.

The Hsingshanchen (Xingshanzhen) and Chaok'e (Zhaoke) fortified regions were located on the main attack axis of Second Far East *Front*. These were modern, heavy, permanent fortifications that would enable the defenders to offer stubborn and prolonged resistance.

Formations and units of 15th Army and 5th Rifle Corps had detailed sketches of firing positions, minefields, and other defensive elements of each fortified zone. Tactical reconnaissance assets had conducted continuous, careful monitoring of the regimen of activities at Japanese garrisons.

By the evening of 8 August our observation posts noted a modest but strange repositioning of forces in some eastern sectors of the Hsingshanchen fortified region. This kind of movement had not been observed earlier. Reports soon began to arrive from listening posts located along the banks of the Amur River: by all indications the enemy was withdrawing units from the forward edge into the depth.

At this time the *front* chief of intelligence, Major General

Nikolay Aleshin, was at 15th Army headquarters.[5] Army reconnaissance reported the incoming data to him. It was exceptionally important information that had to be reconfirmed. For this purpose, General Aleshin ordered the immediate organization of searches on a broad front and the capture of prisoners where possible.

In turn, army headquarters made available to the *front* commander, General M. A. Purkayev, the information that had been acquired. The decision was made that after the searches had been conducted, their results would be rapidly reported to the Supreme Commander of Soviet Forces in the Far East, Marshal of the Soviet Union A. M. Vasilevskiy.

Ninety minutes later the situation was clarified. The Japanese had abandoned the first defensive line of the fortified region. The first-line troops had been taken back to the second defensive position. An immediate report went up to Marshal Vasilevskiy. It was said later that the marshal, having read the report, pondered it for several moments. Then he announced: "The Japanese would not abandon positions that cost them so many resources to construct. They are planning some sort of deception against our command." He next gave an order: without delay, the chief of intelligence of Second Far East *Front* was personally to confirm the intelligence assessment and then immediately report the outcome.

General Aleshin understood that such a categorical demand on the part of the supreme commander was dictated by the unusual circumstances. By this time the Soviet government's declaration concerning its entry into the war against Japan, as well as the proclamations of the *front* military councils, had already been read to the troops. Only a brief time remained until the initiation of hostilities.

"Search group Aleshin," eight stalwart dismounted scouts of 15th Army's separate motorcycle battalion, went out on reconnaissance with a squad of *avtomatchiki* on each flank to provide security for the high-ranking officer's foray into enemy lines. If help were needed, it would be close at hand. In all likelihood the history of the Great Patriotic War has not recorded another such patrol involving a general officer.

They quickly crossed the Amur River and on the opposite bank met scouts who had been dispatched earlier. It was pouring down rain, and visibility was limited to just a few meters—a situation both good and bad in that it ensured the security of the actions but at the same time created the enormous risk of unexpectedly encountering the enemy. However, "playing with fire" was an entirely normal act for scouts.

General Aleshin and his escorts walked along the enemy-fortified region first defensive line for more than an hour. They came upon and examined trenches and dugouts. Permanent fortifications were closed. They did not see a single enemy soldier. They did pick up some material indicators—newspapers, magazines, books, and cooking utensils. Thus they confirmed that the extremely important information reported earlier was indeed correct.

Not wasting time, they returned to their own lines. A portion of the scouts remained in the Japanese-fortified position with a radio. In the event of any kind of change in the developing situation, they would immediately render a report. General Aleshin reported the results of the reconnaissance to the *front* commander, who in turn sent it on to the Supreme Commander.

General M. A. Purkayev decided to cross the Amur River with the lead battalions and occupy the abandoned Japanese fortifications surreptitiously. This task was accomplished by the close of 8 August.

Taking into account the repositioning of Japanese troops that had occurred, the staffs managed to make all the adjustments: artillerymen in the overlays for their preparatory fires and aviation staffs for air support to the initiation of the offensive. In accordance with these corrections, all artillery and air strikes were shifted to and concentrated on the second defensive line of the Hsingshanchen fortified region. Thanks to the boldness of the tactical reconnaissance plan, boxcars full of ammunition were saved. But more importantly the lives of hundreds of soldiers and commanders were preserved.

After the defeat of the Kwantung Army, the concept of the Japanese commander regarding the maneuver of the fortified region forces before the beginning of the Soviet offensive was revealed. It turned out that the enemy was more convinced with each passing day that combat operations would begin soon. The Kwantung Army planned to carry out a withdrawal of its units in two stages—on the night of 7–8 August and the night of 8–9 August.

The Japanese knew well that with the beginning of the artillery preparation for the breakthrough, the first powerful fire barrages would be conducted against the forward edge of the defenses. Subsequently fires would be shifted into the depth, to the second line. The Japanese command calculated that the garrisons that had been withdrawn from the first line of resistance would succeed in reoccupying their temporarily abandoned positions before the beginning of the ground attack. And they would meet the advancing Soviet infantry with a storm of fire from all weapons.

Under the given circumstances our reconnaissance had its eyes open, and the enemy's scheme—though correct and original in principle—was defeated. All the scouts who participated in the disruption of the enemy's plan were recognized with high awards.

Difficult Mission

War places a heavy burden on the shoulders of any participant and often assigns to him a mission that has many unknown elements. Yet war demands the most rapid, most precise, and most careful execution of that mission. It is a hundred times more difficult to carry out such missions at the highest levels of military authority. Here, as in no other environment, thoughts, words, and deeds are blended together in the tightest possible manner. All assigned tasks must carried out with the highest standard of attention to duty.

This is a story of such a mission, one associated with the capitulation of militarist Japan in September 1945. It is the account of the former deputy chief of the intelligence section of a *front* staff, who was in charge of a radio-communications center for special communications. At the time the incident occurred, Colonel (Retired) Roman Romanovich Gonchar was a major.

The Manchurian strategic offensive operation, which had begun on 9 August, was developing successfully. In five or six days the *fronts* had advanced into the depth of the enemy dispositions: Transbaykal *Front* to 250–400 kilometers, First Far East

Front to 120–150 kilometers, and Second Far East *Front* to 200 kilometers.[1]

The powerful attacks by Soviet forces had been catastrophic for the Kwantung Army. The Japanese government made the decision to capitulate on 14 August: it informed the governments of the USSR, the United States, Great Britain, and China of the fact that Emperor Hirohito had accepted the conditions of the Potsdam Declaration. The Suzuki cabinet fell on the following day.

However, the Kwantung Army had not stopped offering resistance. In connection with this, on 16 August the General Staff of the Soviet Army published an interpretation that stated that the communiqué of the Emperor of Japan concerning the capitulation was only a declaration and that he had not issued an order for the cessation of military activities. Consequently Japanese forces had not, in truth, capitulated. "In view of this fact," the document stated, "the Armed Forces of the Soviet Union in the Far East will continue their offensive operations against Japan." After this statement the headquarters of the Kwantung Army appealed to the Soviet command to stop the offensive, but in a diplomatic sense they were silent about capitulation. To this, the commander in chief of the Soviet Forces in the Far East, Marshal A. M. Vasilevskiy, replied to General Otozo Yamada in a radio message on 17 August: "I suggest to the commander in chief of the Kwantung Army that as of 1200 on 20 August the army cease any military activity against Soviet forces on all fronts, lay down its arms, and surrender. Soviet forces will halt their own combat actions only when the Japanese forces begin to lay down their arms."[2]

This message had to be transmitted quickly to the commander in chief of the Kwantung Army, and a reply received. In order for this to be accomplished, radio communications had to be established. [The remainder of this story is in the voice of Colonel Gonchar.]

On the morning of 17 August the *front* chief of intelligence, Colonel Yakov Nikiforovich Ishchenko, summoned me to the *front* field-command post, located in a forest eight kilometers southwest of the village of Dukhovskoye.[3] He handed me the typed appeal, signed by Marshal of the Soviet Union A. M. Vasilevskiy, and a certificate attached to it signed by the chief of staff of First Far East *Front*, Lieutenant General A. N. Krutikov. The certificate authorized Major R. Gonchar to utilize any radio equipment of the organizations and departments situated on the territory of the Primorskiy Kray for the purpose of accomplishing the command's mission.[4] Yakov Nikiforovich informed me that the *front* chief of communications, Lieutenant General Dobykin, had that morning consulted with his own radio operators concerning what communications means might be used to solve this problem quickly. They were unable to recommend a solution. In light of this fact, Ishchenko strongly emphasized that at this stage of military activities, this was my radio-communications center's principal mission and I was personally to see to the mission's accomplishment.

The assignment was a great responsibility, and I did not have a clue about how to carry it out quickly. I had never been in such a predicament before. I pondered. I considered various scenarios that would result in contact with the enemy.

Before departing for my own communications center at Voroshilov-Ussuriysk, I met briefly with the chief of the radio intelligence department, Lieutenant Colonel Viktor Ploshayev. I requested that he instruct the commander of the separate OSNAZ radio battalion, Lieutenant Colonel Nikolay Gamratov, to give me assistance and cooperation.[5]

I should note that we constantly maintained close contact with the radio intelligence service, which was immensely useful in providing valuable information about the organization of enemy communications and about the activities the enemy was engaged in. Our motto was "It is no disgrace to learn from the enemy." But of course we did not blindly mimic the enemy.

I spent the two-hour drive back to my own unit absorbed in thought, ultimately outlining two possible ways of accomplishing the mission. The first was to enter the communications net of the Kwantung Army headquarters in place of one of its net stations. The second was to transmit the appeal over a broad-band broadcasting station in the city of Voroshilov-Ussuriysk, with our transmitter on the wavelength of the Chanchun (Sintszin) Japanese broad-band radio station.

I stopped by the radio battalion to see Lieutenant Colonel Gamratov. Together we listened to the chief of his operations section on the state of the current radio communications of the Kwantung Army. It was lamentable. Command and control of the forces had been completely lost. Kwantung Army headquarters

did not have radio communications with its fronts and formations, let alone with lower echelons of its forces.

This fact was later confirmed by the commander of the Japanese First Area Army, General Seiichi Kita, during interrogation:
"Communications with divisions and even armies were disrupted
in the first days of combat actions, and we lacked complete and
timely information on the situation at the front. I learned of
Japan's capitulation from the emperor's 15 August radio address."

I paid special attention to the information provided by the
chief of the operations section of the OSNAZ battalion about the
persistent efforts of the Kwantung Army headquarters to communicate with a whole series of subordinate formations, which from
the beginning of our offensive had not answered the center's net
calls. One could suggest that the Japanese command was quite
interested in establishing contact with them. While I was at the
OSNAZ battalion, I also made note of the radio operating data of
two net stations—perhaps the Japanese would continue attempts
to establish contact with them.

We analyzed in detail the nature of the work of the subscribers
that concerned my particular mission. It turned out that they had
earlier employed the international Q-code and radio jargon for
official traffic. However, they transmitted letters and numbers not
in Morse code but in their own Katakana code. We did not know
this code.

Our lack of knowledge required me to exercise the special
authority I had been given to utilize any asset for ensuring the
transmission of the appeal of the commander in chief, Soviet
Forces in the Far East. I commandeered two interpreters—for
English and Japanese—and a radio operator who knew how to
transmit characters in the Katakana code. The appeal was quickly
translated into both these languages.

The interpreters, the radio operator, and I arrived at my radio-
communications center at approximately 1600 on 17 August. A
call from Chanchun (Sintszin) to a distant subscriber was anticipated at 1700. And indeed a call went out to that subscriber at
the appointed hour. Operating on a whip antenna at ten percent
output power, we quickly tuned the transmitter of an American
SCR-399-A radio set to this wavelength.[6]

The reason we were using this specific transmitter and not
some other piece of equipment needs to be made clear. First,

the tone of this transmitter corresponded to the tone of the subscriber that was being called. Second, it had the capability of
broadcasting initially at low power, which would not alarm the
Japanese. As a result of this caution, communication was established with good audibility. We announced that we had a radio
message and questioned the readiness of the Japanese to receive
it. After receiving their confirmation, we implemented our plan.
We immediately turned the American transmitter up to 100
percent output power and transmitted the commander in chief's
appeal in Katakana code in the Japanese language with a speed of
fifty to sixty characters per minute, repeating each word.

Upon completion of the communications session, we asked
the Japanese to confirm receipt of the message. There was no
response. Then I again turned on the transmitter and personally
transmitted the appeal in international Morse code in English. In
the first and second instances, after the signature "Marshal of the
Soviet Union Vasilevskiy," we added in our own words that we
anticipated a reply by the Chanchun (Sintszin) broad-band radio
transmitter.

We had no doubt that the appeal had been received in the
headquarters of the Kwantung Army—a confidence we based on
the inarguable fact that our radio transmitter had entered the
special network of the Japanese headquarters. Just the same, I
made the decision that we would duplicate the broadcast to be
completely sure. Having arrived at the broad-band radio station
in Voroshilov-Ussuriysk, I presented the certificate of special
authority issued by the *front* headquarters and requested that a
spare medium-band transmitter be tuned to the wavelength of
the Sintszin radio station. We checked—the setting was ideal.
We transmitted the appeal by voice in Japanese and in English.
Then the transmitter was switched over to tonal telegraph, and I
transmitted the document demanding capitulation in Morse code
in English.

The difficult mission was executed by 2100 on 17 August. I
reported to Colonel Ishchenko: "Contact was established with the
Kwantung Army headquarters. The appeal of the commander in
chief was transmitted using various means and special communications."

The operations duty officer of the radio-communications center received the instruction: "Organize continuous monitoring

of the work of the Japanese broad-band radio station in Sintszin beginning at 0001 on 18 August."

Morning came, the day led toward evening, and no response was received from General Yamada. I understood the mental state of my superior officers—I was extremely anxious myself. We had good reason! Everything had been handled in the soundest manner but without result. Yakov Nikiforovich called me three or four times on 18 August. Not shy in his expressions, in heightened tones, he "blew up" over the fact that up to that moment the important mission had not been accomplished.

Meanwhile the Soviet forces' offensive was developing successfully. The formations of Transbaykal *Front* had reached the central region of northeastern China by the tenth day of the operation. The cavalry-mechanized group had linked up in the Chzhantszyakou and Chende areas with units of the KNOA that were to meet them in the northern provinces of China.[7] Having crossed the eastern Manchurian mountains, the forces of First Far East *Front* had reached the central Manchurian plain. The forces of Second Far East *Front* had advanced 150 kilometers on the Tsitsikar axis and had penetrated to 300 kilometers on the Sungariy axis.[8] It had become clear to the Japanese command that subsequent resistance was out of the question.

Finally, at 1700 on 18 August, through the Sintszin (Chanchun) broad-band radio station, we received a radio message from General Yamada, the commander of the Kwantung Army, addressed in Russian to Commander in Chief of Soviet Forces in the Far East, Marshal of the Soviet Union A. M. Vasilevskiy. General Yamada's message indicated that he had given the order to Japanese forces to capitulate and to cease military operations. The general reported in this same radiogram that he was sending a delegation of generals and staff officers of Kwantung Army headquarters by passenger aircraft to conduct talks on the capitulation procedure. His Kwantung Army chief of staff, Lieutenant General Hikosaburo Hata, was the head of this delegation. The message indicated the number of aircraft they would be flying, as well as their recognition markings and the type of antiaircraft fire–avoidance maneuvers the planes would use when crossing the front. We immediately retransmitted this radio message by telephone to Colonel Ya. N. Ishchenko.

The Japanese delegation landed in the city of Harbin on 18 August and fell into the hands of our assault force, which had landed there several hours earlier.[9]

The mass surrender of Japanese soldiers and officers began on the morning of 19 August. General Hata and his entire delegation were delivered to the command post of First Far East *Front* on that same day. Lieutenant General Hata was presented to Marshal of the Soviet Union K. A. Meretskov, commander of First Far East *Front*, and to Marshal of the Soviet Union A. M. Vasilevskiy, commander in chief of Soviet Forces in the Far East. Marshal Vasilevskiy presented the specific demands, the locations of the prisoner-of-war assembly points were stipulated, and the march routes to them and the time were indicated. Hata agreed to comply with all the instructions of the Soviet command. He complained that the Kwantung Army headquarters had been unable to pass down the capitulation order to its subordinate formations in a timely manner because communications with these formations had been lost from the very beginning of combat operations. They had been forced to use aircraft for this purpose.

A. M. Vasilevskiy sent a message with Hata to the commander in chief of the Kwantung Army containing the following ultimatum: "To the Commander in Chief of the Kwantung Army Yamada. The chief of staff of the Kwantung Army, Lieutenant General Hata, received instructions from me on 19.08.45 concerning the procedure for capitulation of the Kwantung Army and its disarming." The message went on to lay out the remaining points in greater detail. Communications were maintained with the Japanese through the Chanchun (Sintszin) radio station until the complete capitulation of the Kwantung Army.

Strong-willed Nature

From time to time, difficulties—be they large or small —arise in everyone's life. This is a completely normal occurrence. But what about the person whose life has been a unbroken series of tribulations, every hour of every day, month after month, year after year?

The town of Klimovsk is on the southern fringe of Moscow, about thirty miles from the Kremlin. On the edge of this town lives Viktor Sergeevich Karelin, a war veteran about whom I can boldly say, "He emerged unbowed from the flames. He is from the generation of Meresev!"[1] Born in 1925, Karelin is a first-category war invalid.[2]

Having learned the story of his life quite by accident, I was seized by an enormous desire to become acquainted with him. Accompanied by Lidiya Nikolaevna, Viktor's first cousin, I walked up to a single-story house, in the right half of which the Karelin family had resided for the past seven years. We went into the apartment and introduced ourselves. Our appearance was apparently unanticipated, and our host was somewhat dismayed. I managed quickly to disarm the situation, however. It turned out that Lidiya had not told her cousin anything about our visit. She had only asked by telephone if he and his wife, Tatyana Mikhaylovna, were home to receive her.

I told him about the purpose of my visit, and I was impatient to begin the interview. But it had to wait: we have a long-standing tradition in Russia that guests must first be served food and drink. And only after the repast can one get down to the business at hand. The table was laden with food—garden-grown vegetables and all sorts of poultry. There was also home-made wine made from black currants.

I sat at the table next to Viktor Sergeevich, prepared to come to his assistance at any moment. The fact is that as a result of traumatic wounds, Karelin is missing both of his hands. I monitored his actions out of the corner of my eye, trying to see if my unusual neighbor could serve himself or if he would need my help.

I admit he surprised me from the moment we sat down at the table. He wore a soft rubber cuff on his right stump, under which he had slipped a fork. After having filled his plate with all sorts of treats, as if nothing were unusual, he pressed his glass between his two stumps and quietly raised it to his mouth.

We finished lunch. When everything had been removed from the table, we began an interesting conversation that lasted many hours. This is what the war veteran told me:

They drafted me as this eighteen-year-old into the army in January 1943. Fourteen months of intensive training: basic, followed by sniper and junior leader-development schools. I received the rank of sergeant and went to the active army in March 1944. They made me the commander of a platoon in 7th Company, 3d Rifle Battalion, 180th Rifle Regiment, 329th Rifle Division. It was a position that carried heavy responsibilities and difficult duties and was normally filled by an officer.

After a number of successful battles on Polish soil, I was promoted to senior sergeant. And the silver medal "For Courage" glistened on my soldier's tunic. It was one of the country's highly respected combat decorations.[3]

On 13 February 1945, 180th Rifle Regiment units had captured several eastern sections of the town of Glogau, on the west side of the Oder River. It was the 1,333d day of the Great Patriotic War. Viktor Sergeevich remembers the following about this day that was so significant for him:

My platoon had seized a large building that contained a saw mill. Three of its windows opened out onto a somewhat broad street. We knocked the frame out of one of them. We were preparing for a rush to the next building on the opposite side of the street. The company commander ordered us to continue the attack. Our squad machine gunner fired a dense burst at the enemy stronghold. The first group of riflemen jumped through the window opening from the cover we were occupying and, rushing across the street, burst into the neighboring building. A number of the Germans were killed and the rest dispersed.

The first and most important mission had been accomplished relatively easily. We had gained a toehold in the enemy position. We now needed to build up our strength for the subsequent storming of this section of the town. As everyone understands, in urban combat we had to fight the enemy step-by-step, one room after the other, floor after floor, structure after structure. Stubbornly, persistently, we had to "sink our teeth" into the German defense.

I rushed into the attack with a new group of soldiers along the same path as the first group. [*Loza:* This was a grievous error by the platoon commander. Never should all the soldiers have attacked toward the enemy along the same path.] I made it to the middle of the street in two or three leaps. And suddenly a burst of fire flashed in front of my eyes. I remember it well. I came to some time later, lying on my side. I began to move a bit. At that moment my left forearm began to burn with pain. A round had passed through it. In all likelihood an enemy sniper had shot me, attempting to finish me off. Two mines exploded not far away. I understood—the enemy was covering the street with dense crossfire. My glance fell to the fist of my left hand. Then I looked at my right hand. The fingers on my gloves had been mangled into unrecognizable shreds, like the frayed ends of a rope. I was covered in blood. I tried, unsuccessfully, to move my fingers. They were lifeless, unresponsive. To lie there in full view of the Germans meant to be in death's crosshair every second.

Viktor Sergeevich was silent for several seconds. I did not press him. He was collecting his thoughts and also catching his breath. This was stirring up his memories and emotions:

I summoned all the strength of my will, all the energy left in me. I got up off the ground in a jerk and ran headlong back toward the sawmill. A mine detonated several meters behind me. Fortunately at that moment I fell like a sack of potatoes inside the building. The situation was no less complicated for me there. Twice my comrades had tried to drag me out from under fire, each time unsuccessfully. One Soviet soldier was killed, the other seriously wounded.

They gave me first aid in the platoon. The bandages they wrapped around my hands were immediately soaked with blood. Litter bearers carried me to the regimental aid station without delay. The doctors shook their heads in futility. I had a whole assortment of serious wounds. Both of my hands were mutilated; a shrapnel fragment had penetrated into my left eye;

1. Fold down the upper right corner of 8 1/2 x 11-inch paper.

2. Fold upper left corner down; a slot is formed.

3. Fold up lower left and right corners.

4. Fold up bottom portion, tuck into slot formed by 2.

5. A triangle envelope results.

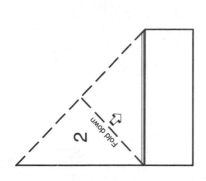

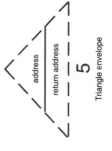

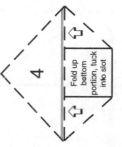

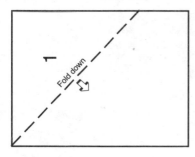

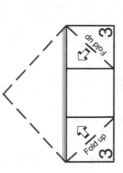

Folded triangle envelope

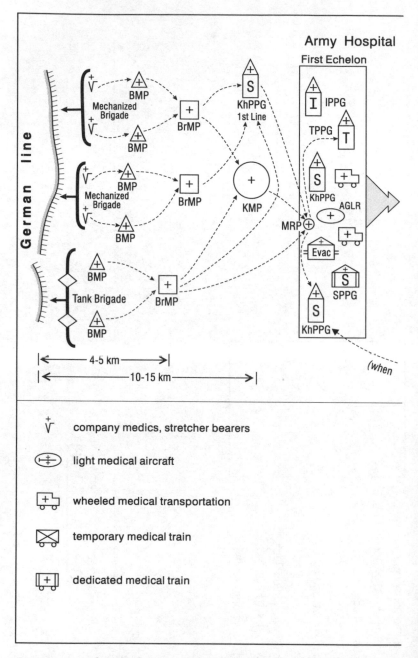

Organization of medical support in Soviet army units and formations

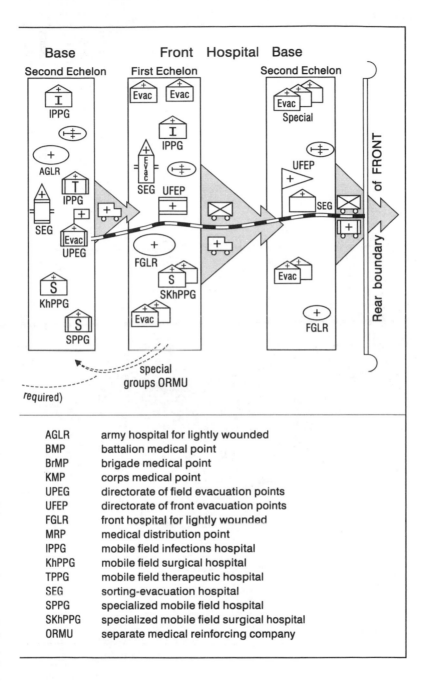

AGLR	army hospital for lightly wounded
BMP	battalion medical point
BrMP	brigade medical point
KMP	corps medical point
UPEG	directorate of field evacuation points
UFEP	directorate of front evacuation points
FGLR	front hospital for lightly wounded
MRP	medical distribution point
IPPG	mobile field infections hospital
KhPPG	mobile field surgical hospital
TPPG	mobile field therapeutic hospital
SEG	sorting-evacuation hospital
SPPG	specialized mobile field hospital
SKhPPG	specialized mobile field surgical hospital
ORMU	separate medical reinforcing company

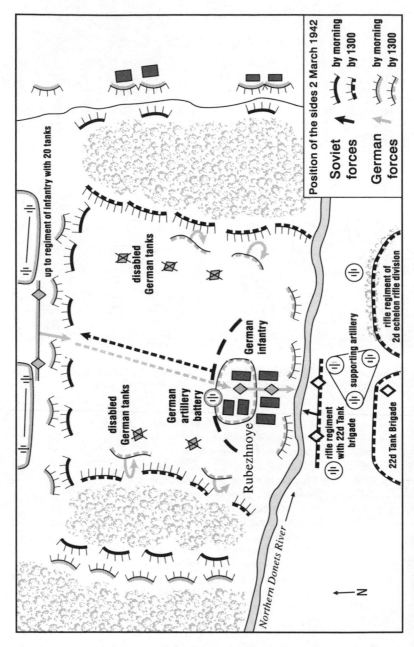

Counterattack by units of 1st Guards Division, March 1942

Map labels:

Position of the sides 2 March 1942

Soviet forces — by morning / by 1300

German forces — by morning / by 1300

up to regiment of infantry with 20 tanks

disabled German tanks

disabled German tanks

German artillery battery

German infantry

Rubezhnoye

rifle regiment of 2d echelon rifle division

supporting artillery

rifle regiment with 22d Tank brigade

22d Tank Brigade

Northern Donets River

N

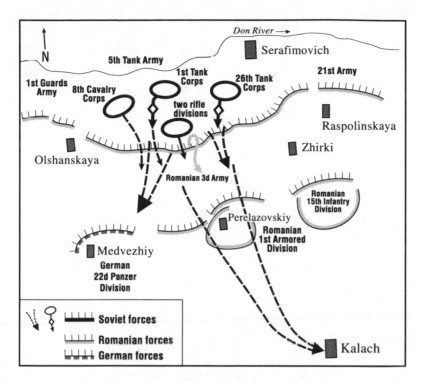

Breakthrough of enemy defenses near Stalingrad, 19 November 1942

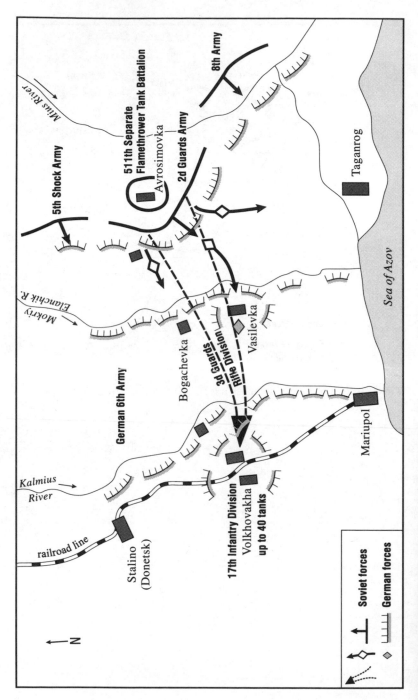

Mius River

5th Shock Army

511th Separate
Flamethrower Tank Battalion

Avrosimovka

2d Guards Army

8th Army

Taganrog

Sea of Azov

Mokriy Elanchik R.

Bogachevka

3d Guards
Rifle Division

Vasilevka

German 6th Army

Kalmius
River

17th Infantry Division
Volkhovakha
up to 40 tanks

Mariupol

railroad line

Stalino
(Donetsk)

N

Soviet forces

German forces

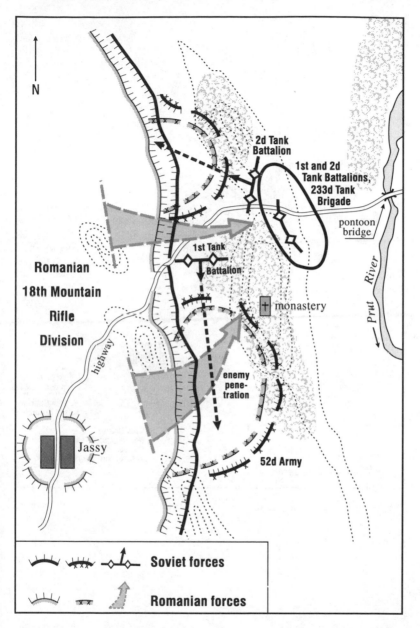

N

2d Tank
Battalion

1st and 2d
Tank Battalions,
233d Tank
Brigade

pontoon
bridge

1st Tank
Battalion

Prut River

Romanian
18th Mountain
Rifle
Division

highway

monastery

enemy
pene-
tration

Jassy

52d Army

⎯⎯ ⎯⎯ ⎯⎯ Soviet forces

⎯⎯ ⎯⎯ ⎯⎯ Romanian forces

Situation near Prut River, Romania, 31 July–1 August 1944

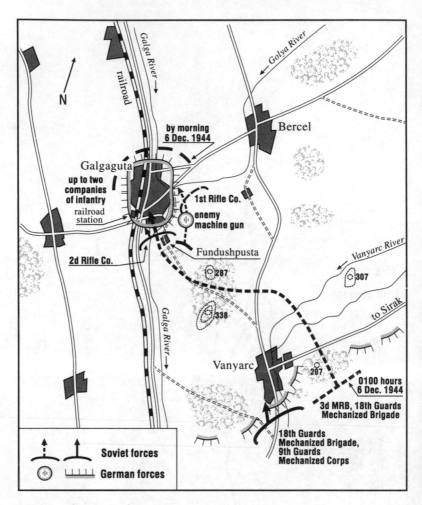

Night raid, 6 December 1944

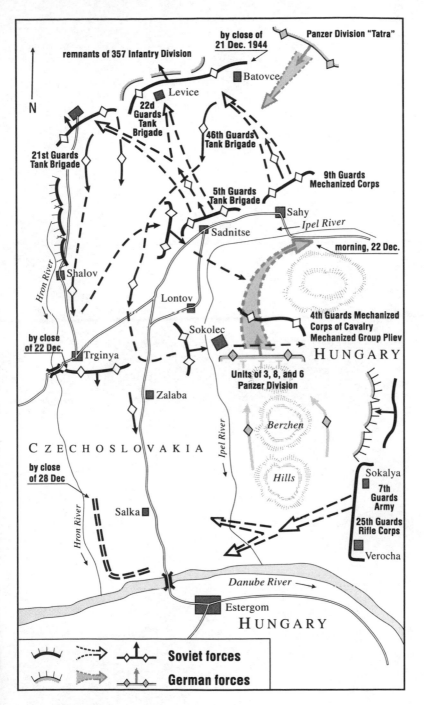

Battle at Lontov, December 1944

my left toe was broken; bullet holes went completely through my left forearm. The war had pitilessly half-blinded me, both literally and figuratively. Later, in the hospital, one of my ward-mates said, "Such wounds and mutilation are enough for an entire human generation!"

Any delay was dangerous. I continued to lose blood from the large common area of open wounds. There was a great likelihood of infection. They put me back on a litter and carried me to the division medical battalion, where a group of doctors quickly surrounded my litter. After examining my wounds for several minutes, a surgeon announced, "Into the operating room."

They carried me up to the second floor. A nurse wiped my face and head with a wet washcloth (bathing me in a tub was not even considered). Then they put a mask over my face and started administering an anesthetic. "Count!"

I remember counting to twenty-one, and then I passed out. I slept. When I came to, I was in a bed. I raised my arms to my right eye and could see that the ends of my forearms were tightly bandaged. My hands were gone. They had been amputated.

I asked Karelin what his mood was at that moment. His response was, "I understood one thing—I would fight my way back! To be sure, protracted treatment lay ahead of me. I had to prepare myself for this every day."

Viktor Sergeevich was right. He was later moved to a *front* hospital in Chenstokhov, where he underwent a second operation. They removed his left eye, along with the mine shrapnel fragment.

Four days after the second operation, a medical train carried him and other recuperating soldiers and officers deep into the USSR. The train stopped in Yerevan, the capital of Armenia.

The psychological state of this young man crippled by the war continued to interest me. The disposition of his spirit, his behavior. Did he fall into hopelessness? I got him to talk about this aspect of his recovery:

Collapse of spirit? You could not have found anyone lower! But hopelessness? It didn't happen. The single most vexing problem was that I lost my appetite. I almost didn't touch food for several days. The patient in the next cot told my doctor that

I wasn't eating. Scolding me severely, the doctor spent much time convincing me that behavior like this caused great harm to my health and prolonged the healing process of my wounds. He then prescribed a brewer's yeast that I had to drink before taking solid food. I began to eat everything they placed on my tray, and I even started to gain a little weight.

In order to push troubling thoughts out of my mind, I began to read and read and read. The days and nights flew past, leaving time only for sleeping and eating—and thinking about what I had read.

At the request of my ward-mates, the hospital staff made a simple stand for supporting the book and keeping the pages open. It allowed me, without the aid of the hands I no longer had, to hold the book in a comfortable position for reading. In the predicament I was in, books were my best friends, genuine comforters. Reading, it turned out, was a miracle-working drug that helped me drive importunate and unbearable thoughts from my head.

Six months passed. On 2 September 1945, I arrived home— Kaluga oblast, Vorov *rayon*, the village of Ermolino.[4]

On 13 February 1945 the pitiless fires of war had literally divided Viktor Sergeevich Karelin's life into two parts: before he was wounded and after. The twenty-year-old had been deprived of two of the primary body parts that a person needs in order to work—his hands and an eye. From his earliest childhood this country boy had been taught that work and only work would bring him a better life. What path would he take now? How would he build his future?

Viktor Sergeevich's entry into his unusual new life is worthy of the highest praise and admiration. Reading books in the hospital, he was drawn to the words of Ernest Hemingway, the American author: "Work is the main thing in life. Against all unpleasantness, all misfortunes, one can find a single deliverance—in work." This statement came as no revelation for Karelin, but it once again forced him to think and to contemplate, here in his parent's home. He was compelled, one could say, to become a designer, an inventor of various devices that would help him become a working man again.

Without hesitation his friends brought his concept to life— they sharpened, they welded, they drilled. Viktor Sergeevich

showed me what they created for him: crude—but so necessary
for amputated hands—"handles" on a sledge hammer, an ax, a
scythe, a rake, and a shovel. These iron loops were fastened to the
handles of each tool with clamps or bolts. Karelin inserted the
stumps of his forearms into them and began to work—breaking
rock, cutting or splitting firewood, turning over the soil, cutting
grain, mowing grass, or spading the garden. He bragged about
his first "handicrafts" on a wood-working lathe—an egg, a large
wagon, and a small one.

Viktor Sergeevich spent the next five years in this "home
university," working every day. Giving himself no respite, he
often continued until he was exhausted, stubbornly and persistently learning to use his tools. But he also was trying with all
his might to live and not just to exist. He helped his parents with
everything around the house, inside and outside. He recalled
with pride his first achievements in the field, the garden, and the
meadow. Success, as everyone knows, empowers one—especially
a person in Viktor's physical and psychological condition.

"Did you, perhaps, get quite tired?[5] Did you have a desire to
abandon this heavy work and take up something easier? Or in
general, to do nothing at all? I don't think anyone would have
criticized you for such a decision," I said to him. Viktor smiled:

One of the great poets said, "Life and work are firmly joined,
like fire and light."[6] I can't imagine one without the other. This
is the first thing. And I never forgot whose son and grandson I
was. My loss did not give me the right to become weak, throw
up my arms or hang my head.

Yes, it was three times as hard. Our Karelin ancestors were
constantly guided by the iron rule that the more difficult life
is for you, the stronger you become. I don't mean to brag, but
all the men and women in our family have always been work
horses.

The history of the Karelin family is somewhat unusual. By
decree of Catherine II, a large group of expert cabinet makers
were resettled from Karelia [the lands adjoining Finland north
and northeast of Leningrad] to the Moscow area. By a command of the government, they were given the surname Karelin, perhaps so that they would not forget their roots. The
settlers were provided with good homes, with various imple-
ments and outbuildings, and with land that was marked out for

each family to grow crops for their own needs. However, they were categorically forbidden to engage in any business other than filling government orders for cabinets and furniture. My father was an excellent furniture maker.

Viktor Sergeevich pointed at the wall between the windows, where hung an elegant bookshelf made from walnut:

This is the work of Sergey Gavrilivich. He made it some time in 1927. Our home was not plush, but we had everything necessary for normal life — an adequate food supply, good clothing, and shoes. My parents worked in the field or in the shop from dawn to dusk. When I was young, I helped my father prepare materials to make furniture. I planed boards and sanded the finished articles. From the moment we three boys could walk, they taught us to work. We grew up in a family of workers.

All that I have described about my family and my childhood, you understand, gave me strength. It demanded that I be a worthy preserver and progenitor of the traditions of my forebears. We are not Ivanovs, who don't know our ancestry.[7]

I asked him what kind of education he had, and he replied:

During the war, before I was drafted into the army, I managed to complete seven grades of rural school. The work experience I gained under my father's tutelage gave me unusual courage and self-confidence. Though there was a special institution of a similar type in the *rayon* for disabled veterans, in 1950 I enrolled in a two-year normal school for gardeners and apiculturists. By that time I was physically and psychologically ready for any endeavor that is considered appropriate for a normal person. It was my fervent desire to keep up with everyone else, step for step, and I accomplished that goal.

In school they selected me as the class leader and, a little later, as the *Komsomol* guide. I was twenty-five years old, and my classmates were fifteen and sixteen. I completed training in 1952 and immediately went to work in the "Ermolino" *sovkhoz* as the lead gardener. We raised fruit-tree saplings.

Every person has his or her own lot in life and his or her own road to travel. And sometimes fate wishes that the two distant roads of people previously unacquainted join together and remain as one for an entire lifetime. This is what happened with the current life-mates Tatyana Mikhaylovna and Viktor Sergeevich. After completing the fruit and vegetable curriculum at the

Timiryazevo Agricultural Academy, Tatyana Medvedeva received a diploma with qualification as an agronomist. She was assigned to work at the "Ermolino" *sovkhoz* in the position of agronomist-nursery supervisor.[8] The two specialists in the same profession worked shoulder to shoulder in the garden and in the office, compiling various records and documents. On 22 April 1952, they married.

When I asked Tatyana Mikhaylovna, "What attracted your attention to Viktor Sergeevich? What touched your heart?"[9] she laughed and responded, "It's our secret!"

"We were able to do everything!" said Viktor.

"Not everything. We couldn't do everything!" exclaimed Tatyana.

Perhaps it was true that in young Viktor's mutilated arms, everything had not been perfectly handled for Tatyana. But you could not tell it now. The apartment, which had its own central steam-heating system, was in excellent repair, a large portion of all of the work having been done by the master of the house, with the help of his two sons. And frankly I was amazed by what they had accomplished out in the yard. The soil around Klimovsk is extremely swampy, and in order to get a good harvest of a variety of vegetables, one must find a way to dry out the soil. In fact, one must carry out large-scale drainage work, and Karelin had done this. He dug several large trenches by hand and laid cement-asbestos pipes in them. Before he laid the pipes, he drilled scores of holes in them for draining water from the soil and carrying it into the town drainage system.

The Moscow Prosthetics Factory created a special device that fits over the stump of Viktor's right arm. A metal claw on the front allows him to grasp any tool—hammer, screwdriver, saw, file, and so on—and manipulate it. With the aid of this device, he and his sons converted a normal bicycle into a three-wheeler with two hinged (ball-and-socket jointed) prostheses mounted on the handlebars. Now Viktor Sergeevich is able to move about freely on any road, maneuvering with relative ease even in traffic.

In the Karelins' yard are a shed and a garage for their Zaporozhets.[10] These are solid structures, for which Viktor prepared all the materials—sawing, planing, chiseling. His sons put up the frames, and together they installed the roofs. Viktor did the wall sheeting and ceiling himself, along with laying the floor.

As so often happens, a man who has been seared by grief is prepared at the first opportunity to help others who have fallen into
a similar circumstance. He strives because of his own experience
to lessen the suffering of others. For Karelin, it became a creed
that he, who had known great misfortune, would go to the aid of
any fellow amputee without hesitation or hope of recompense.

In the period of the combat actions in Afghanistan (the mid-
1980s), this disabled veteran wrote a letter of appeal to doctors
who were treating the wounded soldiers and commanders. He
mailed it to the editor of *Pravda*. In the letter, Viktor shared the
story of his recovery from amputation to become a gainfully
employed working man. And he pleaded with surgeons to listen
to some advice he had to give them, something he wanted them
to remember if they were ever confronted with a situation in
which they felt it necessary to amputate someone's hand. It was
advice based on his own personal experience.

During his surgery at the division medical battalion at the
front in 1945, doctors either accidentally or intentionally left Karelin a portion of the upper palm at the base of the thumb on one
of his hands. It is these soft areas that a person uses to transmit
impulses to a tool during various tasks—pushing or nudging,
pressing, striking, turning, twisting, and so on. The small pad on
his right stump is what permits Viktor Sergeevich to accomplish
work that would seem impossible in his condition: chopping,
sawing, digging, turning soil, planing, drilling, and chiseling.
If he did not have this pad, he would not be able to accomplish
the things that he has. Karelin thus told the doctors to leave an
area of the pad as wide and as complete as they possibly could
in order to ensure the fullest restoration of the patient's working
capability.

Viktor Sergeevich's activities have generated a deep respect
in virtually everyone who has worked with him. The disabled
veteran was employed in a civilian occupation for thirty-six years.
He was initially a leader for a mixed crew on the *sovkhoz* and
later of a garden-field crew. He was named chief of the living
quarters and barracks section, where he was responsible for the
complete maintenance of buildings. Later he was made responsible for two village steam-boiler plants.[11]

The legislature of the Russian Federation found it necessary
to recognize this category of workers who serve in collective

farms. Not long ago, the State Duma passed a law that permits disabled veterans to accrue both military and civilian pensions. A civilian pension is paid to any disabled veteran who, after leaving military service, works in a civilian occupation for twenty-five years or longer. Because of this legislation a disabled war veteran and retired civilian worker now enjoys a significantly improved situation. Our country has also honored the accomplishments of V. S. Karelin as a soldier and a laborer by awarding him several decorations: the Order of the Patriotic War 1st Degree and the medals "For Courage," "One Hundred Years since the Birth of V. I. Lenin," "Veteran of Labor," and "Fifty Years since the Victory over Fascism."

When I was in the Karelin home, I quickly bent down and glanced over their small but carefully selected library. It contained many classics, both Russian and foreign. I asked Viktor Sergeevich what authors he most liked to read, and he answered: "Those who correctly describe the most terrible war of the Soviet people with fascist Germany, those who depict the difficult lives on the *sovkhoza* and the *kolkhoza*,[12] in the plants and the factories, truthfully and realistically. I do not accept those authors who denigrate and find fault with every nuance of our glorious Russian history. Some writers whine about everything and everyone; they misrepresent some facts and events and simply invent others."

Karelin stood up and opened the lower doors of the book cabinet. There were piled stacks of journals for the past several years: *Roman-gazeta, Nauka i zhizn, Tekhnika molodezhi, Vokrug sveta, Rabotnitsa, Krestyanka,* and *Selskaya molodezh.*[13]

This story about Viktor Sergeevich would be far from complete if I did not talk about Tatyana Mikhaylovna, his wife, friend, helper, and advisor—a mother and now a grandmother. The enormous will of Karelin in overcoming virtually every possible difficulty is underpinned by the decades of devotion she has given to him. Their forty-five-year marriage itself confirms the truth of this.

I found out a great deal about this unusual woman from Lidiya Nikolaevna, Karelin's cousin who accompanied me to his home. What has been Tatyana Mikhaylovna's contribution to society? What kind of burden has she carried? How has she managed to endure? It is difficult to imagine how she was not beaten down, broken. Yet she continues to generate the family's energy, to provide drive to all the Karelins, adults and little ones alike—a clear example for them to emulate.

At home I listened over and over to the tapes of our several hours of conversation. Not once was there a word or nuance of complaining on Tatyana's part about her husband. An enormous love of life echoed in their voices. They talked with great warmth about the land as a source of food—about working it, about garden and field concerns and efforts—and about their grandson and two granddaughters.

In my life I have encountered all kinds of people, but this particular meeting left a special mark in my memory and in my heart. It was as if I had touched upon something beautiful, something splendid. As though I had been drinking water from a healing source, I felt I had carried away with me an element of enormous vital energy. Unprecedented gift! I am thankful that such inflexible, strong-willed natures exist on this earth. For me to have encountered them is a boundless joy.

Leaves Are Canceled

By order of the People's Commissar of Defense, commanders of all ranks were called in from leave at the beginning of the Great Patriotic War. Ordinary leaves were canceled for the duration of the war.

Despite this administrative prohibition, however, wounded commanders and soldiers managed to find their way home, even if only for a few short days. They were able to embrace their mothers and fathers (if these men were not at the front themselves), their wives or sweethearts, and the rest of their families. These brief excursions were possible in two circumstances: if a soldier's relatives were not living too far from his unit and if his town or village was not temporarily occupied by the Germans.

Wounded personnel who were recuperating in frontline and rear-area hospitals were able to take advantage of this ostensibly unauthorized opportunity to go home. Enlisted soldiers, sergeants, and senior sergeants were to report to collection points at times specified in their orders, and officers were to report to reserve regiments, normally five or six days after being released from the treatment facility, for return to their units.

In individual cases, particularly after a soldier's recovery from serious wounds, a medical board could authorize a convalescent leave at his or her home for two or three weeks. I personally took advantage of such a brief leave after recuperating from my wounds in a hospital in the town of Shuya, 265 kilometers east of Moscow. It was December 1943, and I went to visit relatives in Dzerzhinsk, a few kilometers from Gorkiy.

Passenger trains were running irregularly at that time, and it was almost impossible to obtain a train ticket. I jumped aboard a reserved seat car and laid down on an upper bunk. I rode this train like a "squatter" all the way to Gorkiy. After a brief stay, I traveled by the same method to a reserve regiment in Vyazma.

Although this was the extent of leaves during the Great Patriotic War, there remain a few interesting incidents in this regard that merit attention.

It was April 1945, and battles were raging in the Bratislava-Brno area of Czechoslovakia. General Pliev's First Guards Cavalry–Mechanized Group was pushing its offensive toward the Morava River, intending to force it from the march. The enemy was offering stubborn resistance in the town of Malatska, located on the approaches to the river. General Pliev's forces had fought an entire day to capture this important settlement, though without success.

Marshal of the Soviet Union Rodion Yakovlevich Malinovskiy, commander of Second Ukrainian *Front*, was demanding the rapid defeat of the German forces in this area. There was sufficient artillery, and we also had enough tanks. But there was no forward progress. The cavalrymen raced into the attack more than once and, suffering losses, withdrew to their start positions.

The group commander, Issa Aleksandrovich Pliev, decided to inject a clear incentive into this situation. He issued a call: "To those who distinguish themselves in the attack on Malatska, I promise a medal and a short home leave. To the soldiers among you with the longest time at the front, I promise demobilization!"

The general's troops took him at his word. "If Issa said it, it is rock solid!" They defeated the enemy with an energetic night attack, and the offensive was renewed.

Staffs began assembling award recommendations and preparing lists for discharging longer-serving soldiers. The awarding of decorations preceded home leave. A soldier going home must be wearing a shiny medal on his fatigues.

General Pliev's unusual order reached the attention of Moscow. Someone had reported him, perhaps in order to gain favor. One day the telephone rang. It was the Supreme Commander himself. Joseph Stalin exploded into the telephone and categorically ordered, "Cancel the leaves! Stop the demobilization!" Issa Aleksandrovich, grudgingly and curtly responded, "Yes, sir!"

The war rolled on to the west, but Pliev did not forget his promises. Delaying the leaves to a later time, he quietly implemented his demobilization plan. Not every general could permit himself such defiance of Stalin's orders—the Kremlin did not forgive disobedience. Perhaps the central government did not punish Pliev for his willful acts simply because his presence was crucial in the planned operation against imperialist Japan. He was later to command the Soviet-Mongolian Cavalry-Mechanized Group, designated to launch a supporting attack in the general direction of Kalgan.

During the period of transferring the 6th Guards Tank Army from the West to the Far East, the issue of leaves—or more precisely of brief flights to home to visit loved ones—became especially acute. Our trains were wending their way across the entire length of our enormous country, through towns large and small. Frontline soldiers had not seen their homes for two or three years, or even longer.

We would be passing close to some of these hometowns. How could we not let our men visit their families? Our unit and formation commanders well understood the longings of their subordinates. So they made it happen. Of course they did not authorize mass leaves, but neither did they create impediments. They issued documents for two-, three-, and four-day leaves.

There was no doubt that these men would be able to catch up to their units. Troop trains were flowing toward the Far East in a steady stream. A soldier returning from leave could hop aboard an available train and ride it to some large station two or three stops down the line—dozens of trains were stacked up at these large marshaling yards. After a brief halt here, the solider could continue on his journey to another such yard. The key to this "train-hopping" system was for each soldier to know the train number of his unit and to find his train at one of these stops.

Only one category of soldier had the privilege of authorized ordinary leave during the war: any serviceman who was awarded the rank Hero of the Soviet Union. After having received this high award, a soldier was given three to four weeks of leave, depending on the distance to his home.

Rest and Relaxation

We were able to consider rest and relaxation only in breaks between battles, when our units had been pulled back for reforming or refitting. The longest period of combat action for our 6th Guards Tank Army, and for its subordinate formations and units, was in 1944, from early April to mid-August. There was no time for pleasure or relaxation from late August of that year to the end of the war in the West. Large-scale offensive operations— Jassy-Kishinev, Budapest, Prague—followed one after the other. Our 6th Guards Tank Army played a leading role in each of them.

Just the same, our tankers found some time for rest and relaxation. Time was an all-powerful task master that dictated to us the nature and place of our rest and the means of our relaxation. The first and most important task after a unit's withdrawal from combat was for the troops to bathe and then dress in clean underwear and fatigues, stocks of which clothing were maintained at brigade and battalion levels.

The bath has always been a matter of great importance in Russia. It might seem trivial, but when one goes for weeks, even months in continuous fighting, this issue becomes one of the highest priority. We never neglected to furnish showers for our troops at the front. A clean body and disinfected uniform meant a happy soldier!

Shower-disinfecting companies came down to the units from

corps and army levels. A shower point was typically set up near a water supply, and the soldiers' clothing was "cooked" in special containers to kill parasites. Only after this process was the clothing sent through the laundry—although sometimes we tankers did dip our underwear in diesel fuel and then carefully wring it out and put it back on. For while the louse, a carrier of typhus, was quite a serious problem for the infantry, it was a rare guest among tank crews.

The infantry's fight against lice was particularly important in right-bank Ukraine in early 1944. The war had swept through this particular terrain on two occasions, from west to east, and now it was moving in the reverse direction. The epidemiological status—that is, the likelihood of the outbreak of an infectious disease and its spread—of this area was borderline dangerous. The Germans had burned many villages to the ground. The winter had been quite warm, with slush forming in the day and freezing temperatures at night. Civilians and military troops had been crowded together in available shelter.

Yet while the possibility of disease was enormous, Soviet Army medical personnel did manage to keep the situation under control. My purpose in emphasizing the inherent danger in the situation is to stress the fact that if we had not addressed the issue, our troops would never have been able to rest or relax during lulls in the fighting.

Not any less important than bathing and cleanliness is sleep: how often do soldiers in war have to go days without proper rest? So it was also with us. Therefore every soldier at the front had to learn to catch up on lost sleep and to store up sleep for the future. Having rested, we could all turn our thoughts to other activities. Soldiers and officers who were away from the front line wanted and needed to "unload" psychologically, to release tension—and to forget, if only for a little while, the cruel face of battle.

The forms of rest and the means of relaxation for us were varied. Some activities were conducted in small groups—crews, squads, or men of the same nationality. Other activities were conducted at platoon or company level. Officers frequently passed their time with other officers. Frankly the forms and methods of our entertainment were not quite as rich as those of enlisted men.

Every day at 1200 Moscow time, wherever tankers were located, representatives of our units assembled, listened, and took notes from *Sovinformburo* [Soviet Information Bureau] broadcasts concerning the situation at the front and life back home. After the broadcast they passed this information along to the troops in their companies. The battalion deputy commander for political affairs was in charge of this process. Not everyone who had access to a radio receiver in wartime was authorized to turn it on. Our procedures for using communications devices were quite strict.

Here are some specific episodes in the life of a tanker during breaks in combat.

In mid-December 1943, units of 5th Mechanized Corps were concentrated in the area south of Belyy Tserkov. Our 233d Tank Brigade was assembled in the village of Volodarovka. We were doing maintenance on our vehicles after a difficult road march from the Fastov area on extremely muddy roads.

In the first days after we had arrived in the land of the ancient Kievan Rus, several of the battalion's officers came to me asking that I arrange a feast for them—one consisting solely of vareniki, the famous Ukrainian fruit dumpling. I fully sympathized with their request. Many had heard of, but never tasted, this Ukrainian delicacy. There had been no time for such things before—but now the possibility existed. I had to satisfy my fellow officers.

I approached the lady of the house where my ammunition-supply platoon was staying: my request was that she assemble a small group of women in the village to act as temporary cooks for our dumpling banquet. But where would we find the flour to prepare this dish? It would require no small amount. There was barely a handful in either the battalion or the brigade. My efforts to purchase flour from local villagers or to barter with them for canned meat went for naught. There was no flour to be found anywhere in the village of Volodarovka. Each household had a small supply of wheat that they had managed to hide from the Germans. As a rule they buried it in the ground and then covered it with any available rubbish as a camouflage.

I had to go to the mill. For the villagers this was a daunting task in itself. They had first to find the transportation, and then they had to wait in a long line. It took a while to mill the grain. I decided to become involved in the flour business: I received the battalion commander's permission to travel to the mill in the *rayon* center, and then I announced in the village that I could get their grain milled. My proposition was well received: they quickly drew up a list of the farmers' names and the amount of grain each one was contributing. Early the next morning we loaded the grain into a truck, and I departed. By evening the flour was delivered back to the village and turned over to its owners.

Smoke from the village's ovens filled the air for the first time in ages. The women rolled out flat pancakes, cooked up *pampushki* [a kind of fritter], and boiled the fruit dumplings. But a genuine dumpling contains cottage cheese: where would the cottage cheese come from? There was not a single milk cow in Volodarovka because the Germans had slaughtered them all for meat or taken them to Germany. So they prepared the dumplings with potatoes—tasty but not as good as the ones with cottage cheese or with sour cream or butter.

The Russians ate the dumplings with great gusto nonetheless. For a long time after this, they recalled that supper in Volodarovka and the exceptional culinary skill of Ukrainian peasant women.

From March to July 1944, units on the southern wing regularly received Moscow newspapers two or three days after their publication, and our own army newspaper arrived fresh in our units every morning. Interruptions in the delivery of our paper were not permitted, but if they occurred, it was not healthy for the persons responsible. We relaxed in various other ways, too. Once or twice a month, for example, a frontline singing and dancing ensemble visited corps units, and occasionally we were treated to performances by artists from Moscow. These groups traveled from unit to unit, performing several concerts a day to bring their entertainment to the maximum number of troops.

Our most common form of entertainment, however, was movies. We did not have theaters, of course. So we constructed a special viewing area, always in a patch of woods. Movies were shown at night under the stars, but we took special precautions to conceal this activity from air observation. The audience sat on the ground. We had no benches, which was fine because they also could have given our position away. These open-air theaters were always set up in close proximity to the deep shelters that had been constructed to protect the troops in the event of an enemy air attack. The manager of this field theater maintained telephone communications with the antiaircraft unit. If enemy aircraft appeared, an appropriate order was issued and the theater was shut down. After an appropriate interval of time, on signal, the theater was reopened. Such interruptions were rare, however.

The center of our leisure time remained the unit. Senior Lieutenant Dmitriy Niyakiy was known as the best accordion player around the battalion. At any time, day or night, without much coaxing, he would walk among the soldiers and sergeants playing his instrument. A frequent performer among the officers as well, he had a broad repertoire of songs.

Each platoon normally had its own choir—three to five young men with good voices. They often serenaded us with their quiet music before supper. We heard songs from Ukrainian, Russian, Georgian, Armenian, and Tatar traditions—indeed, more than ten different nationalities were represented in our battalion.

Despite our ethnic diversity, I don't recall our ever having any tension on that score. The determining factor was not a soldier's nationality but what kind of soldier he was on the battlefield. The succinct but weighty expression "You can go on reconnaissance with him!" was the highest praise one could render a fellow soldier. It meant that he knew his job, that he was cool and clever under fire, and that he would not abandon a friend in need, always coming to one's aid.

We had one very special old friend in the battalion: a prewar phonograph manufactured in the Soviet Union that we had found in a destroyed German tank around Smolensk back in 1943. The Germans had taken it from some Russian family. Now it gave us joy and comfort. Unfortunately, we had only a few records for it, but we cherished it anyway.

We also enjoyed an unusual pair of sergeants who served in the 2d Tank Battalion of 233d Brigade. To everyone's envy, they played their music on two trophy German harmonicas. Their repertoire included vocal and dance themes of the various nationalities that populated the Soviet Union. The two sergeants were known throughout the brigade and were frequently given newly confiscated harmonicas in return for their impromptu concerts. I remember how, in the years immediately after the war, these "liberated" harmonicas were readily available in our flea markets and secondhand stores. But the foreign instrument never quite took root in Russian soil. We soon forgot about it.

War and misfortune brought us young men—from cities, villages, and settlements—together and formed us not only into crews and squads but into a family. We had a natural desire to get acquainted with our comrades, to learn about one another: we might go into battle tomorrow, and we wanted to know who was going with us.

This "sounding out" normally occurred in the first days of the formation of a combat unit, in the deep rear of the country during the creation of replacement units for dispatch to the active army and at the front after one's assignment to a specific tank crew.

The moments when new replacement tankers arrived in the brigade were particularly animated. And it was no surprise that later those same tankers, before they drifted off to sleep, spent long hours in quiet conversation. They exchanged stories about their families, their villages and towns, and their youth. They talked about the young girls who had promised to await their return from the war—somewhere there was a young girl waiting for every soldier taken by the war.

In 1944 our brigade spent almost four months in the second echelon, resting, refitting, and regrouping after the bitter winter and spring battles to recapture the right-bank Ukraine. In early April in preparation for the Soviet strategic offensive into Romania (the Jassy Kishinev operation), Soviet authorities evacuated the entire civilian population of Moldavia from a zone along the front line to a depth of 100 kilometers. For those who were being resettled in the rear, this was an enormous catastrophe. By this time of year, vegetables were beginning to grow in their home gardens, and crops were emerging in the fields. There was much work to be done in tending these young crops: watering, weeding, and cultivating. The farmers were all being taken away, and no one knew for how long. They left with tears in their eyes and a heavy weight in their hearts.

They had been forced to abandon what they had planted and sowed with their own callused hands. The crops would die of neglect, or the military units would tear up the fields with their movements. The civilian populace, faced with empty cellars in the coming winter, would be hungry for sure. The population of the village of Skulyany left with these troubling thoughts on their mind. They led their cattle and sheep away, loaded up their poultry and small bundles of the most necessary clothing and bed linens, and left in a hurry.

We understood the villagers' predicament. It was difficult for us to look at their downcast faces, their worried stares. They were being torn away from their roots, from the source of their sustenance, and were worried about the hunger that lay ahead of them. The village fell silent. No cocks crowed. No carefree children's laughter was heard. Just the voices of soldiers, the infrequent clanging of metal of a tank hatch closing, and the sounds of truck engines.

The commands at *front*, army, and all lower subordinate levels understood the difficult position in which the local populace had been placed and what awaited them in the autumn if emergency measures were not taken to protect their crops. An order was issued to all forces of Second Ukrainian *Front*, which was immediately distributed to the armies and corps, that measures be undertaken to preclude the possibility of even the slightest degree of harm to the gardens and fields of the Moldavian people. The most severe punishment was prescribed for violation of this order, including trial by military tribunal for looting.

The order further required commanders of all units located in villages and settlements to create crews of ten to fifteen men each whose task would be to work the gardens and fields adjacent to the village as an important official mission. Along with this, the order required that continuous educational work be conducted among the soldiers to explain to them the utmost importance of protecting the harvest for the resettled villagers: "These are Soviet citizens who have been liberated from German occupation. It is the duty of each soldier to assist them in this difficult hour. We will replace them in the gardens and fields."

At this time I was the chief of staff of 1st Tank Battalion. The brigade commander summoned me and said, "You are a peasant son, well-versed in agricultural issues. From this moment forward you will fulfill the temporary position of chief of all the field-garden teams that the units are now creating. Lists of these working parties will soon be drawn up and submitted. Your task is to develop and then implement the work plan, the sequence of tasks, and the time schedule for work in the fields and gardens. Bring it to me for approval. Report to me on its execution at the end of each day."

One could receive almost any type of instructions from one's commander. What I received fell on my head like ice water. The tasking was not only unusual; it also carried a great responsibility. The commander added a strict warning: "You must not only grow everything but fully protect it. Your tankers should not touch a single cucumber, tomato, apple, or anything else!"

How were we supposed to accomplish this mission? That, he did not say. We had to resolve our unique problem ourselves. We could hardly position a guard at every garden and field, yet we also had to acknowledge the enormous desire of every man to eat fresh vegetables and fruit in this period of postwinter vitamin deficiency. Had there been a local population in Skulyany, we would have purchased our greens and fruit from them. In the existing circumstances, however, this option was not open to us.

It had now been several years since my prewar life as a peasant in my father's house. We rural children, even when we were small, helped our parents with the field chores: we herded cattle, worked in the garden, mowed grass for the cows, fed the chickens and ducks, and helped milk the cows. The size of our workload grew as we grew until we occasionally took the place of our father or mother in the *kolkhoz* fields for a day or two.

Yes, the prewar school of the young farmer would be of great use now. In the first place, we had to organize our soldier-farmers for the cultivation of quick-ripening vegetables—radishes, lettuce, dill, parsley, and carrots. The time for planting cucumbers and tomatoes had not yet passed. One thing concerned us: how much time would be allocated to us for working in the fields? When the senior commander arrived to inspect the execution of his agricultural order, we did not hesitate to ask him, "Will we have time to grow these crops?" He told us that we would—perhaps someone had told him the approximate date of the beginning of the offensive. This gave us some comfort.

This new and unusual duty did benefit our soldiers in that we were allowed to cultivate narrow strips of ground along roads and fields for our own use. Various greens were added to our army rations in great quantities. Every time, and for whatever reason, something was picked from a garden, the typical soldier looked to see if it had come from his "supplementary plot." No one was in a hurry to be accused of being a looter, with the dangerous consequences attached to this label.

I suggested the following procedure for expediting the arrival of greens to the battalion kitchen: while our own troop-planted gardens were still growing, we would consume greens from the villagers' plots. If the local inhabitants should return home on short notice, we would compensate them with produce from our own harvest or pay them with cash. The brigade commander approved my suggestion. Our experience was copied in other corps units. With the permission of the battalion commander, I took the headquarters clerk Sergeant Pavel Nizhnik as the bookkeeper. He would keep track of our food requisitions.

Without going into great detail on our farming activity, I will say that the tankers worked with enormous enthusiasm. They fully understood that their conscientious labor was an enormous unsolicited gift to the inhabitants of Skulyany. Of course, upon their return they would not simply be surprised by what they saw but, as one of the soldiers expressed it, "dropped in their tracks." This fact alone was sufficient to disprove the immense lies that official German propaganda had drummed into the heads of the Moldavians for years: the Red Army was a band of thieves, its soldiers were aggressors, its commissars were without mercy.

We farmer-tankers did not ignore our normal soldier duties, however. We worked to maintain our equipment, and we attended training. Units of 5th Guards Tank and 5th Mechanized Corps of the 6th Tank Army in the second echelon of Second Ukrainian *Front* engaged in the farming activities for approximately four months, with almost the entire enlisted component of the corps' units working the fields on a weekly rotational basis. Working in the fields was not a hardship for our young soldiers; rather, it was a break. The weather was warm, and as a rule, both soldiers and sergeants worked in shorts. As they irrigated the rows of vegetables, they poured water on each other. They also worked on their tans.

On the evening of 18 August 1944 the order came down to cease work in the field gardens and return all tankers and motorized riflemen to their unit assembly areas. This was a clear indication that the start of the offensive was approaching.

Brigade commander Colonel Nikolay Mikhno summoned me to his headquarters on the morning of the following day and informed me of the following: "On the night of 20 August, corps units will depart to start positions on the other side of the Prut River. You will remain in Skulyany to hand receipt of the livestock and crops of the gardens and fields back to the local inhabitants. A truck will bring representatives here tomorrow. Try not to be delayed too long, and then catch up with us!"

Ten villagers arrived in Skulyany early on the morning of 21 August. After completing an inspection, the senior member of the group was to sign a document for receipt of the houses and all the fields and gardens belonging to the village inhabitants. The peasants hurriedly jumped down from the bed of the truck and quickly dispersed throughout the village. We did not delay them, allowing them to satisfy their strong curiosity as quickly as possible.

Among those who had arrived was the lady of the house in which I and my small staff had quartered. She immediately headed for her garden. Not more than twenty minutes passed when the peasant woman returned, walking with a light, brisk step. Her face was lit up with joy. She approached me and, not speaking a word, kneeled down, wrapped her arms around my legs, and kissed my boots. I was frozen for several seconds in surprise—no one had ever before shown me such a gesture of deep gratitude. Recovering, I bent over sharply, grasped the woman under the arms, and raised her up from the ground. "You have done so much!" was all she was able to get out, still not having regained control of herself.

They say that when people are frightened, their eyes open wide. I have every reason to affirm that a person's eyes also open wide for joy. The pupils of the Moldavian peasant woman's eyes were large, and streams of tears flowed down her cheeks. These were tears of joy. What she had seen had stunned her, and her face turned bright red from her excitement. Everything in the village was just as they had left it. Along the edges of their gardens and fields were additional rows of leafy carrot tops, greens and lettuce, parsley, cucumbers, and mounds of tomatoes. It was as if a magician had tended their crops.

Loud, joyful voices rang out along the main street and in the alleys of Skulyany. The village was alive with animated conversations. The village representatives came up to me singly and in groups, shaking my hand again and again and offering heart-felt words of appreciation.

We concluded all the formalities of signing the village back over to its representatives in the afternoon. All ten persons signed the document, at their own request. We did not object. The battal-

ion sergeant major, Grigoriy Nesterov, took two of the representatives back to their temporary accommodations in the rear in his
motorcycle's sidecar. Eight Moldavians remained in Skulyany to
guard everything that we had planted, preserved, and turned over
to them.

As it had done many times before, the combat situation forced
us frontline soldiers to forget about rest and relaxation from
August 1944 until victorious May. During this period, 6th Tank
Army (later 6th Guards) was the leading force in Second Ukrainian *Front*.

Field Mail System

The postal system employed by the Red Army during
the Great Patriotic War was called "field military mail" [*polevaya
voyennaya pochta*]. The almost melodic title *polevaya pochta*
[field mail] was a loaded term: it was in fact a system of coded
numbers representing military units. For example, my 233d (46th
Guards) Tank Brigade had the field post number 34484.

There was an additional peculiarity in the work of the field
mail system: strict censorship had been imposed on it literally
from the first days of its creation. Official opening and reading of
correspondence was permitted. Anything in the letters that was,
in the opinion of the censor, a state or military secret was blotted
out with a special black marker. It was impossible to read lines
that had been eliminated in this manner.

We knew that certain information would never reach the
reader: the sector of the Soviet-German front we were fighting
in, our military specialty, any information concerning our unit's
combat actions—even our everyday concerns and other problems.

In the letters from relatives and friends to troops at the front,
one would not be able to read about certain information as well:
how much and what kind of food they were receiving from ration
cards, where they were working, and what the mood of the factory or *kolkhoz* workers was like. All lines containing such information were ruthlessly struck through. The censor was con-

cerned lest such information adversely affect the mood of the soldier at the front.

Frequently, all that remained in letters to and from home were greetings to relatives and acquaintances and wishes for good health. But even this abbreviated and shortened news was quite welcome, both by the families and by the soldiers. It was particularly well received in homes where the father, son, brother, or husband was far away at the front, alive and fighting the Germans.

We soldiers at the front found means of breaking through the censor's barrier: we reported to our relatives and friends our location in the active army.[1] Russian soldiers have dealt with this problem for generations. A soldier or officer has written a letter, let us say, to a friend in a neighboring *front*. He wants to let his friend know where he is stationed, so he designates a prearranged sign that will say "read where I am now located." The prearranged sign is the repetition of one word at the beginning of the letter's text.

For example, "Hello, Kolya-Nikola!" [This repeat of the name in two forms was the cue to look for the code.] Then, in the first five to seven lines of the text, the author placed dots above the relevant letters. How could the censor cut these out? He had to open and check hundreds, perhaps even more letters. I informed a comrade from the Saratov Tank School using these barely noticeable marks that my unit was located around Yelna (on the approaches to Smolensk). And in the same fashion he told me he was stationed around Kursk. Our family and friends also knew our "secret" frontline key.

The war made its mark on the shape of the postal envelope as well. This was the famous triangle (see figure 1), which became a right of citizenship in this trying time for the simple reason that factories could not produce the required volume of envelopes for the millions of troops who were at the front and for the significant numbers of civilians who had been moved eastward. There was also a paper shortage. Industry was struggling to produce weapons or parts for weapons, or shells and mines. Even small factories were fully involved in war production.

In addition the unsealed triangle permitted the censor to freely and quickly open the mail and check its contents. This system, which was used throughout the war, justified itself. The triangle

envelope even became the motif for a war memorial in a field
near Volgograd that was dedicated in 1982.

Normal envelopes also went out through military postal channels during the war, though their arrival was constantly feared
in the far reaches of the Soviet Union. For families, this envelope
brought shock, grief, and tears, for it contained the official document that notified next of kin of the death of a loved one at the
front. Among the people these envelopes were known by one sor-
rowful, grieving word—*pokhoronka* [death notice]. The document
in this envelope reported the last name, first name, patronymic,
time of death, burial place, and the date any entitlements to the
family would begin. Such envelopes have been preserved and are
in millions of homes to this day, passed down from generation to
generation.

The military field mail system delivered packages from the
rear to the front lines. The population, which itself was experiencing enormous hardship, made an effort to assemble and send
modest gifts to the defenders of the Motherland on holidays.
This was a deeply patriotic impulse, not a response to an order
from above. The parcels contained warm socks and mittens,
embroidered tobacco pouches with tobacco, handkerchiefs, and
hand-knitted scarves. These packages also frequently contained
brief but warm letters. In regions that lay close to the front, these
gifts were prepared at factories and offices, the workers bringing
the contents to the workplace and assembling the parcels there.
The *rayon* leadership then selected a representative delegation
to travel to the military unit to hand out these parcels to soldiers
and commanders.

This was a common practice, as the following facts attest. Millions of warming items were donated for soldiers from September
to November 1941: 1.75 million pairs of felt boots; approximately
3 million kilograms of wool; over .5 million sheepskin coats;
over 2 million sheepskins; millions of pairs of woolen gloves and
mittens, fur mittens, and wool socks, as well as quilted jackets
and caps. More than 3,400 train cars of individual and collective
packages arrived at the front for Soviet soldiers from November
1941 to May 1942.[2] Each of these parcels always contained a letter
either from the workers at a plant, a factory, or an office, or from
the *kolkhozniki* [collective farmers], or from individual citizens.
These letters expressing sincere and heartfelt wishes for the

holiday and for combat success had an enormous psychological impact. They mobilized the efforts of the soldiers to a still higher level of duty in their difficult combat missions.

I will recount an unusual story of one written insertion into one of these packages that was sent to the front. I know it well because it is a story about two friends of mine.

The workers of the Bauman district of Moscow were preparing holiday gifts for the soldiers of the Western *Front* for the May Day holiday (1 May) of 1942. A nineteen-year-old clerk, Tamara Epifanova, was participating in this worthwhile project. Her gifts were handmade: socks, mittens, and embroidered handkerchiefs. She wrote a brief letter to the command with the request, "Give these to the bravest soldier!" and she included her Moscow address.

A delegation from Bauman district arrived at Yuknov (170 kilometers southwest of Moscow) in the latter days of April. As representatives of the factories, plants, and offices, they traveled around the units, handing out the parcels to soldiers and commanders. They also put on several concerts for the largest audience of soldiers they could assemble. The tireless diva Lidiya Ruslanova, who accompanied the group, entertained everyone with her rich repertoire of national songs and music by Soviet composers. The holiday was a success! The soldiers were satisfied, and the Moscow visitors left happy.

Tamara Epifanova's parcel was given to a brave tank company commander, Lieutenant Gevorg Avakovich Chobanyan, whose company had operated with very good results in a series of recent battles. Along with their infantry, these tankers had driven the Germans from two important villages and advanced almost fifteen kilometers into the enemy's dispositions, losing only two т-60 tanks in the process.

Chobanyan quickly wrote a letter in reply, fervently thanking the young girl for the gifts she had sent and asking her for a photograph. After some hesitation and with advice from her friends, Tamara fulfilled the request of this unknown tanker. She informed him that her brother was also at the front, just in case they might be able to meet. A little later, Tamara had a small picture of Gevorg, and they began a regular correspondence. I have asked my two friends, "How many letters did you write to each other during the war?"

They laugh. "We do not know exactly, but a great many!"

Chobanyan replies. "Perhaps three letters went to Moscow every month, and the same number were sent to my field postal number." Chobanyan later fought on Sherman tanks in the right-bank Ukraine and continued to maintain regular contact with Tamara. His elderly father wrote him infrequently. Tamara's warm letters gave him strength to endure the trials of frontline life in the heavy, continuous fighting.

Chobanyan was seriously wounded in the right leg on 1 June 1944 and remained hospitalized in Sverdlovsk until January 1945. He was suffering from gas gangrene. The frequent and affectionate letters from Moscow, from a dear person whom he had not yet seen, were a miracle-working cure for him. They made it possible for him to surmount the pain and the multiple surgeries. He waited for her letters every day and did not fail to write his own letters to her. He was sure that Tamara eagerly awaited his letters.

Gevorg Avakovich, receiving a month's convalescent leave when his medical treatments were completed, arranged his travel home through the capital to meet his girlfriend at long last. Three years of writing letters had given him the right to call her that. However, fate played a trick on them: Tamara was not in Moscow, having traveled to a *kolkhoz* to work for a while.

His leave was quickly over, and in March of 1945 Chobanyan arrived at the Directorate of the Commander of Armored Forces. Since he had been evaluated and declared a third-category invalid, he was not permitted to return to the front. Instead, he was sent to serve at base 404 of tank and mechanized forces.

The two "unacquainted" young people who had come to know each other through the mail met for the first time on 1 May 1945. They were married after the victory salute on 17 May. More than fifty years have now passed since this brave soldier and a simple Moscow girl joined their lives together. They raised a son, who in turn gave them two grandchildren, now adults themselves.

I have to tell about letters of another kind—ones that were extremely difficult for me to write because I had to relate the entire truth in them, holding nothing back. These were the letters I had to send to the relatives of fallen soldiers, who would typically ask the friends of their sons or brothers about the circumstances of their deaths and the locations of their graves. Using our standard triangle-envelope stationery, we wrote out several accounts— those of the witnesses, the crew members, and the friends—

regarding the death. We did not leave out any details, for we understood how important it was for these people to know the truth about their relatives.

After the war I visited many families of our fallen comrades. I saw our collective narratives about the last moments in the lives of their sons and brothers. I was surprised, and very grateful, that the censors had not blacked out a single word.

A blizzard of letters from the front poured in when *Sovinform-buro* reported the liberation of new western oblasts and *rayons* of the Soviet Union. The military field–post office (eight persons in all and one truck in our tank corps) worked under an enormous overload, but they did not grumble. So that no one would delay the delivery of a letter, senders would very often write on the triangle in clear letters, "to a liberated city or village" or "on liberated soil!" This helped.

This precaution was a reflection of the craving of frontline soldiers to be informed as quickly and as often as possible about the lives and circumstances of their family members. Many of these civilians had lived under German occupation for two, three, or more years. How were they? Who was still alive? Were they healthy? And the families, having just been freed from slavery, had no less desire to know about their soldiers at the front.

The field mail system never let us down. Letters from home, from girl friends, from close friends—these were the same as shells and cartridges, and perhaps of even greater significance, to us. We received them without delays, and they helped us to achieve our victory.

Ammunition Resupply

As tankers, we followed a rigid practice of carrying a large ammunition supply on our vehicles. This was particularly the case during deep offensive operations, as were all of the campaigns we conducted on foreign soil in southeast and central Europe (specifically the Jassy-Kishinev, Budapest, Vienna, and Prague offensive operations). We were certain that we would find food and fuel when we captured enemy stockpiles. But ammunition was another matter altogether. Without ammunition, a tank is not a powerful force but only a heavy piece of metal.

It was the end of 1943 and the beginning of 1944, and we were fighting for the right-bank Ukraine. We had received our Shermans in the late fall of 1943, and during this period we were learning how to use them. These tanks had both positive and negative qualities. Insofar as ammunition was concerned, the Sherman showed its best side. The main-gun rounds came exceptionally well packed, each round in a cardboard tube and three tubes strapped together with a carrying handle. If the tank should happen to burn, these rounds did not detonate.

This packing method enabled our crews to load and carry extra main-gun rounds on the floor of the fighting compartment. The cardboard tubes were strong enough for us to walk on. We also carried extra ammunition strapped to the outside of the tank, wrapped in pieces of tarpaulin and firmly strapped with twine to the grills and the tops of the fenders.

The basic main-gun ammunition load of a Sherman was seventy-one rounds. We carried approximately one and a half times this basic load. We would have liked to carry more, but that was not possible. It must be recalled that the M4A2 was carrying other cargo: auxiliary fuel drums and approximately ten *tankodesantniki*. We had to maintain some semblance of seating room around the outside of the turret for our infantry brothers. Their presence was crucial to our combat success, and we could not be dropping them along the road. The most important thing was always to maintain freedom of movement for the turret, for firing.

Our tank formations had their own logistic support units. When 6th Guards Tank Army formations were acting in the capacity of the *front* mobile group (in the Jassy-Kishinev and Manchurian operations), the logistic units of the forward brigades always moved with the tanks. If brigade logistic units were located some ten to fifteen kilometers from the line of contact of the opposing sides, then battalion logistic units were not more than three to five kilometers back from this same line. This was actually quite close, normally a separation of one terrain feature from the fighting units.

The battalion support platoon was equipped with nine Studebaker trucks, three of which were always loaded with ammunition. They carried one-fourth of the battalion's basic load of main-gun rounds, coax and antiaircraft machine-gun ammunition, and rounds for the Thompson submachine gun that came with each Sherman for the crew's personal defense. The ammunition load carried on these three trucks was in effect the "second echelon" of tank ammunition resupply.

Because the support platoon was equipped with high-frequency tank radios—cannibalized from battle-destroyed Shermans— it could deliver ammunition to the Shermans whenever they needed any. We had no iron-clad delivery schedule. During brief or rapid-maneuver combat actions, deliveries of ammunition and other supplies were not preplanned; the "on-call" method was preferred.

As soon as the battalion support platoon had dropped off its ammunition cargo, it would head immediately to the brigade transportation platoon—a unit made up of two squads, each equipped with eight trucks and manned by twelve personnel, that carried one-fourth the brigade's basic load. At the brigade the battalion support platoon vehicles would draw a full load of ammunition and then return to the battalion. The brigade logistic unit sometimes brought a load of ammunition forward to the battalion. This frequently occurred during particularly fierce combat, with the brigade logistic element providing backup to the battalion. When the ammunition supply at the brigade transportation platoon began to be depleted, its Studebakers were sent to the corps exchange point and loaded with the required quantity of ammunition.

In March 1944, during the attack on the town of Beltsy (midway between the Dniester and Prut Rivers), the forward battalions of our 233d Tank Brigade received a parachute delivery of ammunition. It was the only case in which this means of delivery was used in our Second Ukrainian *Front*. But in the difficult conditions of the spring thaw, there was no other way to accomplish the resupply.

One of the additional duties of our support platoon was to recover all serviceable ammunition from battle-damaged or destroyed tanks. This ammunition was brought forward to fighting units, saving both scarce resources and time and reducing somewhat the distance traveled by the trucks themselves. When viewed over the course of eighteen months of combat with the Shermans, the savings were significant.

Another responsibility of the support platoon was to pick up expended brass—a practice that was not as strange as it may seem. The German army established special units for the collection, confiscation, and outright theft of metals, particularly copper and brass. These units ripped out window and door handles and even made off with the statue of Samson from Leningrad. All this metal was shipped back to Germany. Brass and copper were, are, and always will be valuable, even strategic, metals. The strictest instructions existed in the Soviets' active army: collect all fired cases and deliver them to the supply points from which ammunition was obtained.

Of course in tanks—even in ones of such large internal dimensions as the Sherman—the crews could not save fired cases for long. As soon as the coax spent-cartridge bag was half full, the crews emptied it. We threw the cases out, but not simply in the fields and forests; we collected them all at one location. When possible, an entire tank company would pass by a single point and dump all expended machine-gun brass and main-gun round casings. The battalion support platoon picked up the cases and delivered them to the brigade transportation platoon, which in turn trucked them to the corps ammunition supply point, and so on, until the cases reached the ammunition plants in the deep rear of the country.

Before the start of the Manchurian operation, we also took on a greater than normal supply of main-gun rounds and machine-gun cartridges. We carefully wrapped the main-gun rounds in canvas and secured them on the upper portion of the Shermans' hulls. We had no problem with this supplementary ammunition supply during our crossing of the Gobi Desert, where the thick dust that settled on the canvas wrappings caused no harm.

However, when our units moved into the southern reaches of the Grand Khingan Range and its torrential downpours, our commanders began to worry. The canvas covering on the supplementary ammunition supply was not hermetically sealed, and thus water began to leak through to the cardboard tubes, soaking them. If the rounds themselves were exposed to excessive moisture, the cases might begin to oxidize—a condition that could lead to extraction problems when the rounds were fired, leaving expended cases stuck in the breech. We brought some of the supplementary ammunition supply into our turrets and wrapped the remainder with additional layers of canvas.

After overcoming the mountains, units of 9th Guards Mechanized Corps were delayed in the area of the town of Lubeya by a fuel shortage. We used this time to clean and dry our ammunition. Our tankers carefully prepared for the possibility of combat with the Japanese in the course of subsequent movement to the southeast.

Our fears were not realized, however. We did not have to employ our weapons. For a distance of over 1,500 kilometers our *gvardeytsy* had carried a large quantity of ammunition that was intended to be used to launch a massive tank attack in a region where the enemy considered it possible to move only a few camels.

Radio Communications

Our tank units were powerful. They had four fighting qualities: armored protection, heavy weapons, maneuverability, and radio communications. Who could compare with us in that now long ago war? The artillerymen and aviators were close, but not on the same level, in radio communications. In this respect, tankers were always better equipped, especially when our 233d (46th Guards) Tank Brigade began to receive their Sherman tanks. Other units envied us. We had enough radios to give them away as precious gifts for special purposes, particularly to our friends in the artillery.

Each M4A2 Sherman came equipped with two radios, one very high frequency (VHF) and one high frequency (HF).[1] The VHF radio was used for communications within the platoons and company to a range of one and a half to two kilometers. The HF radio—used for maintaining communications with our higher commander (battalion or brigade)—was an excellent piece of equipment. We liked the fact that it allowed us to establish reliable contact with a subscriber and then solidly maintain the set frequency. No more worries! No jolt or vibration of the tank would dislodge this radio from the frequency.

I must also say a good word for one other indispensable piece of equipment in the American tank: the auxiliary generator unit for recharging the vehicle's storage batteries.[2] Located in the left rear of the crew compartment—with an exhaust pipe that exited the hull along the right side, between the upper and lower runs of the track—this remarkable device could be started up at any time. Unfortunately our Soviet T-34 tanks were never equipped with such a component during the Great Patriotic War. They had to start their engines to keep their storage batteries in working order. Five hundred horsepower to charge batteries was not only noisy, but it used up both fuel and engine hours.

The superior technical capabilities, especially of the HF radio, led Lieutenant Aleksandr Morshnev, 1st Battalion communications chief, to make a suggestion after the battles on the Dnieper River. With the battalion commander and the staff supporting his idea, he suggested that the HF radios and the auxiliary generator unit be removed from tanks that were unsalvageable due to battle damage, if these items were still serviceable. The equipment was subsequently installed in the battalion's supporting wheeled vehicle fleet, beginning with the ammunition and POL [petroleum, oil, lubricants] trucks. On the impassable winter and spring Ukrainian roads, and in rapidly changing combat situations, the radio-equipped support platoon could now receive orders to deliver necessary supplies to forward tank units.

In short, after the Korsun-Shevchenkovskiy operation and offensives on the Southern Bug and Dniester Rivers, and toward the Prut River, battle-destroyed Shermans gave the battalion approximately ten extra working HF radio sets and auxiliary generator units. These were priceless gifts!

We used wire communications during the March–April period of 1944, when we were in a temporary defensive posture in the bridgehead northeast of Jassy. This was my single experience using wire at the front. Tank units generally did not use wire communications in a combat situation. It was another matter when units were in the rear for reforming or refitting. In these situations the telephone was an irreplaceable means of communication, and the radio was turned off.

We were normally forced to use telephones in the defense because strict radio silence was imposed on us. German signals intelligence was constantly searching for tank-unit radio nets. Using direction-finding as a means of determining our tank units' locations, the Germans passed the coordinates off to their artillery or aviation units.

The wire line extended from the battalion commander to the brigade commander. Visual signals were used to communicate between defending companies. A battalion of 122-mm howitzers was designated to support our battalion. The artillery forward observer team (an officer and a radio operator) was located at our battalion command post, which was the battalion commander's tank with a deep shelter dug beneath it. With a radio as a backup, this team used wire as the primary means of communication with its firing batteries. There were no artillery forward observers at the tank company level.

The enemy methodically rained artillery fire on our positions, frequently disrupting the wire links between our tank battalion and the supporting artillery battalion. The artillery forward observer switched over to his radio during the time that the wire links were being restored. His radio communications were unreliable, either for technical problems or other reasons. After several days, Major Gorodilov, the battalion commander, had seen enough of these communication lapses with the supporting "gods of war." With good reason he harbored some concern that radio communications might fail during a battle. He therefore ordered Aleksandr Morshnev to give the artillery battalion a tank radio set with an auxiliary generator unit and to teach the artillery communications section how to use it. The order was carried out, and three days later the new means of communication was tested with complete success. The artillery battalion could now maintain reliable radio contact with their forward observer team at the tank battalion.

This gift we tankers gave to our friends in the artillery played an important role in the events before the launching of the Jassy-Kishinev operation, when the enemy made a serious effort to destroy our bridgehead on the west side of the Prut River. Our supporting artillery unit commander used his new radio set to maintain continuous command and control of artillery fires in support of our local counterattack.

At the request of the battalion maintenance officer, Captain Aleksandr Dubitskiy, a second similar gift of a radio and an auxiliary generator unit was given to the corps' mobile tank repair base chief. This enabled the captain to maintain uninterrupted contact with the brigade maintenance team. Our experience of removing HF radios from combat-destroyed tanks was copied by our corps' mechanized brigades, using the Sherman losses in their own tank regiment.

Communications also worked without interruption in offensive battles in Romania, Hungary, Czechoslovakia, and Austria. Voice or key (if the terrain was broken) was used when forward units became separated from main forces by distances of fifteen to twenty kilometers; at distances in excess of this, Morse code was used.

The relative "richness" of the battalions and the brigade in HF radio-equipped vehicles raised the issue of strict control over their employment. Counterintelligence officers from the SMERSH service accomplished this control. No one took violations of this organ's instructions lightly.

It must be noted that by the end of 1944, SMERSH personnel paid little attention to the way our radio communications were being handled. Perhaps they felt the war would soon end, or perhaps they were busy with more important tasks.

As I have mentioned, enemy signals-intelligence units continuously monitored our transmissions and carried out direction-finding activity against working radios in tank units, both at brigade and battalion levels. I personally experienced their activity.

In mid-April 1945, 46th Guards Tank Brigade was developing success in northern Austria. My battalion was attacking toward the town of Gaweinstal (twenty-five kilometers north of Vienna). Several minutes prior to this, I had concluded a radio conversation with my brigade commander, Guards Lieutenant Colonel Nikolay Mikhno, during which he had given me some vital instructions. Suddenly someone was calling me on the radio, not by my call sign but by my last name. I thought, "Nikolay Mikhaylovich forgot to tell me something"—he frequently called battalion commanders by their last names rather than by their call signs. So I picked up the earphones and responded, "I am listening!" In reply an unfamiliar voice said in the purest Russian, "Loza, Loza, you prick, you are still alive!"

I burst out immediately, "You scum! I am alive and will remain alive! It will soon be over for you, you fascist scum!" There was no response on the other end of the conversation. And in the end, the fascists got what they deserved.

Soon after the conclusion of combat activity in the west, our battalion, which was near Prague in Czechoslovakia, handed its Shermans over to another unit. We kept our extra radios and auxiliary generator units, however, because we thought they would be useful to us in peacetime—we would find an application for them. Then we began to assemble for the long trip to the Far East. We had one more war to fight, against imperialist Japan.

In the complex conditions of the offensive in the Gobi Desert, while passing over the southern reaches of the Grand Khingan Range, and on the Manchurian plain, we used only our tank

HF radios. Neither the VHF radios nor any radios that we had mounted on our battalion support vehicles worked. The majority of our Studebakers went only as far as the western slopes of the Khingan, remaining there with all their equipment. We did not have sufficient fuel for them to proceed farther. We never saw these trucks again, however. They were sent somewhere and given to some other unit. We were ordered to drop them from our hand receipts.

When the Shermans were turned into tractors after the war and sent out to work in the civilian economy—a fact that caused great consternation among our crews—we grudgingly gave up our radio sets. These fine instruments, originally recovered from damaged tanks, saw their final service in the forests of Siberia, where they are still remembered.

Combat Vehicle Maintenance

The tank is a great iron beast, but in combat it's a friend! Like any other asset, it has to be prepared carefully for an enemy engagement. The modern armored vehicle requires complete maintenance of its armaments, steering gear, gauges, engine, suspension, communications gear, and its various other components. During World War II all of this was accomplished by tank maintenance support elements, which existed in every troop formation, from the bottom to the top of the force structure.

Appropriate maintenance organizations were created as the scope of their work grew significantly over the course of combat actions. Their priority missions were to provide comprehensive assistance to combat units through the evacuation of disabled tanks from the battlefield, the replacement of parts and components with the crews' assistance, and the supplying of fuel to the vehicles.

Depending on the number and location of the damaged and destroyed tanks, repair parties and facilities were moved to them, or the vehicles were moved to the repair sites. The experience of the Great Patriotic War indicates that 75 to 80 percent of disabled vehicles were returned to service, and 20 to 25 percent were written off as total losses.

Commanders exercised control of their tank-maintenance support through their deputies for maintenance, or maintenance officers. The following forces and means existed to carry out the various maintenance tasks and related services within the several echelons.

The TOE [table of organization and equipment] of a tank battalion provided for a support platoon (25 men) of four squads: automotive repair (with a type-A mobile repair shop), weapon repair, transportation (9 trucks), and supply. Tank and mechanized brigades had a technical support company (125 men) of three platoons: wheeled and combat vehicle repair, electrical equipment repair, and artillery and rifled weapon repair. This company was equipped with 25 vehicles, including 3 fuel trucks, type A-2 and B-1 mobile repair shops, and 2 mobile generators. The transportation platoon (3 sections and 35 men) included an ammunition section, a fuel section, and a spare parts and food provisions section.

Brigades also had an evacuation section with 5 recovery vehicles. Our 233d (46th Guards) Brigade had more recovery vehicles than our TOE provided for, at times up to 8 extra vehicles. These extra recovery assets came from Sherman tanks whose main guns had been irreparably damaged—when a German solid-shot round had struck the gun tube, for example. If additional personnel were needed to work in repair units, they were brought in from battalion and brigade reserves—a measure that helped reduce the amount of time combat vehicles spent in repair.

The TOE of a mechanized corps included a mobile tank repair base (PTRB—*podvizhnaya tankoremontnaya baza*) and a field wheeled-vehicle repair base (PARB—*polevaya avtoremontnaya baza*). The PTRB (107 men) consisted of an inspection section, platoons for disassembly and assembly work, a special tasks platoon, an evacuation platoon, and support elements. The PARB (70 men) included platoons for disassembly and assembly work, repair and restoration of components, and technical and supply support.

The tank army had one separate repair-restoration battalion and two mobile repair bases, with a total of seven companies among these three establishments. The units were capable of accomplishing 316 medium and routine repairs in a month's time. The army also had two evacuation companies with 30 recovery vehicles in each and an armored vehicle supply facility.

Equipment monitoring points (PTN—*punkt tekhnicheskogo nablyudeniya*) were established in the tank corps at battalion level and above, and in the mechanized corps beginning at the regiment, for continuous monitoring of the battlefield. Created during periods of combat actions, their purpose was to determine the location of disabled combat vehicles, what unit they belonged to, the nature of their damage, and the means of evacuating them.

Maintenance and evacuation groups (REG—*remontno-evakuatsionnaya gruppa*), a non-TOE organization, were created from the assets of the technical support platoon of the battalion and brigade maintenance units. Their mission was to evacuate damaged vehicles from the battlefield or repair them at the closest protected position.

Frequently an army repair group (ARG—*armeyskaya remontnaya gruppa*) was designated in a tank army. This was the case with 6th Guards Tank Army in the Korsun-Shevchenkovskiy operation (January 1944), during the Jassy-Kishinev operation (August 1944) and later that month around Bucharest, when we had to accomplish a massive exchange of Sherman road wheels (they had not withstood the August heat after prolonged road marching).

The ARG consisted of five to six type-A repair shops, two type-B repair shops, and a mobile compressor unit for filling truck tires. The type-A and type-B repair vans conducted routine and medium repair of tanks and wheeled vehicles in field conditions. They were equipped with a variety of tools, instruments, devices, and materials that allowed for all types of repair work, either at a collection point for disabled vehicles (SPAM—*sbornyy punkt povrezhdennykh mashin*) or at any place where they encountered an individual vehicle.

The SPAM was a facility designed to support armored forces during a combat operation. It was created in armies, corps, and brigades as a center for the concentration of damaged (inoperable) vehicles, their inspection, and the transfer of disabled vehicles to higher echelons of repair. The SPAMs were established in areas that had the greatest accumulation of disabled tanks but that were also close to the evacuation routes and water sources. The brigade

SPAM was positioned three to five kilometers from the forward line of troops, and the corps SPAM eight to twelve kilometers.

The brigade maintenance support company could deploy two to three SPAMs in a twenty-four-hour period. Brigade repair assets were not to be out of contact with their supported units for more than ten to twelve hours and corps assets for more than two or three days.

An order of the Chief of Armored and Mechanized Forces of the Red Army of 26 August 1943 required that the locations of brigade and corps SPAMs, maintenance support companies, and mobile tank repair bases be indicated not only in logistic orders but also in combat orders.[1] It was further required that this information be provided to every vehicle crew.

In order to avoid taking a large number of brigade maintenance assets away from forward units, the army frequently sent its own SPAMs forward with several shop vans to receive vehicles from units and repair them. In this case, resources from the army evacuation company recovered the Shermans from the battlefield. Corps and brigade recovery units were not used to recover battle-damaged tanks directly to an army SPAM.

Having described the organizational structure of maintenance units, I will now describe the way these assets functioned in operations of the 6th Guards Tank Army against the German forces. Our tank army conducted two successful offensives in the expanse of right-bank Ukraine in the late winter and early spring of 1944: the Korsun-Shevchenkovskiy and Umansk-Batoshansk operations. These campaigns were executed in the most difficult conditions of the winter and the spring thaw.

The maintenance support of units equipped with Lend-Lease tanks was complicated by a chronic shortage of spare parts. An analysis of the organization and supply of spare parts for tank formations in battles fought in 1942 was used to establish the basis of issue for spare parts later in the war. The quantity of spare parts issued for a tank company was absolutely inadequate to meet demand.

An order of the Chief of Armored and Mechanized Forces of the Red Army issued on 6 January 1943 established a new procedure. Factories were ordered to deliver a regimental (brigade) set of spare parts and assemblies (ZIP—*komplekt zapasnykh chastey, instrumentov i prinadlezhnostey*) for each group of thirty tanks delivered to the forces. We did not have a company, let alone a brigade *zip*, for our Shermans. We did not even have spare track blocks and track pins. In fairness, though, I must say that each vehicle did come fully supplied with tools, lightbulbs, and fuses—*Shermanisti* experienced no worries in this regard.

In connection with this general shortage of spare parts, battalion and, in particular, brigade maintenance personnel quickly began to remove various parts and assemblies from the first group of combat-destroyed tanks. These parts were stored and then issued in a direct-exchange system. For example, by the end of February 1944, our 233d Tank Brigade maintenance personnel had accumulated 3 radiators, 50 track blocks, 6 idler wheels, 5 drive sprockets, and 25 headlights. At corps level were 4 engine assemblies, 3 transmission assemblies, 5 radiators, 12 sprockets, 8 idler wheels, 120 track blocks, and 22 road wheels.[2] These parts were for the support of 80 Sherman tanks in the brigades. By this time our tank army supply depot contained 40 tank engines, of which 15 (new, not from battle-destroyed tanks) were for Shermans.

Considering the particular intensity of combat and the poor weather conditions of January and February 1944, maintenance assets of First and Second Ukrainian *Fronts* were brought as close as possible to the forward units. They were employed in a decentralized fashion—in separate maintenance detachments operating in the tank and mechanized corps. Twenty-nine of these detachments were established in First Ukrainian *Front* and thirty-eight in the Second Ukrainian *Front*. Each detachment had one or two repair-rehabilitation battalions, one or two evacuation platoons or companies, and a supply of spare parts. In each detachment was an officer with the designated responsibility of maintaining contact with the supported units.

The maintenance assets of the army and *front* were thus working in the interests of their subordinate corps. Twenty to twenty-five tanks and self-propelled guns (one battalion) were repaired and returned to units on a daily basis. At the beginning of February, delivery of engine lubricants was interrupted, and our diesel engines were forced to go some fifty to sixty operating hours past their scheduled oil change. It was an abnormal situation, particularly for the M4A2, which required strict observance of its service intervals. We had to resort to an extreme measure: twice we drained and filtered the used oil. And so, to some degree, in our initial combat operations using Sherman tanks, the units of 5th Mechanized Corps accomplished tank maintenance by the method of trial and error. In fact we gradually gained enough experience to be able to perform even difficult maintenance tasks.

One unusual and amusing incident occurred during this period of combat in right-bank Ukraine. The seats in the M4A2 were covered, as a rule, with a thick brown leather substitute. For a long time our infantry friends looked at this attractive material with covetous eyes. Inspecting our "transoceanic beasts," our combat brothers frequently mentioned that the facing on these seats would make good boots. The infantry were always dreaming about good boots as they wound their leg wraps.[3] The crews quickly learned to cut the undamaged seat covers from battle-destroyed tanks before the vehicles were turned in for cannibalization. I recall seeing several good pairs of boots made from this artificial leather.

While planning the Jassy-Kishinev operation, and considering the crucial role that 6th Tank Army would be playing in it, the command of Second Ukrainian *Front* undertook a series of preparatory measures, including making provisions for tank maintenance support. The positive experiences of the previous two operations were fully applied in this case.

The army therefore received in reinforcement: one repair and rehabilitation battalion (146th Separate Repair and Rehabilitation Battalion), two repair and rehabilitation bases (81st and 154th Mobile Repair Bases), and eight evacuation companies and SPAMs. But all these units were subordinated to the *front* and, in view of the expected rapid pace of the offensive, they were supported by two basic loads of fuel and one and a half times the normal issue of spare parts.

Each company in the T-34-equipped 5th Guards Tank Corps was supplied with a company-size ZIP—an advantage that was not possible with our Shermans. By the beginning of the operation, our brigades in the 5th Mechanized Corps were relying on a supply of direct-exchange parts that had been removed from damaged tanks. Large assemblies, such as engines and transmissions, were readied and brought forward with recovery assets during the course of the operation. Later it became clear that the brigades' supplies of spare parts were totally insufficient to meet the demands of subordinate units.

Front and army maintenance and evacuation groups followed behind the first echelon brigades in the first two days of combat operations, always remaining within fifteen to twenty kilometers of the supported units. They conducted routine light repair of damaged vehicles and assisted crews in maintaining their T-34s and Shermans.

In the operational depth the maintenance and evacuation groups initially worked on vehicles at the sites where they broke down, for periods of up to six hours. Then the tempo of 6th Army's offensive subsequently increased sharply. By 27 August, army and attached *front* maintenance and evacuation units were unable to keep up, having fallen some 90 to 120 kilometers behind the forward units. In this situation, all the weight of correcting deficiencies and servicing the Shermans fell on the corps and brigade maintenance units. They were frequently forced to accomplish not only routine but sometimes medium repair, some tasks requiring twenty-four to thirty-six hours.

It must be noted that serious defects were not a problem with the engines, transmissions, and clutches on our foreign-made equipment. But it was a different story with the suspension components. Our rubber road wheels and support rollers did not withstand long road marches in combination with high ambient temperatures. In our 5th Mechanized Corps, 75 percent of our Shermans lost road wheels in these circumstances. With the intervention of logistic organs in the center,[4] new road wheels were delivered from our country's deep rear by air transport. The second problem was the lack of fuel due to our logistic support's having fallen behind. This problem was solved in 233d Tank Brigade by mixing a cocktail made of gasoline and kerosene.

At the beginning of the Jassy-Kishinev operation (20 August 1944), 6th Tank Army formations had 561 armored vehicles (5th Guards Tank Corps, 263; 5th Mechanized Corps, 170; and in other army units, 128). During the offensive operation, unit assets accomplished 407 routine and 18 medium repairs; corps assets 42 and 71; and army assets 19 and 59, respectively. Army assets accomplished major repair of 5 vehicles. A total of 621 vehicles were repaired and returned to units. During the period from

23 to 30 August, army recovery assets evacuated 13
self-propelled guns from the battlefield (138th Arm
Company, 91, and 88th Army Evacuation Compan

The better-equipped evacuation battalions form
were capable of accomplishing all the tasks associ
evacuation, transportation, and loading of tanks o
shipment to repair shops of the Ministry of Defen
These battalions belonged to the *front* and the ce

Tank maintenance support in subsequent ope
Guards Tank Army to defeat German forces in H
slovakia, and Austria remained essentially unch
the modest depth of the offensives of the army's
the well-developed road network in these count
successful resolution of any problems regarding
tion of damaged vehicles, and timely repair. The
cases of interruptions in the supply of fuel to fi
in the mountainous regions of northern and n
gary, primarily caused by breaks in the serpent

Our 6th Guards Tank Army also participate
imperialist Japan in August–September 1945. C
commanders, the higher-level commanders, a
tic services had to operate in conditions that
difficult even to imagine. Operational planne
staff and *front* level understood the complex
liarities of the regions where Soviet forces w
They intended to concentrate 5,250 tanks an
on the three *fronts* deployed in the Far East,
armored vehicles on the single axis coming
Approximately 30 percent of these vehicles
(*BT* and T-26).[5]

In accordance with the strategic plan of
ful grouping of tank forces and support ass
Transbaykal *Front*. Fifteen maintenance a
had assembled by 9 August. In addition, se
joined 6th Guards Tank Army. In subsequ
units continued to arrive by rail from the
battalions and bases detrained from 10 th
another five from 15 through 25 August.
vehicle repair shop and a separate field o

ployed in the *front*'s zone; this station supplied oxygen cylinders to the forces.

It was most unfortunate that among all of these maintenance units and facilities in Transbaykal *Front*, there was not a single maintenance facility dedicated to the repair of Lend-Lease tanks and armored vehicles. Our corps and brigade maintenance units had to conduct every level of repair with their own personnel and equipment.

Taking into account the difficult situation, commanders at appropriate levels devoted serious attention to planning the use of maintenance and evacuation units. They ultimately distributed them in the following manner: 138th Evacuation Company (six T-34T recovery vehicles) and 49th Separate Tank Maintenance Battalion (*OTRB*) were attached to 9th Guards Mechanized Corps;[6] 88th Evacuation Company (six T-34Ts), a maintenance company from 49th *OTRB*, and a shop van from Army Tank Parts Depot No. 3214 were attached to 7th Mechanized Corps. No army assets were attached to 5th Guards Tank Corps.

In addition, army *SPAM* No. 145, Army Tank Parts Depot No. 3214, and two *front* assets—125th Separate Maintenance Repair Base and 66th Evacuation Company—were to follow behind our 9th Guards Mechanized Corps. Strict parameters were established for the interval between tank maintenance support units and supported units during the course of the offensive. Brigade maintenance units were to follow six to seven kilometers behind the forward battalions, in readiness to conduct routine and medium repairs of modest duration and to recover lightly mired tanks. Corps and army maintenance and evacuation units, following at a distance of not more than twenty-five kilometers from the first echelon, performed medium repair of armored vehicles and evacuated vehicles forward along the route of march. When required, these units also were to create intermediate *SPAM*s.

By the beginning of the operation *Front* maintenance and evacuation units had reached the assembly areas of the combat forces and were able to accept all vehicles requiring medium and major repairs. This allowed maintenance units at the troop level to focus their efforts on accompanying advancing formations through the entire depth of the operation.

In the course of combat actions, *front* assets were not to become separated from the troop units by more than fifty kilometers. Using army- and corps-level SPAMs, these *front* assets were to sweep disabled tanks from the route being used by the advancing units and then to deliver the tanks to *front* SPAMs for repair.

These basic measures for tank maintenance support were implemented in 6th Guards Tank Army's zone. The Soviet logistical planning staff had forgotten nothing; they planned for everything. But monsoon rains that began on 10 August prevented the implementation of the plan. The already-bad roads were completely broken up, and the situation grew steadily worse over the following days. All this led to the development of a large gap between upper-echelon maintenance resources and the combat formations. *Front* maintenance and evacuation assets were some 200 kilometers behind the forward forces by 11 August.

Those tank maintenance support units that continued to arrive by rail remained at their off-loading stations, delayed by a fuel shortage. When fuel finally arrived, the units were unable to catch up to the formations due to the poor condition of the roads. By 12 August it had become obvious that *front* maintenance and evacuation units would be halted at the foothills of the Grand Khingan Range. They thus deployed three intermediate SPAMs on the axis of our 9th Guards Mechanized Corps, separated from each other by some fifty to sixty kilometers.

During the operation 6th Guards Tank Army units evacuated 122 tanks and self-propelled guns to these SPAMs. One explanation for the large number of disabled vehicles was the many old-model vehicles (BT and T-26) in use. They had been in Mongolia since the pre-war period, some having participated in the events at the Khalkhin Gol River. Tank brigades equipped with these vehicles had been subordinated to 6th Guards Tank Army before the start of this operation. These vehicles, already worn out, experienced serious breakdowns on the difficult desert and mountain roads in the first days of the offensive. Only a few of them reached the Grand Khingan Range.

On instructions of the commander of 7th Mechanized Corps, General Fedor Katkov, one of these tanks (a BT) was placed in the Tsagan-Dabo Pass. The crew wrote the words "Soviet tanks passed this by point in 1945" on its turret with a gas welder.

To this day I have not forgotten the sad frustration and regret felt by the experienced crews of these worn-out vehicles. We "westerners" watched as, one after the other, the tanks became stuck in the shifting sands of the Gobi Desert and dropped out along the approaches to the Grand Khingan Range and in the early kilometers of the mountain track. Hard-core tank officers were not embarrassed to be seen crying. We could sympathize with them. During the four difficult years of the war in the west they had stood attentive watch on our country's eastern borders. They had experienced much: the skimpy army rear rations,[7] the continuous combat readiness and the intense pressure associated with it, the ban on all leaves, and the colossal efforts they themselves had devoted to maintaining their obsolete vehicles in combat condition.

While I was still sitting behind a school desk, these men were fighting Japanese aggressors in the burning steppes of Mongolia. Wartime fate had now brought us together in this unequal situation: we were on tanks fresh off the boat, while their vehicles were in their final days.[8] When it was time for these tankers to perform in combat, their old equipment was simply not up to the task. As a consequence, experienced officers and crews were parked on the shoulder of our wartime road. How could they not have been disheartened?

At the time this situation was absolutely incomprehensible to us, and even now I ask myself this question: was the technical condition of the T-26s and BTs totally unknown in the Far East Military District and in Moscow? Planning for the Manchurian operation began on 27 April 1945. Initial calculations for concentrating our forces in the Amur River area and the area around Vladivostok had been made back in the fall of 1944.[9] Why had these units not been reequipped with new vehicles? These experienced officers and their trained crews were fully capable of mastering the T-34 in three or four months. Frankly speaking, our leaders let them down, and we paid a high price for their failure.

Only new equipment could withstand the enormous stresses in these unbelievably difficult geographic conditions. Formations of 6th Guards Tank Army moved from 600 to 1,100 kilometers at an average rate of 70 to 90 kilometers per day during the period from 9 to 24 August. The journey required from 80 to 100 engine hours.[10]

Assigned maintenance assets accomplished tank maintenance

support to our units during the crossing of the Grand Khingan Range and on the central Manchurian plain. The *Shermanisti* pushed and towed but did not abandon disabled vehicles, no matter how difficult the route. But whether it was a serious problem or a minor one, these support units were our only hope.

In the Far East Military District the M4A2 was tested under an immense variety of difficult conditions and, with only rare exceptions, showed itself in an extremely positive light. We had no serious breakdowns or accidents. No Sherman tanks failed under the weight of those circumstances.

Feeding the Troops

Of all the aggregate of battalion and brigade logistic services, providing meals to soldiers was the one with the highest priority—the most important and the most urgent. A great military leader from the past is supposed to have said, "The way to a soldier's consciousness is through his stomach." And another, "A hungry soldier is not a fighter. A satisfied soldier is a powerful warrior!" Feeding soldiers has always been uppermost in the concerns of successful commanders.

During the Great Patriotic War, all issues pertaining to food were resolved at the battalion level. The responsibility of logistic services above battalion level was to ensure a steady flow of raw and packaged food supplies down to the battalion, where it was prepared and served to soldiers. The daily menu was the responsibility of those at battalion level entrusted with feeding soldiers.

By the TOE the battalion had a deputy commander for logistics, the battalion sergeant major, and a messing section (six men and a field kitchen). This section was equipped with a Studebaker truck to haul food supplies and tow the field kitchen. At brigade level we had a section for hauling spare parts and provisions (thirty-three men and six trucks) in the transportation platoon. The corps ration distribution point was manned by four men. The corps also supervised a separate field bakery platoon of forty-two personnel and seven vehicles.

In the course of battles in Ukraine, the battalion logistics officer had a HF radio that had been removed from a battle-damaged Sherman tank. With this radio he could deliver prepared meals on call or at a preplanned time and location that had been coordinated with the unit.

Even Peter the Great (the Russian tsar from 1682 to 1725), who first created a regular army, demanded in his regulations that soldiers be fed hot food twice daily. Those found guilty of violating this order were punished by loss of rank. Feeding soldiers was a serious matter!

We did not feed our tankers and *tankodesantniki* two hot meals every day during the Great Patriotic War, but not because we didn't try. Sometimes the combat or weather situation simply made it impossible. Our troops were fed three prepared meals daily only when the brigade was in the corps' second echelon during reforming and refitting. Our *tankodesantniki*, I should say here, were a permanent element of our combat formation. We carried them around on our armor, fed them, treated and evacuated them when they were wounded, and buried them in graves alongside our tankers when they were killed in action or died of wounds. Together we fought, together we died, and together we were buried. This was the reality of the front line.

Our field kitchen had two wood-burning stoves for preparing the first and second courses. We had a problem with fuel when we reached the unforested region of the Ukraine. The solution was a combination of scarce wood and the packing materials from our tanks' main-gun ammunition. The support platoon carried the cardboard tubes to the rear and delivered them to the field kitchens after resupplying the tank companies.

Food supplies were apportioned in the following manner in the battalion. Each crew carried in their vehicles dry rations sufficient for a three-day period. These rations—called the "untouchable supply" (NZ—*neprikosnovennyy zapas*)—included canned items, sausage or suet, sugar, and dried bread. They were unpacked and eaten only in exceptional circumstances, with the permission of a higher or an immediate commander. The battalion mess team maintained not less than a day-and-a-half supply of food products. However, by hoarding our own deliveries as well as captured food, both tank crews and battalion mess teams accumulated significantly higher quantities of food stocks than were required.

Much of what we ate at the front came from the foodstuffs delivered to the Soviet Union through the Lend-Lease program: canned meat, powdered eggs, powdered milk, biscuits, and creamed butter. There was an oft-used expression among soldiers and officers of the active army in 1943 and 1944 (until June): when we picked up a can of Lend-Lease *tushonka* [a Russian Spam-like meat recipe prepared in American packing plants], we said, "I am opening a can of the second front!" It was our reaction to the Allies' slowness in opening a second front, an event for which we longed because we knew that from that moment on, our lives would be easier and the Germans' harder.

The combat situation at the forward line of troops dictated the way that any combat support or logistic issue would be handled. We used a variety of methods to deliver in a timely manner those items that were needed for combat or the welfare of troops. Here are some examples.

Before the beginning of the Korsun-Shevchenkovskiy operation (26 January 1944) our 233d Tank Brigade of 5th Mechanized Corps arrived in the area of the village of Krasilovka. The offensive was intended to begin at 0800. We fed our troops a high-calorie breakfast of buckwheat porridge with *tushonka*, bread with creamed butter, and tea. Serving our men with care and concern, our support personnel knew from past experience that this might be the tankers' last hot meal of the day. Therefore every crew received an extra bit of lard, a kilogram of sausage, and two loaves of black bread. A squad of *tankodesantniki* received a double ration of the same (they had twice as many men as a tank crew). These extra rations were "insurance." Hot food would be delivered if and when possible. If not, the cooks could rest easy in the knowledge that their Sherman crews and *desantniki* had something with which to fill their stomachs.

Several unusual events occurred in the hours before the launching of the offensive, events that had not occurred before and would not occur again during the war. It all centered in the strange gift of a candy bar. I do not know what senior level of command thought of this treat, or where he acquired it, or what purpose it was supposed to serve. But after breakfast, every member of the tank crews and the *tankodesantniki* was given a chocolate bar with filling and was ordered to eat it thirty minutes before the launch of the attack (0730). Then, about fifteen minutes after we had all eaten the candy, information came down that the attack launching had been postponed by one to two hours due to rapidly worsening weather (heavy, wet snow).

We decided use the time for rest. We had gotten up quite early to accomplish the myriad of tasks necessary for combat. So after posting security, we went into Krasilovka and attempted to get some sleep. But it was impossible. We lay with our eyes wide open. Sleep did not come! We could not even doze off for a few minutes.

Later we learned that the candy bar contained a powerful stimulant. Our tankers cursed the fool somewhere up in the chain of command who was responsible for this. Did he not have any notion or knowledge of the undesirable consequences this stimulant might bring? Gun commanders were especially troubled: in this stimulated condition gunners might have difficulty focusing on the crosshairs of their gun sights! Our concerns were passed up the chain of command through our political organs and reported to the army's military council. They discussed the issue there, and this folly was never repeated.

Sometimes we had to use unconventional methods to deliver meals to the front line. From 14 to 24 February 1944 units of 5th Mechanized Corps, defending on the outer encirclement ring, defeated countless attacks by German forces attempting to break in to their own encircled troops in the Korsun-Shevchenkovskiy area.

With most roads being made impassable by the spring thaw, prepared food was delivered to the front line two times each day with rare exception, even though our troops were engaged in fierce battles with the enemy. Our cooks had to resort to some contrivances to keep the "mobile hot food line" (so-called by the *Shermanisti*) working without interruption.

The terrain on which our brigade was defending was open, with some higher elevations in its farther reaches. This topography precluded both vehicle and hand delivery of anything required for battle, including hot meals, in the daytime, for the enemy would immediately open fire on them. The solution was to make supply and food deliveries to the line companies before dawn and in the evening, when visibility was poorer.

Delivery of prepared meals on foot required too much time and too many porters to carry the thermos containers. As good as the Studebaker truck was—our soldiers called it the "king of the road"—it would have difficulty reaching unit positions in the soggy fields. We therefore decided to use a tank recovery vehicle for other than its intended purpose: food catering. Strict regulations could be violated for the sake of such important missions. Our comrades on the firing line, engaged in almost around-the-clock fighting, were in need.

The recovery vehicle—which was used to go forward with mechanics to tow a damaged Sherman from the forward edge to a repair facility or to remove parts or assemblies from a destroyed Sherman—offered two advantages: it was not as tall as a Sherman tank, and it could use concealed routes through ravines, depressions, and gullies where a wheeled vehicle could not travel. So this vehicle would be loaded with fifteen thermos containers of a prepared breakfast or a supper. Three cook's helpers would climb aboard and off they would set, quickly reaching the battalion command-observation post. The thermos containers with food were apportioned out for the line units, and the empty containers were recovered.

Full-course meals these were not. That kind of menu would be too difficult to transport and impossible to apportion properly at the forward edge. Rather, the standard fare under these conditions was porridge with meat, macaroni, goulash, and stew. Infrequently, as a supplement to the main course, the cooks boiled and sent out potatoes in the skin, cold, to the crews and *desantniki*. The men ate these potatoes with great pleasure, but our supply of these vegetables was inadequate—they were also a rarity in Ukrainian villages.

On occasion, there were unforeseen delays at some sector of the front line. If this occurred in the evening, it was no problem. Dawn was far away. The thermos containers would be returned to the field kitchen for delivery of breakfast. And even though sometimes the recovery-vehicle mechanics would be able to tow a destroyed M4A2 or two from the battlefield while the tankers and *desantniki* were eating, the delivery of hot meals even took precedence over that responsibility.

Now a word about our "medicinal" hundred grams of vodka: as a rule it was brought forward with the supper meal. In a regular combat situation the allure of alcohol was not great. However, under the kinds of conditions that I have been describing, the matter was different: the battalion commander gave his approval for the delivery of the vodka.

After the destruction of the encircled enemy Korsun-Shevchenkovskiy grouping, forces of 6th Tank Army participated in the Umansk-Batoshansk operation (5 March–17 April 1944). With a depth of 200–250 kilometers, this was one of the largest offensives in the conditions of spring thaw. The roads were totally broken up, with the sticky chernozem soil reaching a depth of forty to fifty centimeters. Tracked vehicles could move along these muddy roads, though with difficulty. Wheeled vehicles, even the Studebakers, became stuck. The Studebaker trucks did make this trip, but they burned up a great quantity of fuel—an extremely precious commodity. Our units also had to force four rivers: the Gornyy Tikich, Southern Bug, Dniester, and Prut.

Foreseeing the immense complexity—in particular, that of supplying meals—the battalion and brigade logistic services issued dry rations to the crews in sufficient quantity to last for ten days, as opposed to the normal three days. Subsequent events confirmed the wisdom of this decision.

For the first time, we had to use the full "combat potential" of the M4A2—that is, the two-burner Primus stove and the five sets of utensils (large spoons, dessert spoons, teaspoons, forks, and knives) that were included in the Sherman's standard-issue equipment. The Primus stove came in handy for twelve days during the offensive and for a brief period of March in the defense across the Prut River. We heated up our pork *tushonka* and sausage and toasted our stale bread in our mess tins. During modest pauses in the battle, we boiled water for tea. While we were on the bridgehead across the Prut River the Primus stoves were also in continuous use.

Before the beginning of the offensive, Senior Lieutenant Sergey Smirnov, our battalion deputy commander for logistics, proposed to the battalion commander that the field kitchen with equipment not be left behind in the assembly area. The lieutenant suggested it be towed behind one of the battalion's Shermans. At this time we had insufficient gasoline to use a Studebaker truck for this purpose. The battalion commander agreed to this suggestion, and we moved out. Our resident comedians immediately began to tease the tank crew: "You'll have to fire up the kitchen and charge with your tank. The Germans will disperse in fright. They'll think they're being attacked by the cruiser *Aurora!*"[1]

Two days later the units reached a hard road leading to the town of Mogilev-Podolskiy. A captured German diesel truck was commandeered to tow the kitchen. As soon as the battalion stopped on the west side of the Prut River, the cooks prepared and delivered a hot meal to the tankers, who greatly missed having hot food. The neighboring units were still eating their dry rations.

Our stay in Skulyana wrote a special page in the chapter on the feeding of *Shermanisti*. As I have recounted, a portion of our troops worked on field-garden teams in that village, growing vegetables and greens along the edges of the fields. I can assure you that the tankers ate three healthy meals every day during this time, from March until the beginning of August. This period of field work was especially important to those soldiers who had recently been drafted into the army: they grew strong and healthy on army rations, exercise, and sunshine.[2] There were many times in the future, however, when we all recalled these days of plentiful food and the sun.

Two features marked the activities of the battalion logistic services during the conduct of the Jassy-Kishinev operation (August 1944). From the moment of receipt of the combat mission, it was clear that our unit would have to operate to a great depth and at a high tempo. The situation would certainly change frequently and abruptly, daily if not every hour. It was therefore likely that our rear services would fall behind the line companies, a situation that would result in undesired disruptions of materiel and technical support. Based on this analysis of the nature of the upcoming offensive, it was decided that all the battalion logistic elements would be maintained in march order.

It was also clear that the physical and psychological demands on the troops would be great, if not staggering. In this case, we had to do everything possible, and some things thought impossible, so that our *Shermanisti* and their passengers on the armor would be fed normally (two or three times each day). The kitchen had to operate on the move—no one could count on halts. These were demanding times and conditions, without a doubt! The cooks and their volunteer helpers (tankers from reserve positions, and the battalion and company commanders' orderlies) spent about ten days under these conditions, frequently working for twelve to fourteen hours at a stretch and enduring the high summer temperatures and the heat from their field stoves.

As during previous intensive operations, they did not prepare full-course meals but porridge from various stock—groats, buckwheat, wheat, and peas—with copious amounts of *tushonka*. Of course they understood that the tankers and *desantniki* grew tired of this fare. Not hiding their displeasure, the tankers and *desantniki* would mutter, "Porridge, porridge, a hundred times. To hell with it, and you!" The cooks just threw up their hands, but they did make a good effort to transform this hated dish into something more appetizing. When we entered Romania, for example, every kind of condiment (onions, fresh peppers, dill, and others) became available, and the cooks brought them to the table.

The cooks also found another way of improving the cuisine: soon after going into the offensive, the battalion acquired a modest supply of wine from captured dumps and underground storage facilities. The grumbling stopped. Our wine ration was three hundred grams per soldier per meal, and our soldiers appreciated the supplementary fare—the porridge was no longer boring.

Two unusual incidents occurred during the Vienna offensive. On 16 March 1945, the first day of that operation, units of 9th Guards Mechanized Corps reached starting positions on the western outskirts of Budapest. My 1st Battalion, 46th Guards Tank Brigade, was concentrated in a park (almost undamaged from the recent battles for the city) on a large manorial estate. Only two Hungarian women—one elderly and the other middle-aged—remained on the property. The owner of the estate had run off somewhere. I had taken charge of this building for housing the battalion commander and his staff during the three days our units spent at this location.

People were going hungry in the Hungarian capital at this time, so we decided to invite the caretaker staff to one of our evening meals. While the older Hungarian woman flatly refused, the younger one agreed. We shared all that we had with our guest: well-prepared goulash seasoned with paprika, fresh bread, and sweet, strong tea. She ate with a good appetite. Although none of us knew Hungarian, we had mastered a few everyday expressions. At the beginning of supper, someone said a single word to the Hungarian, "*Bor* [wine]," while throwing up his hands. He was telling her, "We have no wine to serve you with this meal." She smiled weakly, but she understood what the tanker was talking about.

At the completion of the meal, the Hungarian woman got up from behind the table, went up to Lieutenant Stepan Khromov, took him by the hand, and led him outside. The room buzzed with approval of her choice. He was a tall, stately officer with a handsome face. One of the men shouted toward his disappearing figure, "Stepan, live up to our guards' reputation!" These young men had only one thing on their minds!

The pair disappeared outside. The Hungarian woman led Khromov to my tank, which stood not far from the house, and pointed at a shovel. With gestures she led the officer to pick up the tool. Stepan carried out his partner's "command." Next she led the tanker deeper into the park, and when they had reached a small clearing, she took Khromov's shovel and began to dig in the ground, continuously repeating the word *bor*. She then pointed at the spot. When he realized the true purpose of his stroll into the park, Lieutenant Khromov summoned assistance.

Several *Shermanisti* hurried over with shovels and began to dig further into the hole. Spelling each other, they quickly dug deep down—a meter and a half, then two meters—into the ground. They found nothing. The *gvardeytsy* looked at the Hungarian woman with dissatisfaction, but she continued to assert, "*Bor, bor!*" Pointing with her shovel into the bottom of the hole, she mimicked the removal of dirt. The men shoveled out another small layer of clay, and suddenly they struck a hard object.

Their efforts took on new energy. Several minutes later they uncovered a large wooden cask, perhaps 200 to 250 liters [52–66 gallons] in capacity. They cleaned the dirt from it. Khromov having sent someone to his tank to bring back a tow cable, they then secured the line around the container and carefully raised the valuable cargo to the surface.

At this moment the interpreter showed up from brigade headquarters; the chief of staff, Guards Captain Nikolay Bogdanov, had sent a runner for him. Through the interpreter the Hungarian woman told us that the baron of the manor had a son and that on the day of the child's birth, in accordance with Hungarian custom, the cask of wine had been put here in the ground. The cask was supposed to stay there until the son reached a certain age in adolescence. We had dug up this "prize" three years before its "maturity." The Hungarian woman also told us that the baron was a bad person, that she planned to work for him no longer. This was her revenge for the indignities she had suffered in his employ.

We poured the contents of the cask into canisters. Three containers were sent to the brigade command. We also gave some to the two Hungarian women, and of course, we had to sample the wine ourselves. It was exceptional! I gave instructions to hand over the remaining wine to the personal care of the battalion deputy commander for logistics. Our *feldsher* [physician's assistant] recommended it be used for the sick and wounded. The *gvardeytsy* had a sufficient ration of legal spirits.

It was the end of March. The offensive of 9th Guards Mechanized Corps continued in the northwest direction, and the forward brigades reached the approaches to the Austrian border. We captured the towns of Shopron and Szombathely. Our scouts had earlier reported that Austrian army troops and border detachments were positioned along the Hungarian border.[3] We received the order that in the event these forces offered resistance, we were to regard them as hostile and to act accordingly.

Fortunately, events unfolded in quite another manner. Austrian parliamentarians with white flags met us northwest of Shopron on 5 April and informed us that their units were prepared to allow advancing Soviet units to pass into Austrian territory without a fight. We were happy to learn this. They also invited us to assemble our tankers and infantry and eat a hot breakfast meal with them. Indeed, we could see field kitchens a few hundred meters away, belching smoke. I accepted this breakfast invitation. Leaving two men on each Sherman, we sent the remainder to the meal site. An hour later we changed over. No one objected to our precautionary measures. We had sampled the cuisine of the Austrian troops and liked it.

The staffs of the army and border guard units gave us complete information on the German forces in the towns of Mattersburg and Weiner Neustadt. The brigade intelligence chief, Guards Captain Yuriy Gluzman, expressed his appreciation. At my request

Nikolay Bogdanov, who knew German well, posed several questions to the Austrians on matters of interest to us: the condition of the roads south of Vienna, the defensive positions of German forces in this area, and the German forces and equipment in the capital. The Austrian commanders generously shared with us all the information at their disposal, and it proved useful to the *gvardeytsy* over the next several days. This openness finally convinced us of the loyalty of these Austrians to the Soviet Army. We did not have a single hostile encounter with a local Austrian troop garrison during our offensive toward Vienna. Our brief, friendly meeting was completed with a mutual exchange of gifts: we gave them chocolate, American *tushonka*, vodka, and some lard; they brought us an assortment of fruits, vegetables, and wines.

We captured one German food cache during our offensive through Austria. Besides all the normal supplies, we discovered bread that had been baked in 1937. It had been carefully packed in heavy, greased paper. We tasted this bread: it was stale but edible. When we heated it on our tank's Primus stove, it became quite normal. Given the bread's age, our soldiers liked to believe that it was probably made from Soviet wheat, large quantities of which had been delivered to the Germans before the war.

Peculiarities in the materiel-logistic system—and in particular, the provisioning of our forces in the Khingan-Mukden operation (August–September 1945)—were a result of the unique natural conditions that the tankers encountered on a daily basis. When units of 9th Guards Mechanized Corps were located in the Choybolsan area, brigade logistics personnel established close contact with Mongolian herdsmen. Tens of thousands of horses and sheep were grazing in this region. Our logisticians reached an agreement on the exchange of commodities: we gave the herdsmen various grains, sugar, tea, and salt, and they gave us fresh meat. The *gvardeytsy* ate well on this new fare, having become quite tired of their pork *tushonka*.

During the course of the offensive into the Gobi Desert and in the foothills of the Grand Khingan range, we ate three hot meals each day: supplies of firewood were carried on our trucks, tanks, and recovery vehicle. We also took steps to protect the meat, salting down approximately three hundred kilograms of it in the two days before the beginning of the offensive. It supported us well until our arrival at the western slopes of the Grand Khingan Range.

Because of the shortage of gasoline, we left all of the battalion's wheeled vehicles, with the exception of the medical vehicles, on the west side of the Grand Khingan massif. We carried our raw food products on the tanks and the recovery vehicle. As in Romania, a Sherman towed the field kitchen. After we had crossed the mountain range, the kitchen would serve us well.

Korablin Pass in the western portion of the Grand Khingan Range was difficult. The first kilometers of the mountain track showed we would not be able to prepare hot meals in these conditions. I therefore gave permission to the crews to use the NZ rations carried on their vehicles. We would exhaust our entire supply of dry rations during the trek across the mountain range. Now the main priority was to move forward and conserve the tankers' physical strength.

The brigade's units awaited the delivery of fuel and lubricants for three and a half days near the town of Lubey. Normal meal preparation was begun immediately. Fresh vegetables were brought to the soldiers' table—enormous Chinese cucumbers, onions, and tomatoes. The battalion logistics deputy arranged for the acquisition of these items from Manchurian and Chinese peasants. We did not have the local currency but instead traded for *tushonka* and grain. There was an enormous desire to make food more tasty for the *Shermanisti*.

The next problem that appeared was the exhaustion of our firewood supply. How would we be able to fire up the stoves of our field kitchen? It was practically impossible to find firewood or coal on the central Manchurian plain. Each of our tanks was carrying two self-recovery logs, ranging in length from four and a half to five and a half meters. Our cooks looked at these logs with envy.

Guards Senior Lieutenant Sergey Smirnov asked my permission to take several of these logs for food preparation. Pressured by the deputy for logistics to consider the importance of fuel for the kitchen, I had to balance this consideration against the possibility that we might encounter swampy terrain in our upcoming movement. We knew from our rich experience in the west that it would be impossible to recover our tanks without these logs. I finally reached a decision that satisfied both the crews and the cooks. I ordered that each Sherman retain one log at least 3.5 meters long. The rest could be sawed up, split, and given to the kitchen. Here is the logic of my instructions. The width of the tank was 2.9 meters (103–105 inches). When the self-recovery log (in its cut-down length) was used, more than 30 centimeters of it would extend out past the edge of the track on each side. This was adequate.

Units of 9th Guards Mechanized Corps launched the concluding phase of their operation on 16 August. They reached Mukden and halted there. This period was no less difficult than crossing the desert and mountains. Natural conditions here in the central Manchurian plain continued to test both the stamina of us tankers and the durability of the Shermans. We were forced to travel along the railroad embankments for a distance of 120 kilometers. Our *gvardeytsy* drove carefully. They endured, overcoming unbelievable physical and psychological stress. We had doubts about our equipment, but it did not let us down. We accomplished the mission.

We subsisted on dry rations during the five days from Lubeya to Mukden. True, we had an abundance of fresh and recently salted cucumbers (we prepared them in the containers recently emptied of water), tomatoes, and onions—which helped our appetites and made our sausage taste better. We also had a supply of eggs that had been boiled before the beginning of the march, sufficient for two days. Later we learned that a Chinese method had been used: the boiled eggs had been placed in salted water for several days. That is what made them stay good for such a long time. One thing about these eggs was most unusual for us Europeans, however: after this process, the yolks had a dark blue color.

Medical Evacuation
and Treatment

Soviet Army medical service units at all echelons
played an important role in the victory over Germany. All of
these personnel were "soldiers in white coats." At the forward
edge they were the medics and stretcher bearers.[1] Farther to the
rear were the *feldshers*, the nurses and doctors, and the support
staffs at the medical stations and hospitals. Without sleep or rest,
these people fought for the lives of the sick and wounded. Tending to our soldiers and officers, they returned tens of thousands of
them to duty.

A successfully functioning system of sanitary-hygienic and
antiepidemic measures prevented among the personnel of the
Soviet Armed Forces the large-scale epidemiological outbreaks
and large-scale infectious diseases that have been intrinsic to
many armies and wars in the past. To accomplish their difficult
mission, troop medical services in 6th Guards Tank Army were
deployed with the following units. Our 5th (9th Guards) Mechanized Corps consisted of three mechanized and one tank brigade.
Each company in a mechanized battalion had a senior medic and
three regular medics. In addition, they were always assigned so-
called auxiliary medics (reserves) from among soldiers who had
received supplementary medical training—five or six to each
battalion, ten or twelve at the brigade (regiment) level, and thirty
at the corps level.

Tank companies had no assigned medics. Each crew member,
however, received some training in providing first aid to his
fellow tankers. In addition, in every type of combat the tank
battalion was reinforced by a company of *avtomatchiki* from the
tank brigade's motorized battalion. This company had the same
number of medics as the companies in the mechanized brigades.
Each tank and mechanized battalion had a *feldsher* and three
senior medics. The corps' separate *Katyusha* [multiple-rocket

launcher] battalion had the same medical component. Medical property and supplies were transported on a single truck.

Tank units were always maintained above the maximum TOE strength in certain specialties (driver-mechanic, assistant driver-mechanic, gun commander, and radio operator). This practice resulted in an additional ten to twenty men per tank company. From five to seven of these tankers were always assigned to the battalion *feldsher* to assist the medics.

A tank brigade had a senior doctor, two surgeons, and a medical platoon—thirty-eight personnel in all. Our 233d (46th Guards) Tank Brigade had three trucks for transporting the medical supplies and three American half-tracked armored troop carriers. From January 1944 onward, we also had two captured German half-tracked transporters. Together these assets allowed for the rapid evacuation of the sick and wounded in any weather and road conditions.

The personnel and equipment of this medical platoon were used to form a brigade medical station (BrMP)—*brigadnyy meditsinskiy punkt*). Then, depending on how many battalions were operating forward, these personnel were divided into two or three groups that followed behind their combat formations on the trucks or half-tracks to ensure the evacuation of the wounded from the battlefield.

There were some peculiarities in the creation of medical support units in the mechanized brigade. By TOE the brigade consisted of three mechanized battalions and a tank regiment (three tank companies, thirty-five M4A2 Sherman tanks total). Within this structure, three battalion medical stations (BMPs—*batalonnyy meditsinskiy punkt*), one BrMP, and one regimental medical station (PMP—*polkovoy meditsinskiy punkt*) were created. Naturally the tank regiment did not have a battalion medical station.

The hub of the provision of competent medical treatment in the mechanized corps was the medical-sanitary battalion (MSB—*mediko-sanitarnyy batalon*). The MSB could process from 450 to 1,500 sick and wounded personnel in a twenty-four-hour period. The role of this treatment facility grew significantly in the concluding phase of the war.

The MSB was comprised of a medical company (which had a processing capacity of 300 patients per twenty-four-hour period), a sanitation platoon, an evacuation-transportation platoon, and a supply platoon. The total strength of the battalion was 101 personnel. The medical company contained a receiving-sorting platoon, a minor surgery–dressing platoon, a dental section, and an evacuation section. The battalion also contained an anti-epidemic platoon during operations in the Far East.

The reception-sorting platoon conducted the tagging of wounded, designating that these troops be sent either to the minor surgery–dressing platoon or to the evacuation-transportation platoon. Minor surgical procedures were limited to twenty-five or thirty minutes. Some personnel returned to their units after their wounds were re-dressed. The medical-sanitary battalion at full strength (a rare occurrence) or with a portion of its strength (more often) was used to create a corps medical station (*KMP — korpusnoy meditsinskiy punkt*).

There was one unique tendency during the last eighteen months of the war in the development of stages of medical evacuation: the effort to replace lower stages with assets from higher levels of medical service, according to the following plan. At the assembly area, and sometimes at specific objective lines in the course of combat, the mobile field surgical hospital (*KhPPG — khirurgicheskiy polevoy podvizhnyy gospital*) of the first line was deployed in place of the *KMP*. The first echelon of the *front* hospital base (*GBF — gospitalnaya baza fronta*) was deployed in place of the army hospital base (*GBA — gospitalnaya baza armii*), particularly the army's second-echelon treatment facility.

The list of measures that should be undertaken in the effort to render competent medical treatment in the *MSB* (at the *KMP*) included transportation immobilization of fractured extremities (securing and fixing). The primary means of immobilization was splints. Plaster bandages and removable casts were almost never utilized. Surgery was performed on a large percentage of patients at this level. Blood transfusions and fluid replacements were also administered, with priority given to wounded who were admitted in a state of shock. As a rule, patients with illnesses underwent treatment at the *MSB* (*KMP*). Almost 50 percent of soldiers, sergeants, and officers who passed through here were returned to duty.

The number of treatment facilities in the tank army was significantly less than in a combined-arms army. Thus in 1945 the tank army had three *KhPPGs*, a mobile field therapeutic hospital

(*TPPG*—*terapevticheskiy polevoy podvizhnyy gospital*), a hospital
for lightly wounded personnel (*GLR*—*gospital legkoranenykh*),
a mobile field infections hospital (*IPPG*—*infektsionnyy polevoy
podvizhnyy gospital*), and an evacuation reception point—seven
facilities with 2,300 beds altogether. Each hospital was set up to
receive two to three hundred wounded, but in actuality it could
handle twice that number.

The army had medical truck platoons and companies (with
twenty-four and forty-eight ambulances, respectively) for the
evacuation and transportation of patients. Frequently the *front*
reinforced the tank formation's medical services with two or
three light medical aircraft.

At army level were a chief of medical service, a surgeon, a
therapist, and an epidemiologist to supervise the tank army's
medical service component. As indicated in figure 2, the basic
equipment and personnel of army treatment facilities constituted
the first echelon of the *GBA*. As a rule, one *KhPPG* of the first line
was positioned parallel with the *KMP* and received a portion of the
wounded directly from the *BrMP*. This hospital also had the mission of ensuring the maneuverability of the *KMP*, freeing the latter
from the receipt of nontransportable wounded and redirecting to
itself the flow of such patients. In a number of cases the *KhPPG* did
not reinforce the *KMP* but replaced it in full. This permitted the
MSB to move quickly behind the corps' advancing units and render
competent medical treatment at the newly captured positions.
The second echelon of the *GBA* was formed from treatment facilities of the army (one *KhPPG*), and the remaining forces were the
front hospitals (figure 2).

Quite frequently the tank army in assembly areas deployed
only half of its hospitals, with the remaining half comprising
the reserve of the chief of medical services. The procedure for
employment of the latter depended on the developing operational
situation in each specific case. In some situations all hospitals
(both reserve and those relocated from initial positions) began to
work in the new area. In other situations, only a reduced number
of hospitals were deployed; they could then be supplemented by
reserve facilities, depending on the influx of casualties.

The *GBA* included a specialized *KhPPG* for patients with wounds
to the head, neck, or spinal column; therapeutic (*TPPG*) and in-

fection (*IPPG*) hospitals; and a GLR. The specialized treatment in the *KhPPG* was provided by groups from the separate medical reinforcement company (*ORMU—otdelnaya rota meditsinskogo usileniya*). This unit normally consisted of fourteen to sixteen reinforcement groups with various specialties (two to four in general surgery, and two each of neurosurgery, dental-facial surgery, ophthalmology, otolaryngology (ears, nose, and throat), toxicology, and radiology). Specialists were assigned to the TPPG's, the *IPPG*'s, and the GLRs.

Before the Jassy-Kishinev operation (August 1944), 6th Tank Army—the *front*'s mobile group—deployed only two hospitals in the initial position. The *front* took upon itself the mission of medical support to this army that was being committed into the breakthrough sector. This permitted the preservation of hospital assets for actions of the units and formations in the operational depth of the enemy's defenses.

Characteristic features of medical support of a mobile group that reached operational depth included: frequent and sometimes abrupt changes of the overall, medical, and logistic situation; high maneuverability of forces; significant separation from the *front*'s main body (from 30 to 60, and at times up to 100 kilometers); open flanks; and overextended ground communications. All of these factors exerted a significant influence on the medical support of the tank army in the August 1944 battles on Romanian territory.

Medical units (primarily army) were brought as close as possible to the first echelon of forces and deployed, where necessary, with other logistic assets under the protection of the second echelon (reserves) and, in some cases, under the protection of specially assigned security units. Medical facilities, along with their sick and wounded patients, were displaced frequently. In connection with the fact that tank units and formations were operating in the enemy's deep rear, it became necessary to protect the stages of evacuation, particularly the medical transportation system.

Supplementary medical supplies were stockpiled in each vehicle, crew, and unit before the beginning of the operation. We also captured and used a large quantity of medical supplies from the enemy. We used German and Romanian bandaging materials and medications in all treatment facilities for some time after the conclusion of the Jassy-Kishinev operation. Special commissions were created to inventory, account for, and reissue these captured medical supplies.

A complex—one might even say the most complex—sphere of medical services for the troops was the timely evacuation of wounded soldiers from the battlefield and their delivery to medical stations or hospitals. Collection and evacuation were two mutually related subsystems of the treatment-evacuation support of the force. The entire medical-support system depended on swift and competent treatment and evacuation of the wounded.

Assigned and attached company medics together with battalion and brigade senior medics played a principal role in the collection and evacuation of wounded from the battlefield. On a number of *fronts*, this category of medical personnel carried 51 percent of all wounded from the battlefield in the last period of the war. The remainder of the injured walked off the battlefield or were evacuated by their comrades.

The work of medics at company and battalion level was accompanied by enormous risk to their own lives. Losses among combat medics were the highest of all medical personnel. Having attached great significance to this lower stage of the evacuation of wounded, the People's Commissar of Defense of the USSR, J. V. Stalin, signed Order No. 281, "Concerning the procedure for recommending combat medics and stretcher bearers for government awards," on 23 August 1941:

The following recommendations are implemented to encourage the combat efforts of medics and stretcher bearers:

1. Recommend the awarding of the medal "For Combat Service" or "For Courage" for each medic or stretcher bearer who carries fifteen wounded with their rifles or light machine guns from the battlefield;

2. Recommend the awarding of the Order of the Red Star for each medic or stretcher bearer who carries twenty-five wounded with their rifles or light machine guns from the battlefield;

3. Recommend the awarding of the Order of the Red Banner for each medic or stretcher bearer who carries forty wounded with their rifles or light machine guns from the battlefield;

4. Recommend the Order of Lenin for each medic or stretcher bearer who carries eighty wounded with their rifles or light machine guns from the battlefield.

The evacuation of wounded and sick was organized on the principle of "evacuation to one's own facility"—this was written into the regulations and instructions that guided the work of medical services. Each medical facility chief, beginning at the battalion medical station and ending at the *front* hospital, was required to collect the wounded from the previous stage and bring them to his or her own place of treatment. However, this principle was not strictly observed beyond the medical-sanitary battalion level—that is, beyond the corps level. At subsequent levels, things worked a bit differently in actual practice: the chiefs of medical treatment facilities generally transported wounded and sick both "to themselves" and "from themselves."

Evacuation was conducted in accordance with the patient's medical condition. Wounded and sick requiring treatment of not more than ten days' duration were left in the recovery unit at the corps medical-sanitary battalion. Recuperation for up to thirty days was allowed in army hospitals and for up to two months in *front* hospitals. Wounded and sick who required prolonged treatment were sent to the deep rear. The exception to this rule was infectious diseases: these patients remained in the infection hospitals until their treatment was completed.

In January 1944 General Andrey Kravchenko, the commander of 6th Tank Army, ordered our medical personnel to treat in an army hospital—and not to send to the rear—all wounded army personnel whose rehabilitation would be complete within three months. The general did this in an attempt to keep the maximum number of troops in the permanent composition of subordinate formations. We wounded were extremely happy with the new regulation because it meant that now tankers and other specialists would be returned to their own units and to their old comrades.

An important goal at all stages of evacuation was to reduce the time involved in transporting the wounded and sick to medical stations and rendering them first aid. At regimental (brigade) levels of management the goal was three to four hours after a patient had been wounded. The majority of injured reached the

KMP or *KhPPG* of the first line in the first six to eight hours after being wounded.[2] The medical service gave special attention to the most rapid transport of the most seriously wounded soldiers.

Troops who had been so seriously wounded that they could not withstand delivery to hospitals by wheeled transportation were generally not evacuated because there were so few light medical aircraft available (only two or three in the army). These troops therefore had to remain at the first-line *KMP* or *KhPPG*. The medical-station or hospital personnel then moved these wounded with them upon displacement behind the advancing forces. Thankfully, these displacements were for short distances.

It was a more frequent practice to leave these seriously wounded troops behind with a group of medical personnel assigned to treat them. Here is one example, from the January battles in right-bank Ukraine. Our 5th Mechanized Corps was participating in the operation for the encirclement of the enemy's Korsun-Shevchenkovskiy grouping. The muddy and torn-up dirt roads prevented the delivery of fifteen seriously wounded soldiers to the army *GLR*. The decision was made to leave them for a time in the village of Tynovka, from which the enemy had recently been driven. One *feldsher* and two nurses from the *KMP* were treating the wounded tankers. A squad of *avtomatchiki* and a trophy Tiger tank with three crewmen were assigned to guard this makeshift medical station. Twenty-four hours later, the wounded were transferred to the first-line *KhPPG*.

A description of the successive stages of medical treatment begins with the crew. The battalion *feldsher* organized the transporting, by foot or vehicle, of injured personnel from the battlefield to the battalion medical station (*BMP*) or to a collection point. The *feldsher* and the senior medics rendered the first treatment.

During the capture of the town of Zvenigorodka (January 1944), the tank of battalion commander Nikolay Maslyukov was hit. The battalion commander was killed, and two men were wounded, one seriously. The uninjured members of the crew extracted the wounded soldiers from the Sherman and bandaged them on the spot. The battalion *feldsher*, Lieutenant Mikhail Parshikov, applied a tourniquet and stopped the bleeding of the seriously wounded tanker.

A group from the brigade medical-sanitary platoon was traveling behind the lead tanks on two American armored half-tracks.

Feldsher Senior Lieutenant Polina Khodoleeva, who was in charge of this group, was an exceptionally brave woman who knew her business well. The tankers and three *avtomatchiki* were under her care in twenty minutes. She and three senior medics carefully worked the wounds and treated for tetanus. They also filled out the yellow frontline medical treatment tag—the primary medical document that stated the last name, then the first name, and then patronymic of the wounded; the year of the patient's birth; his or her rank, position, and field post number; the nature of the wound; and a description of the initial treatment given. These five wounded soldiers and the dead Captain Maslyukov were then transported on the second armored transporter to the *BrMP*.

One American armored half-track of the medical-sanitary platoon and two Studebaker trucks were used for carrying wounded from the battlefield during the period when Soviet forces were battling the enemy's attempts to unblock its surrounded Korsun-Shevchenkovskiy grouping. On 30 January 1944 I was sent to the corps supply point to receive ammunition for tanks and at the same time to lead an armored transporter and a truck carrying twenty wounded to the medical-sanitary battalion.

I should emphasize that problems with evacuation of injured to higher-level treatment facilities did not exist in tank and mechanized forces. If the situation required it, even combat vehicles (tanks or armored personnel carriers) were designated for this purpose.

The command of our 233d Brigade, and other units of 5th Mechanized Corps, gave special attention to providing the medical personnel at the regiment (brigade) level with highly mobile means of transportation. After the defeat of enemy troops in the Korsun-Shevchenkovskiy area, an enormous quantity of trucks, half-tracks, staff buses, and so on were captured. The brigade's medical-sanitary platoon was reinforced with two captured German transporters.

In the course of the Jassy-Kishinev operation (August 1944), the situation required that several adjustments in the system of phased treatment and evacuation be made in a short time. On 25 August, taking advantage of the fact that the combat formations of our 52d Army were insufficiently dense, a large group of forces of the German VI Army with tanks and artillery broke out to the southwest, intending to fight its way across the Carpathian

Mountains into Hungary. As a result, our 6th Tank Army's lines of communication were disrupted for several days. Some of our logistic and hospital facilities were destroyed and the remainder were unable to move behind our advancing formations and units.

In connection with this complex situation on the rear-area roads, the tank army had to stop evacuating wounded and sick to higher-level treatment facilities. Our brigade and corps medical units, along with groups from army hospitals who were following immediately behind first echelon forces, had to organize a form of first-line GBA. It was concentrated on the western outskirts of the town of Focsany. Special infantry units, reinforced with captured tanks and guns, secured the approaches to the area where these treatment facilities were set up. Crews for the combat vehicles and weapons were taken from our own personnel. When the army rear came forward, the entire contingent of wounded and sick was transferred to hospitals.

Wherever possible, an effort was made to reduce the number of stages in the evacuation process of every individual patient so that he could arrive more quickly at the appropriate treatment facility. This was done in my case, and I am thankful for it. On 19 April 1945, on the approaches to the town of Mistelbach in Austria, my Sherman was hit.

A Tiger tank fired at us from close range from behind a railroad embankment. The round struck the left front of the Sherman and passed completely through the tank's hull on a diagonal. Surprisingly, our tank did not burn. However, my driver-mechanic, Guards Sergeant Gennadiy Kapronov, and my radio operator, Guards Sergeant Nikolay Shevtsov, were killed instantly. My gun commander, Guards Senior Sergeant Anatoliy Romashkin, lost both legs. Guards Senior Lieutenant Aleksandr Ionov, Guards Lieutenant Ivan Filin (my tank commander), and I were all seriously wounded. At this time my battalion had seven tanks remaining. Ionov was on my tank because he had only one tank left in his company.

Because I had been sitting in the commander's seat, my head and much of my chest were in the small cupola. Shrapnel had shattered my left knee, but at the time I felt nothing. My first action was to help Ionov get out of the tank. Then I hurried to Romashkin, pulled him from the turret, and placed him on the ground to the right of the Sherman. Only when I went back to the tank to help the others did I see my own wound. I fell on the grill doors of the engine cover but remained conscious. At that moment I heard a pistol shot. I turned my head and saw that Romashkin had shot himself. Not long before the Vienna operation, after supper one evening, he had said, "If I lose a leg, I will shoot myself!" He had in fact lost both legs in this engagement. Having grown up in an orphanage, he knew what kind of fate awaited him as an invalid. He did not want to be a burden to anyone.

Three brigade scouts—who had been following immediately behind us on an armored transporter—ran over to the tank and carried all three of us officers to cover. The battalion *feldsher*, Pavel Denisyuk, was already on the scene. He was a civilian and had no rank. He applied tourniquets and bandaged us. Guards Senior Lieutenant Polina Khudoleeva arrived on her half-track. She gave us tetanus injections, loaded us on her vehicle, and carried us to the rear, past brigade headquarters.

The chief of the brigade staff, Guards Lieutenant Colonel Pavel Kornyushin, gave instructions to send Ionov, Filin, and me to the army hospital. Khudoleeva filled out our frontline medical tags. Summoned by someone, my light vehicle with driver and orderly had arrived, and we were loaded into this vehicle and rushed to army GLR No. 2632, in the Czechoslovakian village of Klobouka, eighteen kilometers southeast of Brno. I should note that during the war, frontline roads were well equipped with signposts that indicated the location of important logistic facilities. In this case the chief of GLR No. 2632 was Guards Lieutenant Colonel Nikolay Chistyakov. We followed signs with his name on them.

Upon my initial examination at the hospital, I was informed that amputation of my leg was unavoidable: my knee joint had suffered too much damage. To my good fortune the chief surgeon of Second Ukrainian *Front*, Colonel Nikolay Nikolaevich Elanskiy, was in the hospital at that time. He said there would be plenty of time later to remove the leg of a young man (I was just days short of my twenty-third birthday). This skilled specialist operated on me and reassembled my knee joint from its several broken parts. They then "dressed" me in a plaster cast, leaving only my right leg and my arms free. My orderly, Guards Sergeant Grigoriy Zhumatiy, and my driver, Guards Sergeant Yakov Zuyev, carried their immobilized battalion commander around for six weeks—to the yard for air, to the hospital clinic for bandaging, and to the doctor for checkups. My room was in the library of a Czechoslovakian dentist.

Fifteen years after my knee surgery, I was fortunate enough to meet Dr. Elanskiy again. I warmly thanked him for saving my left leg.

"Excuse me, but I do not remember you," said Nikolay Niko-laevich, now a professor at First Moscow Medical Institute.

"That's all right," I responded. "I will remember you for the rest of my life!"

Our 6th Guards Tank Army actively participated in the defeat of imperialist Japan as part of the Transbaykal *Front*. All military activities in this theater were unusual because the circumstances were unusual: the dramatically differing climatic and topographic conditions (desert, steppe, the Gobi Desert, southern reaches of the Grand Khingan range, the Manchurian plain), as well as the enormous expanse of the operation itself. From an epidemiological perspective, practically the entire depth of the operation was in unfavorable regions. Even the daily temperatures fluctuated widely.

Our medical personnel, with their wealth of European combat and treatment experience, found ways to deal with the most complex situations they encountered here in Asia. The system of medical-evacuation support that had been developed in the west now underwent significant transformation, especially in the Transbaykal *Front*. The impact of the operational axis was felt in the medical sphere with full force.

The hospital bases of the armies of the Transbaykal *Front* were located as close as possible to the troops. Of a total of 120 hospitals, the *front* had only 7 khppgs and a single ippg. The total bed capacity for the *front* was 65,900. When combat operations commenced, the remaining facilities were still en route from the west or in the process of forming. The medical establishment was at about 90 percent strength.[3] The *front*'s GBF was deployed in two echelons.

In conditions of overextended lines of communication and almost complete lack of roads, the use of wheeled transportation for evacuation of sick and wounded was extremely limited and, in some phases of the operation, totally impossible. Foreseeing this situation, the commander in chief of forces in the Far East issued an order on the eve of the offensive (8 August 1945) authorizing the utilization of return trips of transport aircraft for medical evacuation.

Formations and units of 6th Guards Tank Army, operating in exceptionally difficult natural conditions (the terrain was the principal enemy), suffered minimal losses in personnel and in combat and transportation equipment. Medical losses reached only 16 percent and illnesses only 29.1 percent of the anticipated levels for the *front*'s forces for the entire operation.[4] We had not employed such a closely packed formation of combat, logistical, and medical units in a single operation against German forces.

It was 10 August in the Gobi Desert. Our vehicles were getting stuck in the sand, and we were helping each other to recover them. We moved forward in the hot temperatures. Corps medical units and a forward group of army GLR No. 2632 were in the march column of 46th Guards Brigade. Everyone kept up with the tankers. They knew we would be either reliable protection in the event of an engagement with the enemy or faithful helpers at a time of difficult movement.

Sanitary-epidemiological reconnaissance was organized and conducted continuously for the entire depth of the operation. Mobile sanitary-epidemiological detachments with special anti-plague sections from the army followed immediately behind the first echelon of 9th Mechanized and 5th Tank Guards Corps for this purpose. This was in addition to the epidemiological platoon that existed in the medical-sanitary battalion of each corps. Personnel and equipment of the laundry-disinfecting company were attached to these detachments. In addition, *front* provided mobile laboratory resources to these army detachments to help them should they encounter any particularly contagious diseases. Fortunately this laboratory unit was never required to deploy its assets. After the discovery that withdrawing Japanese forces had poisoned many wells, special attention was given to the monitoring and sanitary protection of this water source.

We "westerners" had our first encounter with an unusual phenomenon in the Gobi Desert: several *tankodesantniki* suffered heatstrokes as the powerful fans under the Shermans' radiators forced through the engine grills the hot winds of an ambient temperature that reached 40° C [104° F]. The *avtomatchiki* sitting on the outside of the tank were also in a tight spot. The sun was burning them from above, and streams of heated air were burning them from below.

I stopped my column for five minutes so that medical personnel could reach the tank where the ill soldiers were. Our battalion *feldsher*, Pavel Denisyuk, and his senior medics brought the sick soldiers back to life while the rest of the column was moving again. Each Sherman was equipped with two twenty-liter widemouth canisters, which had been filled with water. The medics dipped their caps into one of these canisters and put them on the heads of the soldiers who had lost consciousness. Then, after the medics had also given them water to drink, the men came around. On Denisyuk's recommendation, I ordered the company commander of the *desantniki*, Guards Senior Lieutenant Mikhail Kucherov, periodically to wet down his subordinate's headgear and place it under their helmets. We had no further problems with heatstroke.

The most difficult days of the offensive were 11–12 August, when we climbed the southern reaches of the Grand Khingan Range. Our 9th Guards Mechanized Corps was moving through the valleys of the Suti Gol and Talareli Gol Rivers, where the narrow mountain roads pass between steep mountain walls. The weather abruptly changed, and rain fell in torrents. The exhaust fumes from our diesel engines hung low to the ground, making our breathing difficult. In these conditions, movement would be in one direction only: there could be no thought of evacuating the sick and wounded to the rear, if that should become necessary. We would have to carry them with us. But fate was merciful, and no one became sick or was injured. In all probability the war and its physical stress had an enormous psychological effect on the men, focusing their consciousness on the constant external danger—none of the troops had time or energy for difficulties in their internal organs.

The picture of the system of phased treatment and evacuation in formations of the Transbaykal *Front* was unrecognizable by the third day of the operation. The GBF was still in its start position. Corps medical stations were frequently positioned eighty to ninety kilometers from the front line. Army hospitals remained in the foothills of the Khingan Range. The cause of this confusion was a fuel shortage and the impassable roads through the mountains. With our arrival on the central Manchurian plain, medical support to our force was totally in the hands of the corps' brigade assets and forward groups of the army GLR. This situation did not cause any problem to the troops, however. In the area beyond the Khingan Range, the primary load fell on the sanitary-epidemiological units, who had to investigate the areas and sources of water and the captured Japanese food stocks.

With the arrival of the tank army's formations in the Lubeya area, our tanks ran out of fuel. A hasty airfield was set up south of this town, to which military transport aircraft delivered diesel fuel. A medical evacuation point was also quickly established at the airfield. Medical groups that were accompanying the units in our formation delivered their wounded and sick here. The aviators carried these patients to the *front* hospitals on their return trips.

In the course of the subsequent offensive to the southeast, toward Mukden, Darien, and Port Arthur, all TOE medical units, and also larger medical groups from army hospitals, remained in the march columns of units of 5th Tank and 9th Mechanized Guards Corps, as before. These establishments, when needed, would deploy a portion of their personnel and equipment, receive wounded, and offer them treatment. The remainder of the units would continue to follow the force.

In this period of the rapid offensive of the formations of Transbaykal *Front* deep into enemy territory, only a few army hospitals and *front* hospital groups were deployed in Haylar and Vanemyo. By the end of the operation two field hospitals had been brought in to Mukden and Darien on transport aircraft.

The war with Japan was a direct continuation, and thus a component part, of the Great Patriotic War. The Soviet Army's Manchurian operation was one of the largest of that war: it has entered the annals of military art for its enormous scale, rapidity, and decisiveness, despite unbelievable difficulties related to terrain and weather—circumstances felt particularly in medical units at all levels. The fact is, however, that due to the low number of sick and wounded, the medical service at army and *front* level were never required to deploy during the period of combat actions in the war with Japan.

Combat Decorations

Every decoration of a frontline soldier represents a battle, sleepless days and nights, serious wounds or light ones. These decorations are reminders of those long-ago fiery years, of our youth that was tempered by war. The 3 July 1979 Edict of the Presidium of the Supreme Soviet of the USSR was a deeply symbolic act. By this decree the orders and medals of deceased recipients are to remain with or be transferred to their families for preservation. Prior to this date these decorations were returned to military commissions or to local authorities for subsequent transfer to the Presidium of the Supreme Soviet of the USSR.

Before the Great Patriotic War all awarding of decorations was carried out only by the Presidium. Beginning in November 1942 military commanders were granted the authority to award decorations in the name of the Presidium to soldiers and commanders who distinguished themselves at the front in combat against the Germans, with subsequent confirmation of the award by the Presidium. Commanders from the regiment (brigade) to the division level were authorized to approve the medals "For Combat Service" and "For Courage," the Order of the Red Star, and the Order of Glory 3d Degree for awarding to military personnel through the duty position of company commander.

Corps commanders were authorized to approve the awarding of the Order of the Patriotic War 1st and 2d Degree, the Order of the Red Star, and the Order of Glory 3d Degree to military personnel through the duty position of company commander. Army commanders were authorized to award the Order of the Red Banner, the Order of Aleksandr Nevskiy, the Order of the Patriotic War 1st and 2d Degree, the Order of the Red Star, and the Order of Glory 2d and 3d Degree to military personnel through the duty position of regiment (brigade) commander.

Front commanders were authorized to award the Order of the Red Banner, the Order of Suvorov 3d Degree, the Order of Kutuzov 3d Degree, the Order of Bogdan Khmelnitskiy 3d Degree, the Order of Aleksandr Nevskiy, the Order of Ushakov 2d Degree, the Order of Nakhimov 2d Degree, the Order of the Patriotic War 1st and 2d Degree, the Order of the Red Star, and the Order of Glory 2d and 3d Degree to military personnel up through the duty position of division commander.

The procedure for recommending a soldier or commander for a combat decoration in our 6th Guards Tank Army began with the assembling of an award package by the battalion headquarters. Included in it was a brief description of the heroic act or deed (the number of enemy troops the soldier had destroyed, the number of enemy firing positions suppressed, and so on) and the specific decoration being recommended. By statute, certain quantifiable standards applied to each medal or order, both concerning the enemy personnel or equipment destroyed and the rank or position of the recipient. The award recommendation, signed by the battalion commander, was then forwarded to the brigade commander, who endorsed it with a simple statement and added his signature. A unit stamp was then affixed as an official mark of witness.

The award recommendation was next sent to the corps headquarters, where an order was prepared for the corps commander's signature. Generally speaking, the procedure did not require a great deal of time, and everyone tried to expedite the process. War is war. A soldier is here today but may be gone tomorrow. There were more than a few occasions when a soldier who had displayed exemplary courage directly on the battlefield was decorated by his commander on one day and the appropriate documentation was begun to be assembled on the next.

In our tank forces, higher commanders sometimes authorized these immediate decorations by radio. Because of the way our radio communications were set up, all the subordinates learned about such an award immediately. Headquarters assembled the appropriate documentation and signatures for these awards later. This method made a significant contribution to troops' morale, and inspired in them a greater respect for their commanders.

After the corps commander signed the orders for combat decorations, extracts were, as required, made and distributed to subordinate units for their award recipients. A copy of the order for each award was sent forward with all attached award recommendations for preservation in the Archive of the Ministry of Defense in Podolsk. The award recipients received their medals or orders in a ceremony during a lull in battle, at an assembly area or a unit rest location. Wounded personnel received their awards wherever they were undergoing medical treatment.

Of course, each award was "christened." It is common knowledge that each soldier was entitled to a hundred grams of alcohol daily during the war, and the commander dipped into his own supply of these spirits on these special occasions. An unwritten "christening" ritual was practiced: the commander dropped the order or medal into a glass filled with vodka, whereupon the recipient drank the contents of the glass and collected his award. Only after this "christening" did he have the full right to attach the decoration to his tunic.

The packet for my own Hero of the Soviet Union award passed through a lengthy progression of commanders. The initial submission recommending me for the USSR's highest award was drawn up in 46th Guards Tank Brigade on 16 April 1945 (for an action that occurred on 22 March). Guards Lieutenant Colonel Nikolay Mikhno signed his recommendation ("Deserves awarding of the rank Hero of the Soviet Union"), and it was witnessed with the brigade's stamp. The commander of 9th Guards Mechanized Corps, General Mikhail Volkov, wrote the same endorsement, and his signature was witnessed with the corps' stamp.

The recommendation was then forwarded to Headquarters, 6th Guards Tank Army. Here the materials were endorsed in the same manner and signed by two officials: General G. L. Tumanyang, a member of the military council, and General A. G. Kravchenko, commander of the army. Both signatures were witnessed with the army's stamp. The next level was at the *front*, where three officials signed the award recommendation: General V. N. Baskakov, commander of the *front*'s armored forces; General A. N. Tevchenkov, a member of the *front* military council; and Marshal of the Soviet Union R. Ya. Malinovskiy, commander of the Second Ukrainian *Front*. All three signatures were stamped.

From here the packet went straight to Moscow, to the Presidium of the Supreme Soviet of the USSR, where the large-format order was prepared. I received the rank of Hero of the Soviet Union on 15 May 1946.

In our armed forces, as in every other large bureaucracy, mistakes sometimes occurred. During the war we had one particular award for valor—the Order of Glory—that was intended for decorating privates, sergeants, and higher-ranking personnel in the ground forces, as well as officers in the rank of junior lieutenant in the air force. The Order of Glory came in three degrees and was awarded consecutively: one must receive the 3d degree first, then the 2d degree, and finally the 1st degree. Persons who have received this order in all three degrees are known as full holders of the Order of Glory and are entitled to the same privileges as recipients of the Hero of the Soviet Union.

There were several cases of violation of the statute that governed this soldiers' award. Vasiliy Timofeevich Khristenko, for example, received the Order of Glory 3d and 2d Degree. For a subsequent combat feat he was to have received the Order of Glory 1st Degree. Only the Presidium of the Supreme Soviet of the USSR could authorize this decoration. But somewhere along the protracted path, his recommendation for the Order of Glory 1st Degree was downgraded to 2d Degree. It turned out that he eventually received two Orders of Glory 2d Degree, an unforgivable violation of governing statute.

Several years ago a group of war veterans raised the issue of replacing Khristenko's Order of Glory 2d Degree with the appropriate Order of Glory 1st Degree, which was indeed carried out by an edict of the Supreme Soviet of the USSR. The government did not publish an order rescinding his second, erroneous, Order of Glory 2d Degree, however, and thus Vasiliy Timofeevich is now the proud holder of four Orders of Glory.

Graves Registration

A war, be it large or small, has an unavoidable consequence: wounded and dead soldiers on both sides. The wounded
must be quickly evacuated from the battlefield and transported to
a hospital for treatment. The dead are committed to the earth.

The disposal of battlefield dead, both our own and the strangers
on our native soil, is a delicate theme that is infrequently encountered in war literature. This is particularly so with regard to the
dead soldiers and officers of one's enemy in a given war.

I am enormously grateful that I have lived a long, active life,
having now passed into my eighth decade. I have lived through
some difficult times, in everyday life and in war. This both obli-
gates me and gives me the right to speak the honest truth, neither
violating my conscience nor embellishing that which has happened in my lifetime.

I am thinking back. Neither within the walls of Saratov Tank
School nor in the course of my subsequent military service has
the issue ever been raised concerning the funeral rites or details
for the interment of those who have fallen on the field of battle.
The brief clause "Specially designated teams bury the dead"
appears in the field regulations. How? Where? Not a word of guidance. By the Christian tradition, the dead are committed to the
earth on the third day after death. But where is one to set aside a
day for burying the dead when, as the poet wrote, "a sacred and
just battle is being waged, a deadly battle not for the sake of glory,
but for the sake of life on earth."

The duration of this sad ritual and the nature of its form depended on the time available to the living—the comrades who
were still fighting. Sometimes we buried our fallen friends hurriedly and moved on, into the snow, the dust, and the exhaust
fumes. There were other occasions when we had more time.

Speaking about our own troops who perished in fierce engagements with the enemy, I use the words "we buried," "we
committed them to the earth," "we interred," and "we laid them

to rest in the earth," as if in a mausoleum. There is only one expression for the enemy dead: "we buried them."

Throughout the entire war we tankers buried our soldiers ourselves. We did not turn this duty over to any "burial details." If this tragedy occurred during a moving battle, battalion or brigade support units placed the fallen in the earth. But generally speaking we attempted, even if hurriedly, to place our crew, platoon, and company members in the ground with our own hands.

As a rule, we buried our dead close to the site at which they fell. If there was a settlement nearby, we used the village cemetery or the town square. In foreign countries we used Roman Catholic church grounds. If the circumstances forced us to use an open field, we selected a hill or the edge of a forest or grove of trees. Our goal was to be able to associate the grave site with a topographic feature. Our battalion staff drew up a sketch of the burial site that indicated where and at what distance from a recognizable terrain feature the grave was located. These documents are preserved to this day in the Central Archive of the Ministry of Defense of the Russian Federation in Podolsk.

There were occasions when another method was used. Both our armor and our infantry forces suffered significant losses during the battles fought to break the encirclement of the Germans' Korsun-Shevchenkovskiy grouping (February 1944). In this situation we buried the Soviet dead in mass graves. The grave site would be on a hill, near a road. The unit assigned the responsibility for burial also drew up a sketch map that indicated the location of the site, the identity (rank, last name, first name, patronymic) of each casualty, and each casualty's location by row and number (from the left or right) in the row.

There were several of these mass graves along the Simferopol Highway around Kursk and Prokhorovka. When drivers passed by, they "saluted" them with long blasts of their vehicle horns. It is a long-standing tradition.[1]

There were cases when the seriously wounded, dying soldier himself selected the location of his own grave. We attempted to fulfill his final request. I personally know of one such case, which occurred in May 1945. Tank armies were rushing toward Prague, the capital of Czechoslovakia, from the north and south. The Prague offensive operation was beginning. The forward detachment from one of the units, either 3d or 4th Guards Tank Army, had burst into the center of the city. Assisted by the citizens of Prague, the tankers drove the enemy back, block by block, in fierce fighting.

A *tankodesantnik* [infantry soldier who rode into battle on a tank] named Belyakov was seriously wounded in the stomach. They carried him to a small field hospital that had been set up in a monastery. The Czechoslovakian doctors did all they could to save the life of this Soviet soldier, but he was doomed. Experiencing enormous pain, he groaned continuously. The monastery had a set of bells in a small tower, and when these bells rang out at the appointed times, the soldier was quieted. Every time the bells tolled, his face would light up. One day, when he was clearly failing and his death was approaching, he appealed to the Czech doctors, "When I die, bury me close to here so that I can always hear this beautiful ringing." These were his last words. He died that night. Carrying out his request the citizens of Prague buried him in a modest plot near the monastery wall and placed a simple marker on his grave.

How did we send our comrades on their last journey? They were usually in the same clothing in which they breathed their last breath. If there were time, we dressed the body in clean underwear and uniform. We would wrap deceased tankers in pieces of tank tarpaulin, and infantry soldiers, as a rule, in their own greatcoats. We lined the bottom of the grave with pine boughs or straw or whatever was available. We carefully lowered the body into the excavated grave, being attentive always to inter from west to east [head west, feet east]. We did not use caskets. Accompanied by a volley of rifle fire or main-gun salvos, we threw the dirt in on top of our comrade and then installed a simple pyramid with a star. Right there, at the fresh grave, we drank our daily ration of a hundred grams of vodka, in memory of the fallen. And then we returned to battle.

On only two occasions—in January 1944 and almost exactly a year later—did we bury our comrades in caskets: they were our battalion commanders, Captain Nikolay Maslyukov and Guards Captain Ivan Yakushkin. And I do not remember a single case when we sent a body back to the Motherland for burial. No one ever raised an issue about this: they knew we simply had no time. The primary mission of the living was to defeat the enemy, to bring the hour of victory closer. Hero of the Soviet Union Guards

Captain Ivan Yakushkin, commander of 1st Battalion of 46th Guards Tank Brigade, was wounded in battle and died in January 1945. He was buried in the town of Sahy, Czechoslovakia. In June 1945, when the government of Czechoslovakia decided to gather up and re-inter in cemeteries all Soviet soldiers buried in Czechoslovakia, his body was moved to a military cemetery at Zvolen.

Concerning enemy soldiers and officers who met their fate on our land, they rushed onto Soviet soil with sword in hand. And they died by the sword.

Without exception, the people of our great country lived hard lives in the 1930s. It was a time of belt-tightening as everyone in the country worked hard to fulfill Stalin's five-year plans for industrialization. We suffered through a terrible famine in the Ukraine that devastated many villages. Repression followed repression in the later years of the decade. Military conflicts of the prewar years brought death notifications to our villages and men returning as invalids. We did not need any foreign demagogues slandering the Soviet people or igniting new hostilities. This was the opinion of the simple prewar worker, far removed from the policy of the government.

But war did come to us on 22 June 1941, bringing with it blood and tears, concentration camps, the destruction of our cities and villages, and thousands upon tens and hundreds of thousands of deaths. The enemy occupied many western parts of the Soviet Union for a prolonged time and brutally repressed the citizens of these regions. The German army, its soldiers, officers, and generals, brought all of this to us. If it would have been possible to collect all the tears of my fellow Ukrainians that flowed during the four years of the war and to pour them out on Germany, that country would have been at the bottom of a deep sea.

The Soviet people rose up as one in defense of their Motherland. The song "Sacred War" became our hymn, the oath of our national community. The people put up a wall against suppressers, aggressors, thieves, torturers, debauchers, and fascist scum, the dregs of humanity. They threw all their antipathy into the face of this detested, hated enemy! The oath "Beat the Germans!" became a slogan, the burning desire of everyone who took a weapon in his or her hands. For many Germans who had marched triumphantly across Europe, our soil turned out to be the last that their hob-nailed boots would ever trod. Here they found their end.

While the German forces were advancing to the east, they buried their dead in cemeteries in Belorussia, around Smolensk, on the approaches to Moscow, in the Ukraine, and at Stavropol. These and other cemeteries appear in many photographs, with countless birch crosses. When the Soviet Army drove them back to the west, we had quickly to cleanse the liberated cities, villages, *rayons*, and oblasts of the hundreds and thousands of enemy corpses. The tankers, infantrymen, and artillerymen of the first combat echelon of the advancing forces were never engaged in this process, however. Their primary mission was to destroy the enemy, and the more the better! Do not give the Germans the opportunity to leave the Soviet soil that they themselves desecrated, drenched with blood, and plowed up with the tracks of their Tigers, Panthers, and Ferdinands!

The unpleasant but necessary duty of burying the enemy was left to teams assigned to such duty. There were none of these temporary units in tank formations, however; as a rule they were created at the *front* level. The local population was frequently conscripted to reinforce these teams in areas where fierce battles had been fought (for example, at Korsun-Shevchenkovskiy in the Ukraine). If fallen Soviet soldiers were interred in the squares and cemeteries of villages, and on hills near forests and roads, then the enemy corpses were buried in worthless land that was unsuitable for any subsequent use. No documents were ever created for these sites. Perhaps something was done along this line later—I do not know. In all the times I have worked in the archive in Podolsk, I have never encountered such documents.

There are those who would say now that we Russians acted barbarically with regard the burying the Germans. I would not want to level this accusation at the soldiers on the burial teams or at the peasants whose fathers and mothers the Germans shot and whose sisters they took into a foreign land and never returned. At that time a dead enemy was still an enemy, and he was given the appropriate regard.

The soil of many countries that the Germans occupied received the bodies of their dead soldiers and officers, but there are no marked graves in these places. Such total anonymity is the inescapable fate of anyone who invades another's territory.

In the course of the counteroffensive around Moscow, the town of Yukhnov (320 kilometers southwest of the capital) was liberated from German occupation on 5 March 1942. The battles in this area had been exceptionally fierce. Both sides suffered significant losses. The Germans buried many of their soldiers and officers from the period of the offensive on Moscow in several cemeteries in this area, apparently confident that they had captured this Russian land for all time. To these German cemeteries were added the sites where our own teams buried enemy bodies during and after our counteroffensive.

In 1997 the local government decided to commemorate the fifty-fifth anniversary of the liberation of the town from German occupation. Announcements were sent out in anticipation of the event. The townspeople, in preparation for the celebration, invited veterans who had participated in the liberation of Yukhnov. Immediately after the news of the event was announced, three German fast-buck artists showed up with a proposition. They appealed to the local government to allot them a modest parcel of land. It was their intention to establish a cemetery and bring their fallen countrymen to this plot for reinterment. The *rayon* leadership regarded these guests' request with some understanding but laid down one condition: they would have to purchase the land for an amount of money equal to the damage the German troops inflicted here. These funds would be used to construct housing and administrative buildings in Yukhnov and other places in the *rayon*. The applicants departed and never returned.

The third postwar generation of Russians has not forgotten about the war. They recall what kind of materiel and human losses were suffered during those terrible years. I think that ten and even a hundred generations of true patriots will not forget this war. There is a Russian saying: "If you sow the wind, you will reap a storm." The Germans brought incalculable suffering into our land, and themselves experienced grief in ten-fold measure. "Terrible crimes," as Aleksandr Herzen said in the nineteenth century, "entail terrible consequences."[2]

Appendix A

Order of the Presidium of the Supreme
Soviet of the USSR

Concerning the Text of the Military Oath of
the Workers-Peasants' Red Army

In accordance with the Constitution of the Union of Soviet Socialist Republics, the following text is approved for the military oath of the Workers-Peasants' Red Army.

I, a citizen of the Union of Soviet Socialist Republics, entering into the ranks of the Workers-Peasants' Red Army, take this oath and solemnly promise to be an honest, brave, disciplined, vigilant fighter, staunchly to protect military and state secrets, and unquestioningly to obey all military regulations and orders of commanders and superiors.

I promise conscientiously to study military affairs, in every way to protect military and state property, and to my last breath to be faithful to the people, the Soviet Motherland, and the Workers-Peasants' Government.

I am always prepared on order of the Workers-Peasants' Government to rise to the defense of my Motherland, the Union of Soviet Socialist Republics; and as a fighting man of the Workers-Peasants' Red Army, I promise to defend it bravely, skillfully, with dignity and honor, sparing neither my blood nor my life itself for the achievement of total victory over our enemies.

If by evil intent I should violate this my solemn oath, then let the severe punishment of Soviet law and the total hatred and contempt of the working classes befall me.

Chairman of the Presidium of the Supreme Soviet
of the USSR
M. Kalinin

215

Secretary of the Presidium of the Supreme Soviet
of the USSR
A. Gorkin

Moscow, the Kremlin
3 January 1939

**Order of the Presidium of the Supreme
Soviet of the USSR**

Concerning the Procedure for
Administering the Military Oath

The following statute is approved concerning the procedure for
administering the military oath:

1. Upon entering into the ranks of the Workers-Peasants' Red
   Army, Workers-Peasants' Navy, or border troops, each serviceman takes the military oath.
2. Each serviceman takes the military oath individually and
   authenticates it with his personal signature.
3. The following personnel take the military oath:
   (a) young Red Army and Red Navy personnel upon completion
   of individual training and mastery of the regulation regarding
   internal service and the regulation regarding military discipline and significance of the military oath, but not later than
   two months from their arrival in a troop unit;
   (b) officer trainees in military training schools and attendees
   at military academies who have not already taken the military
   oath, by the same time criteria.
4. Young Red Army soldiers and Red Navy sailors, as well as officer trainees and attendees at academies, take the oath under
   the guidance of the commander and military commissar of
   the regiment (brigade) and the chief and the commissar of the
   directorate, department, or institution.
5. The time for taking the oath is published in an order by the
   given unit. All explanatory work associated with taking the
   oath, and concerning the significance of ARTICLES 132 and 133
   of the Constitution of the Union of Soviet Socialist Republics,
   is conducted in units prior to the administration of the oath.
6. At the designated time the regiment (brigade) is assembled in
   guard uniform with unit colors and band. Those taking the

oath are positioned in the front ranks. In a brief presentation, the unit commander explains to the Red Army soldiers the significance of the military oath and the honor and responsibility of the obligation that rests upon those personnel who have sworn their loyalty to the People and Government of the Union of Soviet Socialist Republics and as well the significance of ARTICLES 132 and 133 of the Constitution of the USSR.

After this explanatory speech, the regiment (brigade) commander commands the regiment (brigade) "Stand at ease!" and gives instruction to the unit commanders to begin administering the military oath to their young soldiers.

Company (battery) commanders assemble all those taking the oath in the specified location. Each serviceman in turn reads the military oath aloud, after which he affixes his personal signature to the special list on a line opposite his last name.

Company (battery) commanders hand all lists with personal signatures of those who took the military oath to the regiment (brigade) commander.

The regiment (brigade) is reformed during the retiring of the colors. The commander and the regiment (brigade) commissar congratulate the young soldiers for their taking of the military oath and congratulate the entire regiment (brigade) on accepting these full-fledged soldiers into their ranks. The regiment (brigade) passes in review.

All servicemen who for some reason did not take the military oath on this day take it individually on the following day at the regiment (brigade) headquarters under the guidance of the regiment (brigade) commander and the commissar.

The lists of those who took the oath are stored at the regimental (brigade) headquarters in a special pouch that is numbered, tied with a cord, and sealed with a wax seal. The regimental (brigade) staff will mark in the identification booklet (service record) of the serviceman "Took military oath [day, month, year]."

7. The day on which the military oath is taken is a nonworking day for the unit and is regarded as a holiday.

8. Military-obligated personnel who are assigned to troop units and who have not taken the military oath take it not later than five days after arrival in the troop unit during training assemblies.

9. Upon the declaration of a general or partial mobilization, all military-obligated reserves who have not taken the military oath in peacetime take it upon their arrival in a troop unit.

> Chairman of the Presidium of the Supreme Soviet of the USSR
> *M. Kalinin*
>
> Secretary of the Presidium of the Supreme Soviet of the USSR
> *A. Gorkin*
> Moscow, the Kremlin
> 3 January 1939

Constitution of the Union of Soviet Socialist Republics

ARTICLE 132. Universal military obligation is by law. Military service in the Workers-Peasants' Red Army is an honorable obligation of citizens of the USSR.

ARTICLE 133. The defense of the fatherland is a sacred duty of each citizen of the USSR. Violating one's oath, crossing over to the enemy, inflicting harm to the military might of the state, and engaging in espionage are treason to the Motherland and will be punished with the full severity of the law as a most serious crime.

Appendix B

Order of the People's Commissar of
Defense of the USSR
No. 227
28 July 1942
Moscow

The enemy is rushing ever newer forces to the front and, despite
its enormous losses, is surging forward, tearing into the depth
of the Soviet Union, seizing new regions, laying waste to and
blowing up our cities and villages, and violating, stealing from,
and exterminating the Soviet populace. Battles are being waged
in the Voronezh region, on the Don River, and at the gates of
the northern Caucasus in the south. The German occupiers are
breaking out toward Stalingrad and the Volga River and at any
cost would like to seize the Kuban and the north Caucasus with
their petroleum and grain riches. The enemy has already captured
Voroshilovgrad, Starobelsk, Rossosh, Kupyansk, Valuyki, Novocherkassk, Rostov-on-Don, and half of Voronezh. A portion of the
forces of Southern *Front,* following behind panic-mongers, have
abandoned Rostov and Novocherkassk without serious resistance
and without an order from Moscow, thus covering their unit
colors with shame.

The populace of our country, which has regarded the Red
Army with love and respect, is beginning to be disappointed in
and is losing faith in the Red Army. Many of them curse the Red
Army for handing our people over to the yoke of the German
oppressors, while at the same time its own troops are streaming
to the east.

Some unintelligent people at the front are consoling themselves with the notion that we can retreat farther to the east
because we have much territory, much land, and a large population and will always have grain in abundance. They use this

opinion to justify their shameful conduct at the fronts. But such talk is thoroughly false and deceitful, and it benefits only our enemies.

Each commander, Red Army soldier, and political worker should understand that our means are not limitless. The territory of the Soviet state is not a desert but people—workers, peasants, intelligentsia, our fathers, mothers, wives, brothers, and children. The territory of the USSR that the enemy has seized and is attempting to seize is grain and other products for the army and the rear; metal and fuel for the industries, factories, and plants that supply the army with armaments and ammunition; and railroads. After the loss of Ukraine, Belorussia, the Baltic States, the Donbas, and other regions, we have much less territory, and we have many fewer people, plants, and factories, and less grain and metal. We have lost more than seventy million people, more than eight hundred million poods of grain annually,[1] and more than ten million tons of metal annually. We no longer have superiority over the Germans in human resources or in grain reserves. To retreat farther would mean to squander ourselves and, along with that, to squander our Motherland. Every new patch of territory abandoned by us will surely strengthen the enemy and surely weaken our defense, our Motherland.

Therefore talk about the fact that we can retreat without end, that we have much territory, that our country is great and rich, that it has a large populace, and that grain will always be in abundant supply must be cut out at its root. Such talk is false and injurious; it weakens us and strengthens the enemy. For if the retreat is not stopped, we will be left without grain, without fuel, without metal, without raw materials, without factories and plants, and without railroads.

It follows from this that it is time to bring an end to retreating.

Not one step backward![2] This now should be our principal declaration.

We must stubbornly, to the last drop of blood, defend each position and every meter of Soviet territory. We must stubbornly cling to each patch of Soviet soil and fight for it to the best of our ability.

Our Motherland is living through perilous days. We should stop and then repulse and defeat the enemy, no matter what the cost to us. The Germans are not as strong as the panic-mongers believe. They are straining in their last efforts. To withstand their attack now, in the next immediate months, will mean to ensure a victory for ourselves.

Can we withstand this attack and then hurl the enemy to the west? Yes, we can, for our factories and plants in the rear are now working at full capacity, and our front is receiving ever-increasing numbers of aircraft, tanks, artillery, and mortars.

What do we lack?

We lack order and discipline in companies, battalions, regiments, and divisions, in tank units, in air squadrons. This is our principal deficiency at this time. If we want to save the situation and defend the Motherland, we must establish the strictest order and iron discipline in our army.

We can no longer tolerate those commanders, commissars, and political workers who are abandoning combat positions on their own. We can no longer tolerate those commanders, commissars, and political workers who permit panic-mongers to determine the situation on the battlefield, who are attracting other soldiers into retreat, and who are opening the front to the enemy.

Panic-mongers and cowards should be exterminated on the spot.

Henceforward the requirement *not one step backward without the order of the higher commander* is the iron law of discipline for every commander, Red Army soldier, and political worker.

Commanders of companies, battalions, regiments, and divisions, and commensurate commissars and political workers who retreat from a combat position without an order from above are traitors to the Motherland. We have to treat such commanders and political workers as we treat traitors to the Motherland.

This is the call of our Motherland.

To carry out this call means to fight for our soil, to save the Motherland, to kill and defeat the despised enemy.

After their winter withdrawal under pressure of the Red Army, when discipline was beginning to break up in the German forces, the Germans undertook stern measures, which had fair results, in order to reestablish discipline. They formed more than one hundred punishment companies made up of soldiers who were guilty of violating discipline by cowardice or instability. They placed these companies in the dangerous sectors of the front and ordered them to expiate their sins with blood. In addition they formed approximately ten punishment battalions made up of commanders who were guilty of violating discipline by cowardice or instability. They deprived them of their medals and placed them on even more dangerous sectors of the front and ordered them to expiate their sins. Finally, they formed special barrier detachments, placed them behind unstable divisions, and ordered them to shoot panic-mongers on the spot in the event that any of the soldiers attempted to abandon their positions through their own volition or allowed themselves to be captured. As is well known, these measures had their effect, and now German forces are fighting better than they fought in the winter. And it turns out that German forces have good discipline, though they lack the elevated purpose of protecting their Motherland and have only a predatory goal—to subjugate a foreign country. Our forces, who have the elevated mission of defending their desecrated Motherland, do not have this discipline, and because of this, they are suffering defeat.

Is it not appropriate for us to learn in this matter from our enemies, as in the past our forefathers learned from their enemies and then gained victory over them?

I think it is appropriate.

The Supreme High Command of the Red Army orders:

1. Military councils of *fronts* and foremost of all the commanders of *fronts:*

   (a) unconditionally to eradicate defeatist attitudes in the forces and with an iron hand to halt propaganda to the effect that we can and should ostensibly retreat farther to the east, that there will be no particular harm caused by such retreat;

   (b) unconditionally to remove from positions and send to Stavka for subjection to military court the commanders of armies who permit voluntary withdrawal of forces from occupied positions, without the order of the *front* command;

   (c) to form within the bounds of the *front* from one to three (depending on the situation) punishment battalions (up to eight hundred men) to which to send middle and senior commanders and corresponding political workers of all branches of forces who are guilty of violating discipline by cowardice or instability and to place these battalions on the most difficult sectors of the front so that these individuals have the opportunity to expiate their crimes against the Motherland with their blood.

2. Military councils of armies and foremost of all the commanders of armies:

(a) unconditionally to remove from positions commanders and commissars of corps and divisions who have permitted the voluntary withdrawal of forces from occupied positions without an order of the army command and to send them to the *front* military council for subjection to military court;

(b) to form within the bounds of the army three to five well-armed barrier detachments (up to two hundred men in each),[3] to position them in the immediate rear of unstable divisions, and to obligate them to shoot panic-mongers and cowards on site in the event of panic and disorderly withdrawal of divisional units and in this way to assist the division's honest soldiers in accomplishing their duty to the Motherland;

(c) to form within the bounds of the army five to ten (depending on the situation) punishment companies (one hundred fifty to two hundred men each) to which to send private soldiers and junior commanders who are guilty of violating discipline by cowardice or instability and to place them on the army's difficult sectors in order to give them the opportunity to expiate their crimes against the Motherland with their blood.

3. Army commanders and commissars of corps and divisions:

(a) unconditionally to remove from their positions those commanders and commissars of regiments and battalions who have permitted voluntary withdrawal of units without an order from the corps or division commander, to strip them of orders and medals, and to send them to the *front* military council for subjection to military court;

(b) to render every possible assistance and support to army barrier detachments in the course of strengthening order and discipline in units.

4. This order is to be read in all companies, [ground] squadrons, batteries, [air] squadrons, commands, and staffs.[4]

> People's Commissar of Defense
> *J. Stalin*

Appendix C

Precedence of Soviet Combat Decorations from the World War II Period

TITLE	RECIPIENTS
Rank	
Hero of the Soviet Union	all personnel, valor and merit
Orders	
Victory	highest level commanders, merit
Red Banner	all personnel, valor
Suvorov 1st Degree	all services, higher command, merit
Suvorov 2d Degree	all services, higher command, merit
Suvorov 3d Degree	all services, higher command, merit
Ushakov 1st Degree	Red Navy, higher command, merit
Ushakov 2d Degree	Red Navy, higher command, merit
Kutuzov 1st Degree	Red Army, higher command, merit
Kutuzov 2d Degree	Red Army, higher command, merit
Kutuzov 3d Degree	Red Army, higher command, merit
Nakhimov 1st Degree	Red Navy, officers, merit
Nakhimov 2d Degree	Red Navy, officers, merit
Bogdan Khmelnitskiy 1st Degree	servicemen and partisans, valor

Bogdan Khmelnitskiy 2d Degree	servicemen and partisans, valor
Bogdan Khmelnitskiy 3d Degree	servicemen and partisans, valor
Aleksandr Nevskiy	commanders from platoon to division, valor
Patriotic War 1st Degree	servicemen and partisans, valor
Patriotic War 2d Degree	servicemen and partisans, valor
Red Star	all personnel, valor
Glory 1st Degree	privates and sergeants of
Glory 2d Degree	ground forces, and junior
Glory 3d Degree	lieutenants of aviation (all three degrees)

Medals

"For Courage"	all enlisted personnel, valor
Ushakov	Red Navy enlisted and warrant officers, valor
"For Combat Service"	all enlisted and warrant officers, merit
Nakhimov	Red Navy enlisted and warrant officers, valor
"Partisan of the Patriotic War" 1st Degree	partisans, valor
"Partisan of the Patriotic War" 2d Degree	partisans, valor

Appendix D

Law of the Russian Federation concerning the Status
of Heroes of the Soviet Union, Heroes of the Russian
Federation, and Full Holders of the Order of Glory

This law recognizes the special contributions to the state and to
the people made by Heroes of the Soviet Union, Heroes of the
Russian Federation, and full holders of the Order of Glory.[5] The
government recognizes the necessity to guarantee their economic
and social well-being, and by this law establishes their status and
grants them appropriate rights and entitlements.

SECTION I. General conditions

ARTICLE I. Civil and societal obligations and rights

1. A citizen of Russia who has achieved the rank of Hero of the
Soviet Union, Hero of the Russian Federation, or who is a full
holder of the Order of Glory should bear this high rank with
dignity, serve as an example in the fulfillment of civil and military duty, and carry out other obligations established by the
Constitution and laws of the Russian Federation for citizens of
Russia.
2. Heroes of the Soviet Union, Heroes of the Russian Federation,
and full holders of the Order of Glory (hereafter referred to
as Heroes and full holders of the Order of Glory), regarding
matters that are regulated by this law, are accorded preferential status by the leaders and other officials of organs of
governmental authority and of local administration.
3. Social nonprofit organizations created by Heroes and full
holders of the Order of Glory, and consisting only of persons
in these categories, for the effective fulfillment of their obligations, the actualization of their rights, the resolution of issues
of their social protection and other legal activities not of a
commercial nature are entitled to rights and privileges granted

227

to them in tax codes and other legislation of the Russian Federation and also to the right to receive telephone service at their facilities for carrying out their legal activities, paid for through the budget of the Russian Federation.

SECTION II. Entitlements granted to Heroes and Full Holders of the Order of Glory

ARTICLE 2. Pension entitlement

Increase of all forms of pension for age, years of service, disability, and loss of head of household in amounts set forth in pension legislation and by other legislative and legal acts of the Russian Federation for Heroes of the Soviet Union, Heroes of the Russian Federation, and full holders of the Order of Glory.

ARTICLE 3. Tax exemption entitlement

Exemption from paying taxes, dues, duties, and other payments in amounts set forth by tax legislation and other legislative and legal acts of the Russian Federation for Heroes of the Soviet Union, Heroes of the Russian Federation, and full holders of the Order of Glory.

ARTICLE 4. Medical, sanatorium-health resort service, prosthesis-orthopedic and pharmacy support entitlements

1. Preferential, free personal and free family (spouses and children to age eighteen) services at ambulatory polyclinic facilities of all types and forms, immediate [without waiting in line] free personal and free family (spouses and children to age eighteen) hospitalization and recuperation in hospitals and clinics and also in polyclinics and other medical facilities to which awardees have been attached during their period of employment before retirement. The indicated entitlements are preserved for surviving spouses and children to the age of eighteen.

2. Preferential free provision of medications prescribed by a doctor and the delivery of medications to those who are unable to leave their residence.

3. Free construction and repair of dentures (except those made from precious metals).

4. Preferential admission for Heroes and full holders of the Order of Glory to a polyclinic or place of last employment or free admission to a sanatorium or rest facility one time annually and

for family members (spouses, children to age eighteen) at 25 percent of cost. Passes for sanatorium, health resort, and rest home visits are allocated at benefit rates provided for employees of those ministries and departments to which the indicated facilities belong. All forms of medical service in sanatoriums and rest facilities are free, and meals are provided without charge. Persons who have received passes for sanatorium–rest facility care in accordance with this article of the law are granted the right of free travel to the location of the facility and return by railroad in a two-berth sleeping compartment of passenger trains and in first-class compartments of water and air transportation. These entitlements are maintained for surviving spouses.

ARTICLE 5. Entitlements for obtaining, constructing, and maintaining a residence and for receiving utility services

1. Exemption of Heroes and full holders of the Order of Glory and family members residing with them from paying for utilities (water, sewer, gas, electricity, hot water, central heating, and in homes that do not have central heating, the delivery of fuel required within normal limits established for sale to the population) and from paying for use of residential telephone and alarm services. These entitlements are maintained for surviving spouses and parents of Heroes and full holders of the Order of Glory.
2. Free ownership of occupied residences in state- or municipal-owned apartment buildings.
3. Preferential improvement of living conditions through granting of residence in state- and municipal-owned apartment buildings, with granting of supplemental living space of 20 square meters.
4. Free ownership of land parcel for construction of individual homes, dachas, and gardens with an area of 0.10 hectares in cities and towns, and 0.30 hectares in rural locales.[6]
5. Free major repair of residence irrespective of deed ownership of residence.
6. Preferential distribution of local construction materials for construction of individual residences and for major repair of residence.
7. Preferential use of all forms of communications utilities, pref-

erential and free installation of residential telephones, preferential and free installation of alarm systems.

ARTICLE 6. Entitlements for the use of transportation and payment for passage

1. Free personal travel one time annually (round-trip) by railroad transport in a two-berth sleeping compartment of passenger trains and in first-class compartments of water and air transportation (first-category in some locales) of express and passenger lines, by air, or intercity bus transportation.
2. Free personal use of intercity transportation (streetcar, bus, trolleybus, subway, ferry), light rail in suburbs, and buses in rural areas.
3. Preferential issue of tickets for all forms of railroad, water, air, and ground transportation.

ARTICLE 7. Entitlements to everyday municipal and commercial service, during the use of communications facilities and during attendance at cultural and athletic facilities

Preferential use of all forms of services provided by communications facilities, commercial services, during attendance at cultural and athletic facilities. [This translates to the right to go to the front of the line in all public telephone, postal, and telegraph facilities, in all stores, and at all concert, theatrical, and athletic events.]

ARTICLE 8. Entitlements to obtaining employment, training, retraining, and leave

1. Preferential right of remaining at work during a reduction in force irrespective of seniority at a given institution. Preferential offering of employment upon liquidation of an enterprise or organization.
2. Free training and retraining in new profession at place of employment in courses to improve qualifications in a government-run system of preparing and retraining cadres and in for-profit training institutions and courses.
3. The granting to indicated persons annual paid leave and supplemental leave without pay for up to three weeks annually at a time of their choosing.

ARTICLE 9. Other rights and entitlements

1. Free burial with military honors for deceased (or fallen in battle) Heroes or full holders of the Order of Glory paid for out of the federal budget of the Russian Federation.
2. Placement on the grave of a deceased (or fallen in battle) Hero or full holder of the Order of Glory of a headstone, of a type determined by the government of the Russian Federation, at the expense of the federal budget. Supplementary expenses incurred in connection with a change in the established form of the headstone are paid to the family of the deceased (or fallen in battle) or to the organizational sponsor.
3. Spouses and children (up to age eighteen) of deceased (or fallen in battle) Heroes and full holders of the Order of Glory are each paid a one-time entitlement equal to twenty months' salary determined by established legislation on the day of death (or death in battle).

SECTION III. Concluding provisions

ARTICLE 10. Applicability of this law

This law is applicable to citizens of the Russian Federation who have achieved the rank of Hero of the Soviet Union or Hero of the Russian Federation or who are full holders of the Order of Glory. The rights and entitlements of these persons who live outside the borders of the Russian Federation are determined by treaties (agreements) between the Russian Federation and the states of which they are citizens.

ARTICLE 11. Indemnification for expenses incurred in implementation of this law

Expenditures by organs of state authority and by local administrative organs, enterprises, institutions, and organizations associated with implementation of this law are indemnified by local financial organs on the basis of receipts verified by persons who have received the rights and entitlements in accordance with this law, by means of transfer of assets to the accounts of appropriate organs, enterprises, institutions, and organizations against the assets of the federal budget of the Russian Federation.

ARTICLE 12. Corresponding acts adopted on the basis of this law

1. Organs of state authority and local administrative organs bear responsibility for observance of this law and for legal and other acts adopted on the basis of this law.
2. Organs of state authority of the republic at the level of the Russian Federation, autonomous oblasts, and autonomous districts, and of Moscow and Saint Petersburg krays, oblasts, and cities and local authorities can grant from their own financial resources supplementary entitlements to Heroes, full holders of the Order of Glory, and their families.
3. Any legal acts that limit the amount and enumeration of the rights and entitlements granted by this law are declared not effective.
4. Losses incurred to Heroes and full holders of the Order of Glory, and also their societal organizations, in connection with realization of acts contradictory to this law are subject to full remuneration to them at the expense of organs of state authority or local administrative organs that adopted the illegal act.

ARTICLE 13. Responsibility for violation of this law

Persons guilty of violations of this law bear disciplinary, administrative, and criminal responsibility in accordance with legislation of the Russian Federation.[7]

President of the Russian Federation
B. Yeltsin
Moscow, House of the Soviets
Russia
15 January 1993

Notes

Translator's Foreword

1. Approximately one thousand Matildas were shipped, of which some two hundred fifty were lost en route. David Fletcher, *Matilda Infantry Tank 1938–1945* (London: Osprey, 1994), 23. [JG]

2. At the peak of the war (1944–45) the Soviets were producing about 15,000 T-34 tanks annually, compared to 3,000 in 1941 and 13,500 in 1942. Steven Zaloga and Jim Kinnear, *T-34-85 Medium Tank 1944–1994* (London: Osprey, 1996), 17. [JG]

Author's Introduction

1. World War II began in September 1939 with Germany's invasion of Poland and ended in September 1945 with Japan's surrender. The Great Patriotic War of the Soviet Union began on 22 June 1941, when Germany invaded the Soviet Union, and ended on 9 May 1945, when Germany surrendered to the Allied Powers. This book observes this distinction. [JG]

Audacity and Intuition

1. A forward detachment is a reinforced tank or infantry unit designated for independent execution of a mission. In an offensive they can rapidly penetrate into the enemy's depth, capture an important objective, conduct pursuit, seize a water crossing from the march, and so on. They can also be designated on the march to conduct a meeting engagement. During the Great Patriotic War a division would employ a reinforced battalion as a forward detachment. *Voyennyy entsiklopedicheskiy slovar* (Military encyclopedic dictionary) (Moscow: Voyenizdat, 1983), s.v. "peredovoy otryad" (forward detachment), 548. This source is hereafter cited as *VES*.

2. Georgiy Dmitrievich Ionin was the commander of an antitank artillery battalion in the war. His artillerymen destroyed eleven enemy tanks in one fierce battle in the Balaton [Hungary] defensive operation (January–February 1945). He was recommended for the rank of Hero of the Soviet Union, but for some unknown reason he

did not receive this or any other award. Georgiy Dmitrievich told me about this in 1994. I took up his cause and began to petition for a correction of this oversight. Our efforts were successful. By an order of the President of the Russian Federation, Ionin was finally awarded the rank of Hero of the Russian Federation on 14 April 1995 (in time for the fiftieth anniversary of the victory over Germany). The benefits that accrue to a Hero of the Soviet Union and a Hero of the Russian Federation are the same (see appendix D for a detailed listing of these benefits).

3. Mikhail Emelyanovich is the first name and the patronymic of Colonel Vaytsekhovskiy. Russian patronymics are formed from the father's first name and a suffix according to the person's gender. Use of the first name and patronymic together is polite and respectful. While this convention may be confusing at first to those unfamiliar with it, I have retained its use throughout this translation. [JG]

4. The Order of the Red Banner was established by the Presidium of the USSR Central Executive Committee on 1 August 1924. It was awarded for indomitable bravery, intrepidity, and courage at the risk of one's own life displayed in the defense of the USSR. See appendix C for a listing of Soviet World War II combat decorations. [JG]

Lyuba the Tank Killer

1. Sergey Vikulov, *Parad pobedy: Stikhi o Velikoy Otechestvennoy* (Parade of victory: verses about the Great Patriotic War) (Moscow: Izdatelstvo "Khudozhestvennaya literatura," 1985), 111.

2. Many families perished in the famine of 1933, Lyuba's parents among them. I was eleven years old in that year, and I remember this time well. There were approximately one hundred fifty households in our village of Kolesnikovka; only twenty of them survived the famine intact.

3. The military commission was a military and political institution roughly equivalent to a local draft board in the United States. It issued conscription notices to young men, accepted voluntary enlistments, conducted physicals and other examinations, and determined the branch of service to which an inductee would be sent. [JG]

4. The "active army" was the army in the field, as opposed to the strategic reserve forces and the personnel at the mobilization and training base. This level of medical unit was capable of performing simple surgical procedures, like the removal of shrapnel and the amputation of a wounded extremity.

5. The *protivotankovoye ruzhe Simonova* [*PTRS*—an antitank rifle of Simonov design] was self-loading and had a bore diameter of 14.5 millimeters; it weighed 21 kilograms [46 pounds] and had an effective rate of fire of 15 rounds per minute, a magazine capacity of 5 rounds, a muzzle velocity of 1,012 meters/second [3,320 feet/sec], and an armor-penetrating capability of 35 millimeters at a range of 300 meters. *VES*, 600.

6. The *Komsomol*—*komunisticheskiy soyuz molodezh* (young Communist league)—was the party organization for young adults, with the mission to prepare them for full membership in the Communist Party. A *Komsomolka* is a female and a *Komsomolist* a male *Komsomol* member. [JG]

7. A trophy is any piece of confiscated enemy equipment or gear. [JG]

8. The English translation of *gvardeytsy* is "guardsmen" (singular, *gvardeyets*). The term applies to any soldier serving in a "guards" unit. The closest equivalent to "guards" designation in the American armed forces is a Presidential Unit Citation: an award represented by a gold-framed blue ribbon and granted to a unit by written declaration of the president of the United States, it becomes a permanent award for the unit and for any person assigned to the unit at the time the particular combat action occurred. In a similar fashion Soviet military units designated as "guards" units for exemplary combat performance were honored with the addition of the word "guards" to the unit's name and banner, the word "guards" to the rank of every soldier, and a "guards" badge on every soldier's tunic pocket. [JG]

9. *Tsentralnyy arkhiv ministerstva oborony Rossiskoy federatsii* (Central archive of the Ministry of Defense, Russian Federation), collection 229, index 7077, item 25, sheets 118–20. This source is hereafter cited as *TSAMO RF*.

10. Pronounced *pe-te-er-ovets*, the word *peteerovtsy* is formed from the letters in the acronym *PTR*, which stands for *protivotankovoye ruzhe* (antitank rifle). A *peteerovets* (plural, *peteerovtsy*) is an antitank rifleman. [JG]

Spalling

1. *Perepiska Predsedatelya Soveta Ministrov* SSSR *s Presidentami* SSHA *i Premer-ministrami Velikobretanii vo vremya Velikoy Otechestvennoy voyny 1941–1945gg.* (Correspondence of the chairman of the Council of Ministers of the USSR with the presidents of the United States and the prime ministers of Great Britain during the

Great Patriotic War 1941–1945) (Moscow: Izdatelstvo politicheskoy literatury, 1976), 1:29.

2. In the T-34-76 tank the driver-mechanic and the radio operator–hull gunner were positioned in the hull, and the commander-gunner and the loader were in the turret. The commander-gunner sat on the left side of the main gun, and the loader was on the right side. The T-34-85 added a fifth crew member—a dedicated gunner—whose presence enabled the commander to control the tank's fire and maneuver from a position behind and above the gunner. This repositioning of the tank commander and releasing him from gunner responsibility facilitated tactical control of several tanks if the tank commander happened also to be a platoon or company commander. [JG]

3. SMERSH is a contraction of smert shpionam (death to spies). Every tank battalion had a counterintelligence officer. Each rifle regiment and each tank and mechanized brigade had a SMERSH counterintelligence section. All organizations above the brigade level had SMERSH elements. The mission of this NKVD organization was to round up German infiltrators and spies and to root out personnel among the Soviet troops who maintained or expressed anti-Soviet sentiments. Of course the NKVD maintained analogous organizations in all sectors of Soviet society, including the industrial base. NKVD is the acronym for narodnyy komissariat vnutrenykh del, "people's commissariat for internal affairs," the organization of secret police that was the predecessor of the KGB (komitet gosudarstvennoy bezopasnosti, "committee for state security"). [JG]

4. In this question Loza is not claiming a medical first for Soviet military medicine but simply observing that these eye wounds forced Soviet military doctors to learn new skills. [JG]

5. When referring to land through which a major river flows, Europeans, including Russians, use the terms "right bank" and "left bank." The right bank is the lands to the right when one's back is toward the river's source. In the case of Ukraine, the right bank is the west bank of the Dnieper River. To cite an analogous example in the United States, Nebraska is on the right bank of the Missouri River, and Iowa is on the left bank. [JG]

Not by Rote But by Skill

1. TSAMO RF, collection 601, index 70689, item 5, sheet 8.

2. A full-strength tank brigade would have had forty-two tanks (two battalions of twenty-one tanks each), plus a small number of tanks in the brigade headquarters. That the Red Army would deploy

in combat a brigade with only seven tanks—one-sixth of its normal strength—is a reflection of their desperate condition in the spring of 1942. [JG]

3. The concept of "danger close" exists in all armies. It is the distance from one's own position to which friendly forces are permitted to adjust artillery. The specific distance depends on several factors, including the caliber of weapon being fired, the experience of the observer, the type of cover the friendly troops are using, the gun-target line in relation to the friendly unit, and so on. It is a safety measure intended to protect the lives of friendly troops. Even in war, the violation of the danger-close line is a significant incident. [JG]

4. *TSAMO RF*, collection 758, index 4580, item 9, sheet 139.

5. Soviet tank crewmen received instruction in operating enemy equipment both in their initial specialty training and later in their units. Driver-mechanics and officers learned how to drive German tanks; and using captured ammunition stocks, all crewmen were taught how to fire the main gun. Captured German combat vehicles were infrequently used in frontline units due to the inherent danger of friendly fire. In those cases when they were employed—for example to guard a headquarters or some other rear area facility—their German markings were covered by large red stars, and a red flag was flown on each vehicle. German wheeled and tracked transport vehicles and motorcycles, on the other hand, were widely employed throughout Soviet units. Captured German mobile repair vans, with their excellent tool sets and kits, were especially popular among Soviet tank maintenance units, while supply units preferred the German half-tracks.

Friendly Fire

1. In Soviet military terminology a *front* was a large formation, roughly equivalent to an American or British army group. It was generally commanded by an officer at the rank of army general or marshal and normally was subordinated to the Supreme High Command in Moscow, which exercised its authority through *Stavka*. *Stavka* is the Russian military term for "headquarters," but in literature of the Great Patriotic War the word normally is used to indicate the supreme headquarters of the Soviet Armed Forces in Moscow.

2. A translation of enlisted personnel's oath of service in the Red Army during this period is provided in appendix A. [JG]

3. A coaxial machine gun is mechanically linked with the main gun so that it moves and points where the main gun moves and

points. Universally referred to as the "coax," this weapon is employed to service targets that do not require the destructive power or range of the main gun. While available sources indicate that the Matilda II was normally equipped with a Besa coaxial machine gun, Loza insists that the Matildas issued to 5th Mechanized Corps used the Bren. Dmitriy Loza, letter to translator, 8 February 1997. [JG]

4. The role of this detachment was created in Order No. 227 of 28 July 1942, known as the *Ni shagu nazad* (not one step backward) order. The complete order is translated in appendix B. [JG]

5. *Shturmovik* is a generic term for ground-attack aircraft or helicopter, though the word normally refers to the Ilyushin-2, a single-engine aircraft armed with two 23-mm cannons and one 12.7-mm and two 7.62-mm machine guns. It also carried 800 pounds of bombs. A gunner sat facing rearward behind the pilot to protect the Il-2 against rear attack. [JG]

6. A mechanized brigade had a tank regiment of three companies, totaling thirty-five tanks.

7. These could have been 45-mm antitank cannons or 76-mm divisional guns (ZIS-3 — *zavod imeni Stalina* [plant in the name of Stalin]) employed in an antitank role. [JG]

8. Throughout the text Loza refers to these personnel in three ways: *avtomatchiki* (submachine gunners), *desantniki*, and *tanko-desantniki*. The latter two terms are rooted in the word *desant*, as in "descend" or "descent." In military Russian a *desant* is an assault or attack employing a special means of delivery, such as an airplane (parachute), helicopter, amphibious landing craft, or, in this particular case, the tank. Infantry troops were assigned or attached to the Soviet tank units and rode into battle literally holding onto rails welded to the sides of the tank turrets. When the tanks closed with the enemy, these infantry troops, armed with submachine guns, dismounted and attacked to neutralize enemy infantry and antitank troops. [JG]

Delayed Retribution

1. The selection of an officer to attend the Frunze Military Academy was based on a test administered in the unit, followed by entrance examinations administered at the academy itself in Moscow. Loza was awaiting his call for testing at the academy. He was a student at the Frunze Military Academy from 1947 to 1950. The U.S. Army equivalent of this institution is the Command and General Staff College at Fort Leavenworth, Kansas. [JG]

2. An example of Captain Reshnyak's discretion occurred in March 1944 in Ukraine, when before a battle a crew of tankers intentionally loosened the track adjuster on their Sherman, causing the track to fall off as they moved into combat. They caught up to their unit after the fight was over. This crew could have been sent to almost certain death in a punishment battalion or to a military tribunal, but instead, on Captain Reshnyak's recommendation, it was broken up and assigned to other vehicles with a most stern verbal reprimand.

3. The "punishing sword" is a reference to the NKVD's ability to imprison and otherwise punish those subject to its authority, a fact symbolized in its emblem.

4. An oblast is a political subdivision; the approximate English equivalent of the term is "province." The Smolensk oblast is about 200 miles west-southwest of Moscow. [JG]

5. As the Red Army advanced westward through Soviet territory formerly occupied by the Germans, military commissions rounded up and pressed into military service all able-bodied males of draft age. It is this conscription process that Orlov is said to have avoided due to his existing wound-related injury. [JG]

6. The same military commission that conscripted youth was also responsible for maintaining rosters of reserve and retired officers and for administering pension matters for retired officers and warrant officers.

7. The 11 May 1945 Stavka order establishing approximately a hundred such concentration camps on Soviet and Polish territory for verification of former war prisoners and incarcerated civilians liberated by Soviet and Allied troops is printed in Dmitriy Volkogonov, Triumf i tragediya: I. V. Stalin, politicheskiy portret (Triumph and tragedy: J. V. Stalin, a political portrait) (Moscow: Izdatelstvo Agentsvo pechati Novosti, 1989), bk. 2, pt. 1, 394. These camps, which operated under the auspices of the NKVD, were expected to process a former prisoner in one to two months.

Shooting the Moon

1. The Order of the Patriotic War was established by the Presidium of the Supreme Soviet of the USSR on 20 May 1942 as an award conferred upon servicemen and partisans who had displayed courage, determination, and bravery in battles for the Soviet Motherland and upon servicemen who by their actions had facilitated the success of

combat operations. The award was given in two degrees, 1st Degree being the higher. [JG]

Skill and Daring

1. *Matildovtsy* is a peculiarly Russian way of saying "Matilda tankers."

2. *Yazyk* in Russian, the word "tongue" in this context has always meant a live prisoner, one who can talk. This term was used by all Soviet military forces during World War II and is still in use today. [JG]

3. The "Englishman" is a nickname that Soviet crews used for the Matilda tank.

4. The *TT* (*Tulskiy, Tokareva*) pistol was the Tokarev Model 1930 semiautomatic pistol, which fired a 7.62 x 25-mm cartridge from an 8-round clip. The "lemon" was the F-1 hand grenade, strongly resembling the "pineapple" hand grenade used by American soldiers. [JG]

5. The *PPSh-41* (*pistolet-pulemet Shpagina obrazets 1941*, submachine gun designed by G. S. Shpagin in 1941) fired the 7.62 x 25-mm cartridge from a 71-round drum or 30-round box magazine. [JG]

6. The daily report was a document listing the number of personnel, weapons, and combat vehicles assigned to a given unit on a specific day. The inventory was submitted to higher headquarters at the end of each day. "Active bayonet" is an expression broadly used in the Great Patriotic War: the primary weapon of infantry units was the rifle with bayonet, and an "active bayonet" was a soldier who was able to participate in an attack. The number of such soldiers was thus considered to be the combat strength of the unit.

7. To Soviet soldiers, all Germans were "Fritz," and to German soldiers, all Soviet soldiers were "Ivan."

8. "Misha" is the diminutive form of the name Mikhail. The Russian language, just as English, is full of diminutives for given names (like Bob for Robert, Jack for John, Liz for Elizabeth, and so on). [JG]

9. The *panzerfaust* was a shoulder-fired antitank rocket launcher that fired a shaped-charge warhead.

10. In Russian the singular of "foreign-vehicle tanker" is *tankist-inomarochnik*. The second word is compounded from *innostrannaya marka*, meaning "foreign design" or "brand." Loza's word in the text at this point is the plural, *inomarochniki*. [JG]

Flamethrower Tanks

1. Two official sources provide scant information about this weapon: see *VES*, 729; and *Velikaya otechestvennaya voyna sovetskogo soyuza 1941–1945* (Great Patriotic War of the Soviet Union 1941–1945) (Moscow: Sovetskaya entsiklopedia, 1985), 503–4, 703.

2. Reznichenko was the chief of staff of a battalion during the war. After the war he graduated from the Military Academy of Armored Forces and then began teaching at the Frunze Academy, where he is still on the faculty. Holding a doctorate in military science, he is a member of the Academy of Military Sciences.

3. The military council of the *front* developed a proclamation, which is an essentially political document, before every operation. In general terms, the proclamation described the combat mission and called for maximum effort from the soldiers and the use of those methods that are most specifically calculated to bring about the rapid defeat of the enemy. The military council of any formation consisted of the commander, the deputy commander for political affairs, the chief of staff, and at some levels the chief of the rear (logistics). The council was an institution of collective leadership in both the Red Army and the Red Navy during World War II. Important orders were signed by all the members, not by the commander alone. For a detailed description of the military council, see *Sovetskaya voyennaya entsiklopediya* (Soviet military encyclopedia) (Moscow: Voyenizdat, 1976), s.v. "Voyennyy sovet" 2:272. [JG]

4. A *sovkhoz* (plural, *sovkhoza*) is a farm operated as an industrial enterprise with salaried employees. The word is a contraction of *sovetskoye khozyaystvo* (soviet economy). [JG]

5. A diamond that bore the name "Orlov" decorated the top of the scepter of the Russian tsars. This priceless stone was as clear as water and showed a bluish-green tint. With a weight of 194.8 carats, it was the largest diamond in Russia. An experienced soldier was considered equal in value to this gemstone.

6. Recall that the commander also doubled as the gunner in the T-34-76 tank. Only with great difficulty could this crewman fire the main gun and maintain an awareness of the situation around his tank. [JG]

7. The T-34 tank, in both 76- and 85-mm main gun variants, was equipped with the Degtyarev type-1929 tank machine gun (DT—*Degtyarev, tank*). This weapon fired the 7.62 x 54-mm rimmed cartridge from a top-mounted disk. The machine gun was issued with a

collapsing metal shoulder stock and quick-detachable bipod for use when dismounted from the tank. [JG]

8. "Katyusha" is the popular name for the BM-8 and BM-13 multiple rocket launchers that were mounted on the Studebaker trucks. The BM designation is for *boyevaya mashina* (combat vehicle). The Soviet units to which they were assigned were named *gvardeyskiye minometnyye chasti* (GMCh—guards mortars units). [JG]

Terrible Weapon

1. V. N. Novikov, ed., *Oruzhiye pobedy* (Weapons of victory) (Moscow: "Mashinostroyeniye," 1985), 105.

2. Though this practice was common, the 122-mm howitzer was not in the TOE (table of organization and equipment) for guards mortar units, and its use in this role was entirely dependent on its availability.

3. See appendix B for a complete translation of this order. [JG]

4. Officers in guards units received 1.5 and enlisted personnel 2.0 times the pay of personnel in conventional artillery units. In addition, guards units received new equipment and uniforms before standard units.

5. The M4A2 Sherman had a .30-caliber machine gun mounted in the right front slope. The assistant driver-mechanic manned this weapon.

Death by Fire

1. Julia Drunina, "Ya tolko raz vidala rukopashnyy" (I saw hand-to-hand combat only once), *Stikhi o Velikoy Otechestvennoy* (Verses about the Great Patriotic War) (Moscow: Izdatelstvo "Khudozhestven-naya literatura," 1985), bk. 1, 199.

2. GAZ is the acronym for *Gorkovskiy avtomobilnyy zavod* (Gorkiy automobile plant). *Gazushka*, which appears below, is a diminutive for GAZ (in the same fashion as "Jimmy" for GMC or "Chevy" for Chevrolet). [JG]

3. The basic load of this tank was 71 main-gun rounds, 6,250 rounds of .30-caliber ammunition, and 600 rounds of .50-caliber.

4. The main-gun rounds came individually packed in fiber-board tubes, taped together in threes, with a cloth handle at the top for ease in carrying. This three-pack weighed seventy-nine pounds. [JG]

5. The antitank round in use at this time was solid-shot and relied on kinetic energy to penetrate enemy armor. This projectile

did not contain any explosive substance that would detonate upon striking a hard surface, as did the high-explosive (HE) round. [JG]

6. The Soviet ordnance experts' opinion notwithstanding, another major factor contributed to the salutary outcome of the incident Loza recounts here. The stowed main-gun rounds for the M4A2 Sherman tank were housed in a "wet storage" compartment. The ammunition racks had a "hollow" outer casing that contained a mixture of water, glycerin (or ethylene glycol), and anticorrosion agents. These added ingredients prevented the water from freezing and inhibited the water from corroding the container. The "wet storage" capability was installed in later M4s as a result of earlier combat experience of American crews, whose tanks were often destroyed by on-board fires caused by the main-gun ammunition after the tank sustained a hit. W. F. Atwater, U.S. Army Ordnance Museum, letter to translator, 18 January 1997. [JG]

The Marshal's Embrace

1. Rodion Yakovlevich Malinovskiy (1898–1967) enlisted in the Russian Imperial Army in 1914 and was decorated with the St. George Cross 4th Degree for his combat performance in World War I. Having joined the Soviet Army in 1919, he was made an officer in 1920. After a succession of command positions from platoon to battalion, he began in 1930 a long period of staff service, followed by duty in Spain as an advisor to the Republican Government forces. Malinovskiy was commanding a rifle corps when the Great Patriotic War began in June 1941. He quickly rose through corps and army command positions to become one of Stalin's most trusted *front* commanders. His forces fought on the left wing of the Soviet-German front, from Stalingrad in early 1943 to Budapest in 1945. Malinovskiy became a Marshal of the Soviet Union in 1944 and commanded the Transbaykal *Front* in the brief war against Japan in August 1945. After the war he commanded a military district and, subsequently, all Soviet forces in the Far East; ultimately he was named minister of defense. Malinovskiy is buried in the Kremlin wall on Red Square. [JG]

2. The Soviets have long used a combination of written orders and map overlays for tactical combat command and control. Symbols and lines drawn on a battle map and approved by the commander orally, without any written orders, were considered valid and lawful combat orders. [JG]

3. The word for "commander's reconnaissance" in Russian is

rekognostsirovka. The commander assembles his subordinate commanders at a location from which the enemy position and terrain can be seen and then personally outlines his plan and assigns specific unit missions. [JG]

4. In the Soviet Army the tanks of the brigade commander, the brigade chief of staff, the chief of political department, and the battalion and company commanders were assigned officers as their commanders. If a tank were damaged, the unit commander (chief of staff, and so on) quickly moved to another vehicle. This still left an officer in charge of the damaged tank.

5. The German designation for FW-189 *Rama* was *Uhu* (owl). The Soviets called the twin-boomed aircraft the *Rama* (frame) because of the rectangle formed by the booms and connecting tail surfaces. Powered by two V-type motors and armed with several machine guns, it was originally designed as a tactical reconnaissance aircraft. [JG]

6. After this battle, all damaged Shermans, including those that were sitting between Soviet and German lines, were recovered from the battlefield and evacuated to the Soviet rear. The effort took an entire week and was accomplished completely at night, at times under enemy fire. Several troops were killed or wounded in the process.

7. *TSAMO RF*, collection 19 A, index 2714, item 2, sheet 324.

A Peasant Family's Courageous Deed

1. *TSAMO RF*, collection 339, index 5187, item 1, sheet 124.

2. A covering detachment is a temporary group designated to protect the withdrawal of a unit to a new defensive line. Its composition varies with the size of the parent unit: from a battalion, it is, as a rule, a company; from a regiment (brigade), a battalion. Its mission is to deploy at positions suitable for a brief defense, to inflict losses on the enemy by fire, and to force the enemy to deploy and attack. This tactic delays the enemy's advance and enables the parent unit to break contact with the enemy and withdraw in an organized fashion to a position chosen for defense.

3. The Salashisty were a Hungarian irregular force who supported the Germans. They belonged to the fascist Crossed Arrow Party, led by one Ferents Salashi (Szalasi). Salashi was put to death by the Hungarian government on 12 March 1946 for his war crimes. See *Bolshaya Sovetskaya Entsiklopediya* (Great Soviet encyclopedia) (Moscow: Izdatelstvo "Sovetskaya Entsiklopediya," 1975), s.v. "Salashi" 22:511. [JG]

4. The T-34 escape hatch—oval-shaped, with four locking lugs—was located in the tank's bow, beneath the feet of the hull machine gunner. [JG]

5. A *khold*, the standard unit of area measure in Hungary, is the equivalent of 0.432 hectares or 1.06 acres.

6. In the recommendation signed by Marshal of the Soviet Union S. K. Timoshenko, I had proposed that Geza Onodi receive the Order of the Patriotic War 1st Degree and his wife the Order of the Patriotic War 2d Degree. Somewhere in the administrative bureaucracy, it was reasoned that the medal "For Combat Service" was sufficient for Gezan Onodi. Why, in particular, the Order of the Patriotic War? At that time, only these awards remained with the family after the death of the recipient, and in 1972 these two recipients were already well along in years. Now, by regulation, all awards of the deceased remain with the family and do not have to be returned.

Failure to Coordinate

1. A description of the operational plan is contained in *Velikaya otechestvennaya voyna Sovetskogo soyuza 1941–1945gg.* (The Great Patriotic War of the Soviet Union 1941–1945) (Moscow: Voyenizdat, 1984), 372. This source is hereafter cited as *vovss*.

2. Loza's 233d Tank Brigade was designated a "guards" unit in September 1944 and became 46th Guards Tank Brigade, 5th Mechanized Corps was renamed 9th Guards Mechanized Corps, and 6th Tank Army became 6th Guards Tank Army.

3. The Henschel-126 was a high-winged, fixed undercarriage, single-engine, two-seat tactical reconnaissance aircraft. It had a maximum speed of 193 MPH and a range of 360 miles. It could be armed with a variety of machine guns and cannons and could carry up to 771 pounds of bombs. [JG]

4. The acronym *PVO* is derived from *Protivo-vozdushnaya oborona*, which means "antiaircraft defenses." [JG]

5. Witnesses affirmed in written statements the fact of the destruction of an enemy aircraft by Soviet antiaircraft gunners during the Great Patriotic War. Only because of these documents was the unit credited with the downed aircraft.

Night Raid

1. Not mentioned by Loza is the fact that Guards Captain Avramenko was awarded the title of Hero of the Soviet Union in March

1945 for his actions in the last week of August 1944, when his battalion was fighting in the area of the Romanian city of Jassy. Avramenko retired from active duty at the rank of colonel in 1975. [JG]

2. A bypassing detachment is a temporarily appointed tactical unit whose mission is to seize and hold an important objective in the enemy rear—in this particular case, the town of Galgaguta. The nature of the detachment's actions is to avoid engagement in combat—that is, stealthily to "bypass" enemy garrisons and strongholds in the depth of enemy dispositions—and rapidly reach the objective that it has been assigned to capture. After accomplishing that mission, the detachment reverts to its standard organization, subordination, and mission.

3. The Order of the Red Star was established by the Presidium of the USSR Central Executive Committee on 6 April 1930. It was awarded for outstanding achievement in the defense of the USSR, in times both of war and of peace, in the ensuring of state security and in promoting military science; for the development of military equipment; and for personal courage and valor in battle. It could also be conferred on foreign citizens. [JG]

4. The phrase "stand to" refers to the assembling of all personnel at one or more locations, in large or small groups, for final inspections and briefings before departing on a mission. [JG]

5. *TSAMO RF*, collection of 9th Guards Mechanized Corps, index 274873, item 1, sheets 188–89; collection 18th Guards Mechanized Brigade, index 367302, item 3, sheet 4.

Thank You, Ice

1. *TSAMO RF*, collection 339, index 13262, item 12, sheet 19.

2. "Combat reconnaissance patrol" in Russian is *boyevoy razvedyvatelnyy dozor*. In an armor unit, this was never less than two tanks, so they could cover each other.

3. We decided to attack Zalaba in column. It was dangerous to deploy into a combat formation (a line, for example) at night: the tanks might have gotten stuck in holes and ditches, of which there were many in a village. One might compare this column with the ram of the middle ages, which battered the fortress wall during a siege.

4. The nickname for the Sherman tank comes from the Russian pronunciation of "M4," M *chetyrye*. A crewman was called an *Emchist* (plural, *Emchisti*). [JG]

A Slight Error

1. *Sovinformburo*, or the Soviet Information Bureau, was the government agency responsible for releasing official Soviet government print and radio-broadcast news releases. The information was broadcast over official government radio channels or distributed by *TASS* (*telegrafichnoye agentsvo Sovetskogo soyuza*), the telegraph agency of the Soviet Union. [JG]

2. Until the fall of the Soviet Union, *Pravda* was the official government newspaper; it had the largest circulation of any newspaper in the country. [JG]

3. *Glavno*, the adjective in the compound word *glavno-komanduyushchiy*, means "main" or "supreme"; *komanduyushchiy* itself means "commander in chief." The two words together refer to Stalin's authority over all the armed forces of the Soviet Union. [JG]

4. Loza is being too genteel. In vernacular Russian, *gavno* is also the slang word for excrement, "shit." [JG]

5. "Father of the Peoples" was a beneficent title bestowed on Stalin in the press, the "peoples" being the various nationalities that made up the Soviet Union. "Generalissimus" was one of his official titles, indicating the fact that as Supreme High Commander he issued written and verbal orders to marshals of the Soviet Union. [JG]

6. *Shtrafnik*, the title of address for a soldier in a punishment unit, is perhaps best translated as "punishee." Men in punishment units were typically used to clear enemy minefields, sometimes by simply walking through them, or to attack the enemy as the first unit in a large-scale assault. Assignment to a punishment unit was almost a death sentence in and of itself. [JG]

High-ranking Reconnaissance

1. *Stavka VGK* in this context denotes the fact that forces were being taken from strategic reserves. [JG]

2. *VOVSS*, 481. *SAU* is the Russian acronym for *samokhodno artilleriyskaya ustanovka* (self-propelled gun). [JG]

3. This treaty was signed in Moscow on 13 April 1941 and went into effect on 25 April. In the pact the two sides recognized existing boundaries in the Far East and declared their intention to remain neutral regarding the other side in the event that a third party or more became involved in a conflict with that side. Interestingly, the existence of this pact enabled U.S. Liberty ships, reflagged with the flag of the USSR, to sail from U.S. west-coast ports across the Pacific

Ocean through Japanese-controlled straits in the Kurile Islands to Magadan and Vladivostok in the Soviet Far East with Lend-Lease war materiel that was later used against Japanese forces in Manchuria when the Soviet Union declared war on Japan in August 1945. [JG]

4. *VOVSS*, 473–74.

5. Major General Aleshin was chief of the intelligence/reconnaissance faculty at the Frunze Military Academy from 1949 to 1951. I was a student at the academy from 1947 to 1950, a portion of that time on the intelligence/reconnaissance faculty. General Aleshin personally recounted this story to me.

Difficult Mission

1. *VOVSS*, 485–86.

2. *VOVSS*, 487.

3. Dukhovskoye lies half-way between Lake Khanka and the Chinese border, about 150 kilometers north of Vladivostok. [JG]

4. Primorskiy Kray is a geographic and administrative region of the former USSR, now in the Russian Federation, encompassing the area from the Chinese border south of Vladivostok northward to its boundary with Khabarovsk Kray.

5. *OSNAZ* is a contraction of *osoboye naznacheniye* (special designation or purpose). This adjective is applied to special communications units and special engineer units and, in the Red Navy, to special ground reconnaissance units. The word is a variation of *SPETSNAZ*, *spetsialnoye naznacheniye* (special designation or purpose). [JG]

6. The radio set SCR-399-A was a medium-power mobile station providing voice or continuous wave communications for a distance of approximately a hundred miles under all conditions in the frequency range of 2.0 to 18.0 megacycles. Its principal use was mobile point-to-point and tactical-control communications. The set's components—which included two separate receivers and a transmitter, along with all required ancillary equipment—were installed in a shelter mounted on a two-and-a-half-ton truck. The generator that powered the set was towed behind the truck in a trailer. The total weight of the set (unpacked) was 6,595 pounds. The United States shipped 2,092 SCR-399A radio sets to the USSR through Lend-Lease during World War II. U.S. Army Signal Corps Museum, letter and enclosures to translator, 6 January 1997. [JG]

7. *KNOA* is an acronym for *Kitayskaya narodnaya osvoboditelnaya armiya*, which means "Chinese People's Liberation Army." [JG]

8. *VOVSS*, 487–88.

9. For a brief description in English of this special operation, see William Burgess, ed., *Inside Spetsnaz: Soviet Special Operations, a Critical Analysis* (Novato CA: Presidio Press, 1990), chap. 8. [JG]

Strong-willed Nature

1. Aleksey Petrovich Maresev was a pilot who was shot down in an aerial engagement in 1942. Seriously wounded, for eighteen days he crawled on his hands and knees to Soviet lines. Though both his legs were later amputated below the knees, he mastered his prostheses and returned to his regiment. In subsequent air combat he shot down an additional seven enemy aircraft, for a total of eleven, and flew eighty-six combat sorties. He was named a Hero of the Soviet Union on 24 August 1943.

2. In the USSR (and now in the Russian Federation), law recognizes three categories of war invalid. First-category invalids are those who lost some part of their bodies (arm, leg, eye, and so on) as a result of wounds. Second-category invalids are those who suffered one or more serious wounds. Third-category invalids are those who suffered light wounds or illness during the war. All three categories of invalids are accorded specified rights and entitlements under the law, with first- and second-category invalids receiving the highest level of entitlements. In many ways these entitlements are comparable to those guaranteed to Heroes of the Soviet Union, Heroes of the Russian Federation, and full holders of the Order of Glory (see appendix D).

3. The medal *Za otvagu*, "For Courage"—that is, for personal bravery in combat—was established by an order of the Presidium of the Supreme Soviet on 17 October 1938. The highest-ranking medal in its category, it is worn along the left lapel just below orders. [JG]

4. A *rayon* is an administrative entity for which there is no exact equivalent in the United States. It is larger than a municipality and smaller than a *kray*. Vorov *rayon* is approximately 150 kilometers south-southwest of Moscow. [JG]

5. Initially I addressed Karelin using *Vy* [the plural or polite form of "you"]. But at this point in the conversation he insisted that we frontline veterans address each other using *Ty* [the singular or informal form of "you"].

6. The author of these words is F. N. Glinka (1786–1880), a Russian poet and essayist.

7. Ivan, the English equivalent of which is John, is the most common name in Russia. When the serfs were freed in Russia in the

eighteenth century, many of those who did not take their master's family name for their own resorted to the convention of "Ivan Ivanov." The American equivalent of this would be "John Johnson" or "Peter Peterson." Others, such as the Karelins mentioned here, took their family name from the geographical region of their homelands. The point of his remark about "Ivanov" as a surname is that it lacks any specific origin or root. He is saying, in effect, "We are not John Johnsons; we know who and where we came from." [JG]

8. It was normal during the Communist period for college graduates to be assigned jobs—and not always in a location they had hoped for. This compulsory employment system was mandated by the fact that while the bulk of the population of the Soviet Union was west of the Ural Mountains, much of the country's natural resources were in remote and inhospitable regions to the east and north. Wages and other incentives were insufficient to ensure a qualified labor force where it was needed, so a form of compulsory employment was used. [JG]

9. Tatyana Mikhaylovna asked that I address her with *Ty*. But I would not agree to this for the simple reason that this woman deserves special respect and even reverence. She is a genuine Human Being, with capital letters, and must be addressed only with *Vy*.

10. A Zaporozhets is a small car, resembling a Fiat, made in Ukraine. [JG]

11. The typical village had a central steam-boiler heating plant from which pipes ran (frequently above ground) to heat all the homes. [JG]

12. The word *kolkhoz* is a contraction of *kollektivnoye khozyaystvo* (collective economy). A *kolkhoz* (plural, *kolkhoza*) is a group of farmers who work together and who share the produce of the farm according to the number of days each has contributed to the effort.

13. In order, "Novel-newspaper" (literary works in newspaper format), "Science and Life," "Technology for Youth," "Around the Globe," "Housework," "Rural Woman," and "Youth and Agriculture." [JG]

Field Mail System

1. The active army was the force in the field at the front, as opposed to those units at the training base or in the strategic reserves at the rear. [JG]

2. *Velikaya otechestvennaya voyna 1941-1945, Entsiklopediya*

(The Great Patriotic War 1941–1945, encyclopedia) (Moscow: Sovet-skaya entsiklopedia, 1985), 184.

Radio Communications

1. The VHF radio was an SCR 508 or SCR 528 set (both FM), and the HF radio was an SCR 506 AM set. [JG]

2. This auxiliary unit was a 50-amp, 30-volt generator powered by a 2-cycle, single-cylinder gas engine. [JG]

Combat Vehicle Maintenance

1. *TSAMO RF*, collection 38, index 11362, item 3, sheet 61.

2. *TSAMO RF*, collection 339, index 5179, item 86, sheets 444, 447.

3. Red Army soldiers did not wear socks but wrapped a long piece of straight cloth around the foot and ankle. [JG]

4. In this context the word "center" describes a level of maintenance support provided by the industrial base, controlled by an administrative apparatus in Moscow (the "center"). [JG]

5. The BT, or *bystrokhodnyy tank* (fast tank), was a medium-tank class with many variants. Later models in the series were armed with a 45-mm main gun. The T-26 was a light tank also armed with a 45-mm main gun. [JG]

6. OTRB is the acronym for *otdelnyy tankoremontnyy batalon* (separate tank repair battalion).

7. Soldiers deployed in rear areas were allocated a lower daily caloric intake than soldiers at an active front. [JG]

8. The brigade in which Loza served was issued brand-new Lend-Lease M4A2 Sherman tanks in Mongolia that had been delivered to Soviet Far East ports by ship in the spring of 1945. [JG]

9. A. M. Vasilevskiy, *Delo vsey zhizni* (My life's work) (Moscow: Politicheskaya literatura, 1974), 505.

10. *TSAMO RF*, collection 238, index 77213, item 1, sheet 25. The V-2-34M diesel engine used in the T-34 tank by this period of the war had a service life of 180 to 200 hours. The M4A2 Sherman's twin-diesel engine (two General Motors truck engines assembled together) was tested at 400 hours when it was evaluated for installation in the tank. Richard P. Hunnicutt, letter to translator, 16 April 1997. [JG]

Feeding the Troops

1. The *Aurora* is the cruiser that gave the cannon shot signaling the beginning of the October Revolution in 1917. It now stands at permanent anchor in the St. Petersburg harbor as a memorial,

2. Poor nutrition, and even malnutrition, was the norm in civilian life in the Soviet Union during the war. Even in the armed forces, troops in training or strategic reserve units received fewer calories daily than troops at the front line. [JG]

3. The Austrian army troops were company- and battalion-sized units comprised almost entirely of old men. Understanding full well that the war was lost, many of these units neutralized their German officers by arrest and confinement and ceased to offer any organized resistance to advancing Soviet forces.

Medical Evacuation and Treatment

1. Stretcher bearers, who assisted medics in carrying wounded from the battlefield, were selected from among the physically strong soldiers in the platoons and companies.

2. *Ocherki istorii sovetskoy voyennoy meditsiny* (Outline of the history of Soviet military medicine) (Leningrad: "Meditsina," 1968), 286.

3. *Voyenno meditsinskiy muzey* (Museum of military medicine), collection 1, index 44668, item 76, sheets 11. This source is hereafter cited as *VMM*.

4. Archives *VMM*, index 47167, item 6, sheets 81, 92.

Graves Registration

1. Each mass grave site now has a marker with a number and the date of burial on it; the number is used to indicate the site on topographic maps. Troop units and individual military personnel are required to render honors at the mass graves of soldiers who died for the Motherland.

2. Aleksandr Herzen (1812–70) was a Russian revolutionary, writer, philosopher, and essayist.

Appendixes

1. A pood is 16.38 kilograms, or approximately 36 pounds. This figure of 800 hundred million poods would thus convert to 14.4 million tons. [JG]

2. "Not one step backward" in Russian is *ni shagu nazad*. From this phrase comes the universally known title of this order. [JG]

3. The Russian that translates as "barrier or obstacle detachment" is *zagraditelnyy otryad*. [JG]

4. This order was not published when it was first put into effect. This translation was made from a copy of the order published in

Voyenno-istoricheskiy zhurnal (Military-historical journal) 8 (1988): 73–75. [JG]

5. The Order of Glory was established by a decree of the Presidium of the USSR Supreme Soviet on 8 November 1943. The Order of Glory—which has three degrees, the first being the highest—was conferred on privates and sergeants of the Soviet Army and on air force junior lieutenants for outstanding feats of valor and displays of courage and daring in defense of the Soviet Union. The statute that governed the award listed specific acts for third-, second-, and first-degree status. A full holder of the Order of Glory is one who has earned all three degrees. Out of 2,582 full holders (the number of 1st Degree Orders of Glory awarded during World War II), approximately 700 were living when this law was enacted in 1993, according to the introductory material in the 10 February 1993 newspaper article. [JG]

6. Since one hectare is equal to approximately two and a half acres, these plots are one-fourth and three-fourths acres, respectively. [JG]

7. This legislative act was printed in full in the 10 February 1993 issue of *Krasnaya zvezda* (Red star).

Index

antiaircraft unit, German, 102
antiaircraft unit, Soviet: crediting kills, 92, 245 n.5; fired on German aircraft under Soviet control, 91; provided early warning, 144
artillery, German: against Soviet positions and units, 4, 50, 53, 64, 72, 75, 76, 163; heavy mortars, 45, 64, 66; preparation, 13, 60; tactical positioning, 14
artillery, Romanian: direct-fire against Soviet tanks, 51; indirect fire against Soviet tanks, 76–77
artillery, Soviet: against Soviet tanks, 21, 22; auxiliary generators, 163; danger-close line, 15, 237 n.3; direct support of tank battalion, 162–63; dust raised by, 55, 75; equipped with radios, 163; fired by direct lay, 4; indirect fire against enemy tanks, 15, 54, 74; mortar battery, 96; preparation, 14, 48, 52, 54, 73, 88–90, 97, 120; support of attack, 52, 76; tactical positioning, 3, 18, 73, 89; use of smoke, 45; wire communications, 88–90, 162–63
Austria: combat in, 164, 185–86, 198
avtomatchiki: arrested newspaper editor, 114; combat role, 23, 110, 119, 189; defined, 238 n.8; guarded medical station, 196; rations provided to, 177, 180; suffered heatstrokes, 201–2; surrounded captured German tank, 45; wounded, 197. See also *desantniki*; *tankodesantniki*

barrier detachment: conventional unit employed, 20; defined, 222–23, 238 n.4
BESA coaxial machine gun, 237–38 n.3
Blumentritt, General Gunther, 1–2
Bren coaxial machine gun, 19, 27, 34, 237–38 n.3
bypassing detachment: combat use of, 93–94; defined, 246 n.2

Catherine II, 112–13, 133
censorship of mail, 151–52, 156
close air support, German: to destroy pontoon bridge, 71; during artillery preparation, 60; FW-189 *Rama*, 75, 244 n.5; Ju-87, 35; Ju-88, 18
close air support, Soviet, 20, 49, 120. *See also* Shturmovik
commanders' reconnaissance: described, 71–73; Russian term defined, 243–44 n.3

255

counterintelligence organs: brigade office, 24, 92, 236 n.3; communications channels, 11, 24; control of radio equipment, 164; investigative role, 61; tank battalion officer, 27, 236 n.3. See also SMERSH

covering detachment: combat role, 79–80; defined, 244 n.2

Czechoslovakia: burial of Soviet soldiers, 210, 211; combat in, 104–11, 139–40; Soviet medical facility, 199

death notice, 153, 155–56

deception, 52, 55

Degtyarev coaxial machine gun, 53, 241–42 n.7. *See also* T-34 tank

desantniki: combat role, 26, 51, 106; defined, 238 n.8; rations provided to, 178, 180, 183; suffered heatstroke, 201–2; weary of menu, 183. See also *avtomatchiki*; *tankodesantniki*

desertion, 27–30, 32

evacuation of civilian population, 146, 149–51

female soldiers: antitank gunner, 6; *feldsher*, 196–97, 199; medic, 5; proofreader, 115

flamethrower tanks: KV variant, 47; T-34 variant, 47; combat use, 49, 51, 52–53, 55–56

forward detachment: combat use, 1, 3, 21–22, 105–10; described, 233 n.1

friendly fire, Soviet: artillery against tanks, 17, 21–22; coaxial machine guns against infantry, 19–20; concern to prevent, 50; tanks against artillery, 21; tanks against tanks, 22–23

Frunze Military Academy: entrance procedure, 24, 238 n.1; Malinovskiy's speech, 68–70, 77; Loza an instructor, 70, 110–11

GAZ truck, 63–65, 242 n.2

German tanks: armor thickness, 6; capture, 10, 43–46, 196, 198; destroyed by indirect fire, 54, 74; destroyed Soviet tanks, 49, 53, 198; Panther, 60, 212; Panzer IV, 4, 14–16, 43–46; tactical employment, 4, 7–8, 13, 14, 49–50, 53–54, 60, 64, 198; Tiger, 60–61, 64, 66, 196, 198, 212; vulnerable to antitank rifle fire, 6, 8–9

"Guards" designation: defined, 235 n.8; first unit to earn, 1; pay differential, 242 n.4

half-track, American, 190, 196, 197, 199

half-track, German, 190, 197, 237 n.5

Henschel-126: flight described, 90–91; technical data, 245 n.3

Hero of the Soviet Union: Petr Avramenko, 245–46 n.1; Dmitriy Loza, 206; Aleksey Maresev, 249 n.1; order of precedence, 226; privileges of recipients, 227–32

"Hitler's kisses," 12

Hungary: attacks toward Budapest, 79, 88; combat in, 79–80, 93–104; peasants, 82–88

Jassy-Kishinev operation: analysis by Marshal Malinovskiy, 68; captured medical supplies, 193; designation of army repair group, 167; evacuation of civilians, 146; logistic support, 182; maintenance, 170, 171; medical support, 193, 197; role of 6th Guards Tank Army, 141, 158, 170, 193; unit strength restored, 78

Katyusha: captured, 58, 61; combat role, 48, 53–54; explanation of name, 57, 242 n.8; medical component, 189–90; recovered by tank crews, 62; rigged for demolition, 58, 61; tactics of employment, 58, 61; technical characteristics, 57. *See also* multiple rocket launcher
Korsun-Shevchenkovskiy operation: ammunition supply, 63–64; burial of German dead, 212; burial of Soviet dead, 209; cannibalization of damaged equipment, 162; capture of enemy vehicles, 197; combat description, 60–61, 64; designation of army repair group, 167; food delivery, 179–80; friendly fire, 17, 22–23; goal of operation, 60, 62; medical treatment and evacuation, 196, 197; meteorological con-

ditions, 168; trapped German forces, 60; troops fed, 178
Kwantung Army: capitulation, 127; combat readiness, 118; operational plan for battle, 120–21; radio communications, 124–25, 126; resist Soviet offensive, 122–26

Lend-Lease: Studebaker trucks, 58; foodstuffs, 178, 186; radio equipment, 248 n.6; tanks, 168, 173, 251 n.8; war material to Far East, 247–48 n.3
logistic support, 157–60, 165–88; air delivery of fuel, 187; air delivery of tank road wheels, 171; battalion support platoon, 158–59, 166; brigade transportation platoon, 158–59, 176; food products, 176; parachute delivery of ammunition, 159; position relative to fighting units, 158; radio sets used for, 158, 162, 165; recovery of expended brass, 159; recovery of serviceable ammunition, 159
Loza, Dmitriy Fedorovich: biographical sketch, ix–x; battalion chief of ammunition supply, 63, 143; battalion chief of staff, 71, 147; battalion commander, 116, 164, 199; combat decoration, 32; company commander, 18–20, 25; convalescent leave, 139; famine in the Ukraine, 234 n.2; first combat, 18–20; forward detachment commander, 105–10; Frunze Military Academy,

Loza, Dmitriy F. (*continued*)
24, 70, 110–11; Hero of the
Soviet Union, 206; recovered
damaged tanks, 75; SMERSH
investigation, 24–25, 29, 30;
tank overturned, 109; trapped
under burning tank, 64–67;
witnessed downing of Ger-
man aircraft, 91; wounded in
combat, x, 32, 198–99

maintenance support, 165–76;
radio and auxiliary generator,
163; recovery of disabled or
mired vehicles, 27, 62, 75, 76,
109, 180, 187–88, 244 n.6
Malinovskiy, Rodion Yakovlevich: biographical sketch, 243
n.1; conversation with Loza,
70; *front* commander, 77, 104,
139, 206; conversation with
Stalin, 69–70, 77–78; Minister
of Defense, 68, 243 n.1; speech
at Frunze Military Academy,
68–69, 77
Manchurian operation: communications, 122–27, 164–65;
Kwantung Army, 122–27;
maintenance, 175–76; medical
support, 200–203; role of 6th
Guards Tank Army, 158; supplies, 160, 247–48 n.3; troops
fed, 186–88
Matilda tank: ammunition shortage, 30–31; armor thickness,
25; coaxial machine gun, 237–
38 n.3; destroyed by enemy
fire, 25; destroyed by friendly
fire, 21; destroyed by German close air support, 34–35,

39; Loza wounded in, x, 32;
main gun used against German infantry, 32; nicknamed
"Englishman," 240 n.3;
shipped from Great Britain,
ix, x, 233 n.1; Soviet units
equipped with, ix, 19, 20, 25;
unsuitable for terrain, 26, 31;
use in combat, 25–26, 33–35
medal "For Combat Service":
approval authority, 204; to
Hungarian civilian, 87; to
medical personnel, 194; order
of precedence, 226
medal "For Courage": approval
authority, 204; described, 249
n.3; to medical personnel, 194;
order of precedence, 226; to
soldier, 129, 137
military commission: defined,
234 n.3; induction agency, 5,
239 n.5; postwar role, 24–25,
30, 239 n.6
military council: award approval
authority, 206; consultative
body, 78, 179; pre-combat
check, 50; proclamations,
48, 119, 241 n.3; punishment
units, 222–23; report in archive, 79
multiple rocket launcher: combat role, 48, 53–54; deployed
to Far East, 117; first battlefield use, 57; history, 57; tactical employment, 58, 77. *See
also* Katyusha
mutual recognition signals:
flares, 91; hand-fired rocket,
21, 33; radio, 23

Order of Glory, 253 n.5; approval

authority, 204–5; privileges of full holders, 227–32

Order of the Patriotic War, 239–40 n.1; approval authority, 204–5; to Dmitriy Loza, 32; to double amputee, 137; to Matilda tankers, 46; order of precedence, 226; recommended for Hungarian civilians, 87, 245 n.6

Order of Lenin: to medical personnel, 194

Order of the Red Banner, 234 n.4; approval authority, 204–5; for Civil War combat, 4; to medical personnel, 194; order of precedence, 225; posthumous award, 9

Order of the Red Star, 246 n.3; approval authority, 204–5; to medical personnel, 194; to officer, 96; order of precedence, 226

panzerfaust: fired at German tank, 45; fired at Sherman tanks, 109; technical description, 240 n.9

poncho rafts, 99–100, 101

Primus stove, 181, 186

punishment units: creation, 221–23; editor assigned to, 115; *shtrafnik* title explained, 247 n.6

radio communications, 161–65; American equipment, 23, 124, 248 n.6, 251 n.1; awards authorized via, 205; between Soviet and Japanese headquarters, 125–27; German jamming,

80; infantry unit, 103; Matilda tank, 27, 33, 35; scouts, 120; support platoon, 158, 165, 177; T-34 tank, 80

reconnaissance aircraft, German Henschel-126, 90–91, 245 n.3

Romania: combat in, 68–77, 193; condiments from, 183. *See also* Jassy-Kishinev operation

Romanian Army: combat by units, 48–49, 51–52; linked with German military command, 68, 72, 74, 76; medical supplies used by Soviet Army, 193

Sherman tanks: ammunition issues, 63–64, 65, 158–59, 177, 242 n.3 n.4 n.5; auxiliary generator, 161–64, 251 n.2; cannibalization, 158, 162, 163, 165, 166, 169, 170, 177; coaxial machine gun, 60, 159; combat use of, 22–23, 60, 71–77, 105–10; command tanks, 73, 244 n.4; compared to T-34, 12, 65, 161, 251 n.10; converted to tractors, 165; crew sabotage, 239 n.2; delayed oil change, 169–70; delivery to Far East, 251 n.8; destroyed by enemy fire, 64, 76, 77, 78, 109–10, 198; destroyed by friendly fire, 22–23; *Emcha* nickname, 108, 109, 246 n.4; fire in hull, 64–67; fuel, 157, 171, 174, 203; hull-mounted machine gun, 60, 242 n.5; lack of spare parts, 168–69; in Manchurian operation, 173–74, 176, 188; on-board radio equipment,

83; crew positions, 236 n.2, 241 n.6; destroyed Sherman, 22–23; destruction by ammunition self-detonation, 65; engine failed, 80–81; engine life compared to Sherman, 251 n.10; escape hatch, 245 n.4; flamethrower version, 47, 53, 55–56; plan for destruction, 81; production data, 233 n.2; spalling, 9–11; spare parts, 170–71; tracks used against enemy, 52

ticks, 116

Umansk-Batoshansk operation, 168, 181

Vienna offensive: acquisition of wine stocks, 183–85

wire communications: artillery units, 89; infantry units, 103; tank units, 162–63